GW00382276

POUNAMU

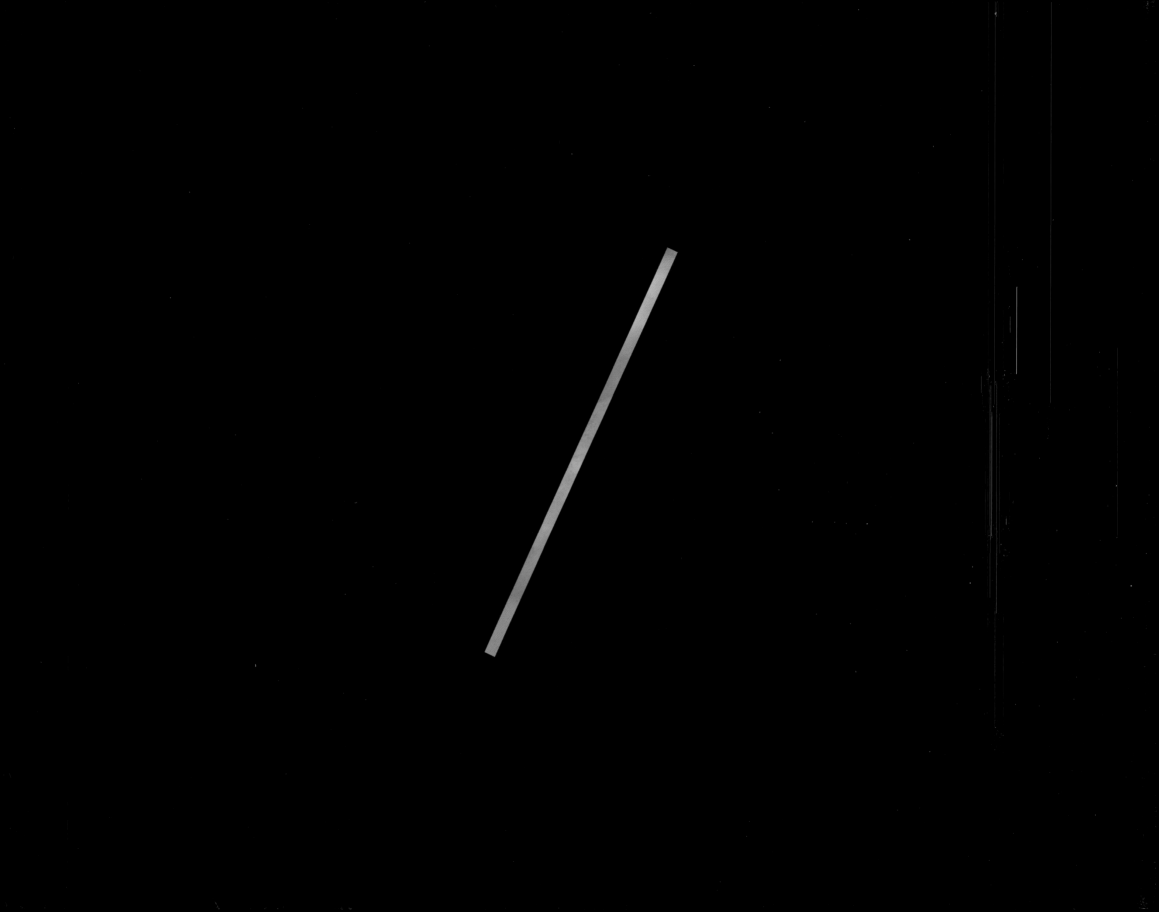

PENGUIN
VIKING

PUBLISHED IN ASSOCIATION WITH
TE RŪNANGA O NGĀI TAHU

THE JADE OF NEW ZEALAND
POUNAMU

RUSSELL BECK *with* MAIKA MASON
photography by ANDRIS APSE

CONTENTS/

KAI TAKU IKA A KĀHUE, KĀI TAHU TAKATA, POUNAMU TAOKA,
KO KOE, KO TĀTOU, KO TĀTOU, KO KOE.

TĀUTI MAI KOUTOU KI TĒNEI PUKAPUKA PUIAKI HAI PUNA
MAHARA O TE AO KOHATU O Ō TĀTOU TŪPUNA. KAI ŌNA
RAU KĀ MAHARATAKA O KĀ KŌRERO MŌ POUTINI RĀUA KO
WAITAIKI, MŌ TE HEKE O RAUREKA ME TE HEKE ANŌ HOKI O
TE RAKITĀMAU NŌ TE TAI O MAHAANUI KI TE TAI O POUTINI.
KA RERE AKU MAHARA KI TE AO KAKARI, KI A MAHINAPUA,
KI TE TAUĀ O TE REHE RĀUA KO TUHURU, Ā, KA TAU KI TE
AWATAPU, KI A ARAHURA TE PŪTAKETAKA O TE AO POUNAMU.

KAI TAKU KURU POUNAMU, KIA NOHO PŪMAU KOE KI TE
MANAWA O TŌ IWI.

PREVIOUS PAGE / Like the emerging
pounamu story, the landscape
slowly reveals itself from the
mists of Doubtful Sound,
Fiordland.

LEFT / The twisted and tangled
fronds of seaweed, resembling
the matted, fibrous structure of
nephrite.

To my sacred fish of Kāhue, Kāi Tahu are the people, pounamu is the treasure, together we are one.

Welcome one and all to this precious book that stands as a spring of memories of the world of our ancestors.
Within its leaves are the memories of the stories about Poutini and Waitaiki, about the journey of Raureka and that of
Te Rakitāmau from the East Coast to the West. My thoughts fly to the ancient times of war, to Mahinapua and the fighting
expeditions of Te Rehe and Tuhuru. They rest now upon the sacred river, Arahura, the beginning of the pounamu world.

To my treasured pounamu, may you always stay in the heart of your people.

FOREWORD/

Half of New Zealand's land mass is named for it: Te Waipounamu. It matters not whether the name is a contraction of 'Te Wāhi Pounamu', the 'place' of pounamu, or whether it should be 'Te Waipounamu', the 'waters' of pounamu. It matters not whether the more common green serpentine should be included among the stones classed as pounamu or whether, as the geologists prefer, it should be excluded. It is the stone, pounamu, that matters. It is a hinge of history. It has been sought after and fought for, wept over and treasured, for almost the whole human story of Aotearoa. Its merits as weapon or ornament, as tool or treasure, are the stuff of proverbial whakatauakī and metaphor. Possession of pounamu has long been a mark of wealth and prestige, a mark of mana.

It would be an overstatement to say that Kāi Tahu migrated southwards into Te Waipounamu in the eighteenth century because of pounamu but it quickly became a major focus of our old cultural and economic life. Kāi Tahu fought with Kāti Tūmatakokiri to block off the old western trade routes for pounamu through Nelson and northwards to Whanganui and the central North Island. When the musket-armed Ngāti Toa invaded Kāi Tahu territory in the nineteenth century, it was against Kaiapoi they threw their forces in their quest for pounamu. By that time, it was the political and economic centre of Te Waipounamu and of Kāi Tahu.

Dominance did not come quickly or easily, however. Kāi Tahu control of pounamu production and trade was contested by Kāti Wairaki on Te Tai Poutini and, for more than a century, Kāi Tahu was forced to trade with them for the treasured stone. It was only in the early years of the nineteenth century that Kāi Tahu dominance became absolute.

In reality, though, Kāi Tahu are the inheritors of pounamu, and its basket of tradition and cultural significance. Those traditions were evolved by more ancient tribes, those who first explored and settled the vast landscape. As those early settlers spread out across the island, they sought – after food and shelter – the stones that made their worlds possible. They were Neolithic people – they belonged to 'Te Ao Kōhatu', the Age of Stone. Their ability to shape stone made both hunting and warfare effective. It led to an ability to cut flesh and fell trees, to catch fish and harvest plants. They gathered and worked stones of many kinds but – quite quickly it seems – pounamu found itself at the pinnacle of their geological 'table of elements'. Their great challenge, though, was developing a method for working it.

Pounamu is not a stone that can be hammered into shape – at least not with any precision. The very qualities for which is valued – density

and toughness, and the ability to hold a sharp edge – come from its 'felted' structure. That structure defied the centuries of Polynesian experience in hammering stone into shape. They found they could shape it only by grinding – 'mahi hōaka'. They had to evolve a whole new stone-working technology in order to cut it and then another to make holes in it. They had first to find and then experiment with the other stones that would make all this possible – the various sandstones for grinding and the even more secretive pāhau flints for drilling. When we contemplate the sheer scale of effort and labour, the journeying, the trial and error of discovery and experimentation, the vagaries of chance, the imagination and skill of artists, all represented by the taoka (treasures) we look at today in our air-conditioned museums and galleries, we can only stand in awe.

That wonder might reasonably fall on things fashioned from other stones or from bone or shell or wood. Pounamu, though, reserves for itself a special wonder simply from what it is and how it is made. It has a history and a character that does not compare readily with any other in the natural world of the Māori. It is little wonder, then, that of all the stones and other treasures of Te Ao Māori it has its own creation myth, its own story, its own unique place in Māori traditional belief.

The Poutini myth, which culminates in the creation of pounamu from the body of the beautiful Waitaiki in the Arahura Valley, is not just another taniwha story. As it follows the lovesick Tamaahua in his search for his abducted wife, it identifies the major quarries from which the treasured stones were extracted in the times of Te Ao Kōhatu. It is an oral map – 'New Zealand's first geological survey'.

Small wonder, then, that when Kāi Tahu entered into the Arahura Purchase with the Crown in 1860, they reserved the Arahura from the sale. Small wonder that for the next 140 years they wrestled with the settler state to get that contractual reservation honoured. Small wonder that as a result of the historic Kāi Tahu Treaty settlements of the late 1990s, pounamu has its own distinct Act of Parliament. It was the historic and cultural place, not its commercial or economic value, of the treasured stone in Kāi Tahu identity that accorded it that status – 'mana pounamu'.

Tipene O'Regan
Ihutai
June 2010

LEFT / To many people, pounamu is not found but reveals itself.

FOREWORD/

Pounamu is a New Zealand icon.

It can be found in every city, town, museum and tourist centre in New Zealand. Sales yield considerable returns every year, as hundreds of thousands of New Zealanders and international guests appreciate its beauty and unique physical properties. Desire is such that even the smallest of pebbles can be of equivalent value to an entire truckload of gravel aggregate. But consumers are commonly unaware that New Zealand pounamu, with its experience of having journeyed through our pristine mountain landscape, sits among imported jade that was obtained and carved into traditional Māori designs in far-distant lands. Economically speaking, pounamu is currently one of our more significant mineral commodities. History suggests the past situation was little different. Coveted for strength, beauty and rarity, it has been utilised for tools, weapons or adornments and widely traded ever since people first inhabited New Zealand.

Formed deep in the Earth's crust at special sites where chemical contrasts and reactions have occurred between different rocks, the concentrated growth of amphibole or serpentine minerals has resulted in these rare rocks with unique physical and chemical properties. As mineral growth progressed over hundreds of thousands of years, erstwhile surrounding rocks contorted and deformed at high temperatures and pressures, each crystal adopted a distinct atomic and chemical signature that varies from region to region. Internal atomic clocks also began ticking and recording pounamu's age. As tectonic forces carried the rocks upwards, away from the heat of the earth's interior, pounamu's whakapapa, or geological genealogy, defined by its age and place of origin, was set.

Pounamu's journey began in geological collision zones where the Earth's shifting tectonic plates buckled and formed mountain chains. As the rocks were uplifted and cooled, erosion peeled layer after layer from the landscape, changing the mountain's shape. Zones rich in pounamu were carried up and eventually exhumed at the surface, surrounded by rocks that are generally softer and less heavy. Today, exposed to gravitational pull, frost action, glacial carving, earthquakes, avalanches and storms, the pounamu now seemingly clings to the mountainsides while weaker neighbouring rock is stripped away. Blocks of pounamu develop local concentrations, but pounamu's fight against gravity in a rugged mountain environment is relentless. Eventually the pieces weather and break, becoming smaller and more rounded as they fall or are carried by ice and water, to be spread out through our streams and rivers. Like attractive fish fighting the downstream current of erosion, pounamu clings to the landscape experiencing all its change and evolution. It is here on its journey towards the

sea that pounamu is typically found, before being plucked and carried into a very different world of humans.

In recognition of the spiritual and cultural importance of pounamu, the New Zealand government vested ownership of pounamu with Te Rūnanga o Ngāi Tahu. It was an unprecedented act in 1997, which not only assigned legal mineral rights but included an unwritten duty of care for our national treasure. But apart from being found in our streams, rivers and some bedrock reefs, there is very little information about the quantity and distribution of pounamu by which to manage the resource.

During the past seven years, GNS Science has been working to provide Ngāi Tahu with a geological perspective of pounamu. Specifically, we have studied the formation and natural spreading processes of pounamu, aiming to quantify the resource and trace erosion and landscape evolution. One aim is to understand a sustainable development limit, whereby pounamu extraction might be matched against the natural supply derived from tectonic uplift and mountain erosion. We have also investigated and defined ways in which the geological age and chemistry of pounamu can used as a tool for archaeology or resource protection.

It has been our great pleasure to have one of the authors of this book, Russell Beck, as a mentor and highly valued member of our science team. Russell's knowledge of pounamu geology is foremost and his enthusiastic fascination infectious, but he also exudes his affinity with and deep understanding of the spiritual connection between people, the land and this iconic resource.

For this book, Russell has joined forces with Maika Mason and Andris Apse. Possessing a lifetime association with pounamu, Maika is an authority on Ngāi Tahu history, values and traditions, and was a leading advocate for the return of pounamu to Māori. Andris is a photographer with almost unbelievable ability to capture moods, shape and changes in our landscape. Their partnership has created this very special book illustrating and describing pounamu, taking it far from its commonly observed occurrence in crowded tourist shops and museums. Their book connects our iconic mineral treasure back to the landscape in which it belongs, gently releasing pounamu's spirit to swim our mountain waters again.

Dr Simon Cox
GNS Science
May 2010

LEFT / Glacial ice, a sculptor of the landscape that has freed and distributed pounamu far from its many sources. Fox Glacier, Westland.

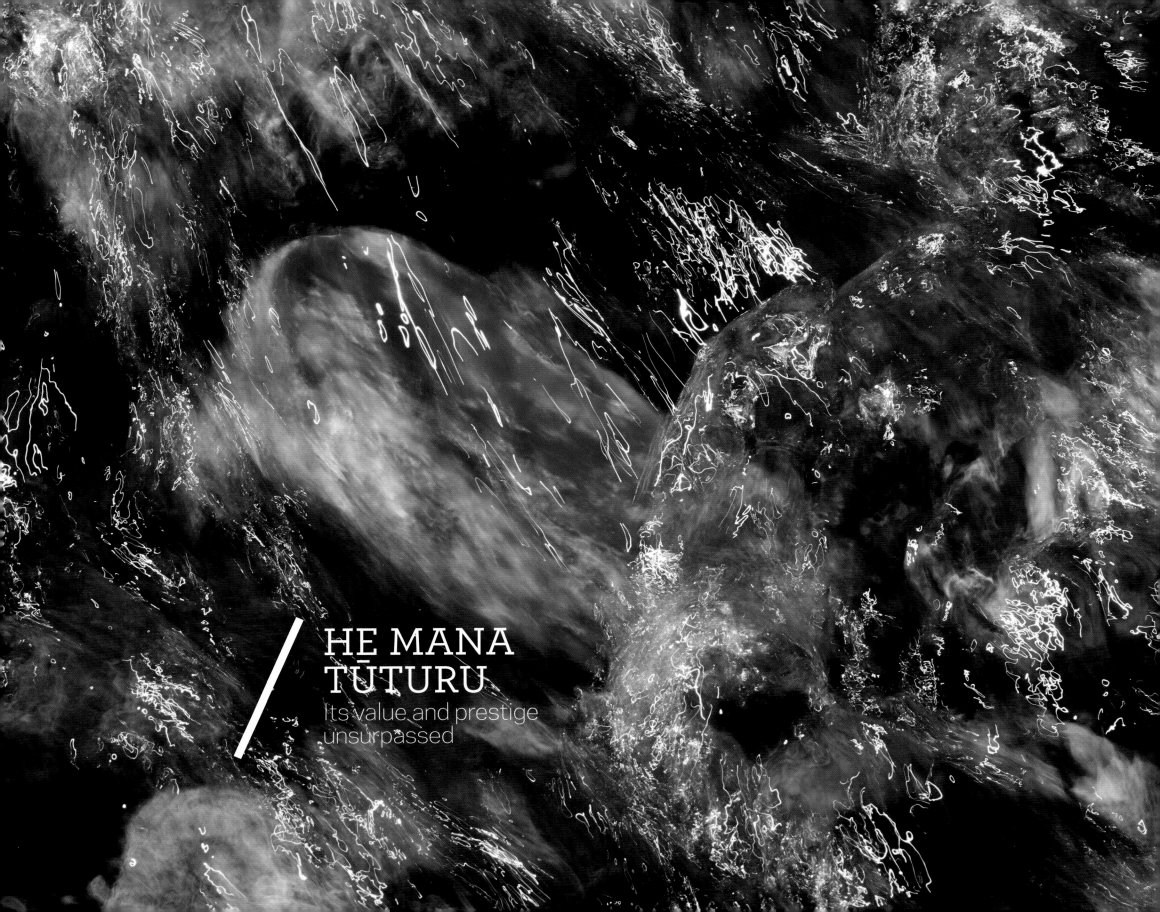

HE MANA
TŪTURU

Its value and prestige
unsurpassed

INTRODUCTION/

For millennia, humans have used jade in a multitude of ways – for tools, weapons, adornment, as currency, spiritual symbol and art medium, and belief in its healing properties. All precious stones are treasured for their beauty and rarity, but the unique practical properties of jade set it apart. Such was the esteem of the material that its physical qualities have been compared to the virtues of life itself.

Deposits of jade have been found in at least twenty-two different countries; twenty of these have nephrite, and five have the much rarer jadeite (see Appendix Two). Jade is a term for two similar-looking but distinctly different rocks: nephrite and jadeite. Nephrite is an extremely tough material. Stone-based cultures with access to nephrite (and there were at least fifteen of them) used it to create implements and weapons that had metal-like qualities while retaining the characteristics of stone. This gave them huge advantages over cultures that were restricted to brittle stone, and allowed them to develop efficient design technology.

Eventually metal was discovered and alloys were developed. But for many societies the appreciation of jade remained, and for some it became their most prized possession and the ultimate medium for the artistic expression of their culture.

New Zealand Māori were no exception to this cultural pattern, and with nephrite (which they called pounamu) they developed in a relatively short time an artistic culture that was notable in the South Pacific. This appreciation for jade was not extinguished with colonisation; instead it was embraced by the European culture, and has continued to the present, although for somewhat different reasons.

Jade carving in New Zealand has developed dramatically to the point where it is valued internationally for its innovative design and craftsmanship. The story has entered a new stage, as the South Island Ngāi Tahu tribe is now the owner of the natural pounamu resources within its boundaries and is developing long-term management programmes that cover all aspects of the stone. Apart from the Nelson field, the six known pounamu fields in the South Island are managed on behalf of the Ngāi Tahu people by nine local rūnanga (tribal councils), either individually or combined where sources were traditionally shared (see Chapters Four and Seven). Mawhera Incorporation – the corporate embodiment of the traditional owners – owns and manages the Arahura River field.

There is much that can be written of the history of jade, and even more to be researched. Those who are unaware of its history may simply view it as an attractive stone or a souvenir. The aim of this, my fourth book on the topic, is to emphasise the important historical role that jade has played in New Zealand and to provide an insight into the special relationship between this stone and the people and landscape of New Zealand. I have produced a more personal aspect, retained some original text and expanded on the story including jade in the Pacific Rim.

It was a visit to Anita Bay at the entrance to Milford Sound in 1958 that first sparked my interest in pounamu. We found beautiful pebbles of 'greenstone' and I was captivated by the clarity of the stone. I soon learned that my pebbles were not jade, but a completely different mineral, bowenite. My interest in pounamu snowballed once I began a career with the Southland Museum and Art Gallery, and my study of this stone has consumed some fifty years of my life and taken me over much of the globe.

Knowledge is not gained in isolation, and I have been particularly fortunate to have had association with other jade enthusiasts both in New Zealand and worldwide. I am grateful to Maika Mason, pounamu researcher for Ngāi Tahu, who has provided a much valued Māori viewpoint. Maika also has a long involvement with pounamu. He and I have worked together on original research projects, and our findings and conclusions are incorporated in this book.

Another person who has influenced and helped me is the late Dr Alfred Poole, CBE, with whom I shared some thirty years of experiences with research and exploring jade occurrences in New Zealand and overseas. Alf and I also enjoyed carving jade together.

With the emphasis being on the relationship of pounamu with the landscape, I invited Andris Apse to undertake the photography. Andris is one of New Zealand's leading landscape photographers, and he has a strong empathy with jade. All photographs, unless otherwise credited, are by Andris Apse.

It is difficult to articulate the deep appreciation for jade that many people the world over acquire. It is not unusual for a piece of this stone to become a treasure, like a family member. There is nothing quite like the excitement of finding a beautiful piece of pounamu which instantly becomes an old friend and invites constant fondling. In time these pieces – be they heirlooms or natural stones – take on a particular patina, charged with mana, and gain a presence unlike that of any other stone.

LEFT / Pounamu, like a fish, never looks better than when first seen in water.

CHAPTER ONE/THE LANGUAGE OF JADE

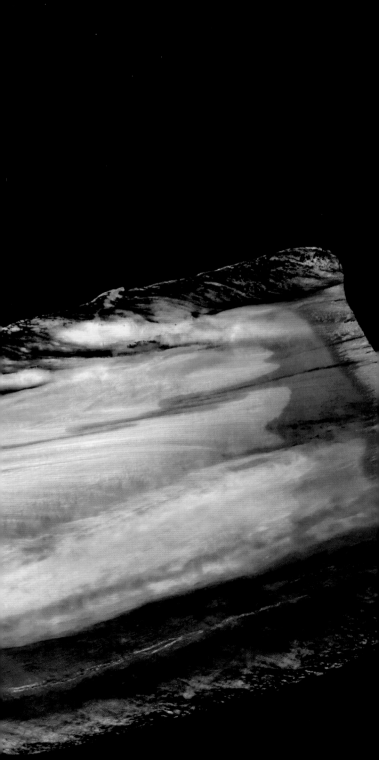

Throughout the world jade has many names, and New Zealand is no exception. Jade, jadeite, nephrite, greenstone, pounamu and bowenite . . . how did these names come about and what do they actually mean? The following is an attempt to simplify and explain these names, including those used by Māori.

JADE

The word 'jade' is a collective term for two rock types defined by the French mineralogist Professor A. Damour in 1863. Before this, all rock specimens and artefacts that looked like jade were named jade, irrespective of their mineralogical differences. Damour actually named three rocks which qualified for his term jade: nephrite, jadeite and chloromelanite. As chloromelanite is now regarded by most authorities as an iron-rich variety of jadeite, the term jade applies to the two rocks nephrite and jadeite. Nephrite and jadeite are similar only in appearance and are structurally and chemically quite different.

Elsie Ruff, a New Zealand jade researcher, traced the origin of the word 'jade' from the Latin *ia*, which became Spanish *ijada*, *yjada* or *hijade* ('loins'), the Italian *iada* or *jada*, and the French *éjade* and *le jade*. It was always referred to in connection with a stone once used as a cure for diseases of the kidney, hence the Spanish *piedra de ijada* (stone of the loins).

JADEITE

Named by Damour from the word jade, jadeite is commercially highly valuable because of its rarity, wide colour range and slightly superior hardness to nephrite. Jadeite is a mineral of the pyroxene family. When it occurs in rock form, often with other minerals such as diopside and albitite, the name is more correctly jadeitite. Jadeite has not

as yet been found in New Zealand; any mention of New Zealand jade applies to nephrite only.

NEPHRITE

The origin of the word nephrite is much older than the word jade, but they have a common meaning. Bright's disease, or inflammation of the kidneys, is also called nephritis – from the Greek *nephros*, meaning kidney; hence nephrite (kidney stone). People who suffered from this disease either ate the stone ground to a paste, or wore it as a charm in the belief that it would heal them. Nephrite is essentially composed of the mineral tremolite, a member of the amphibole group.

SEMI-NEPHRITE

The term 'semi-nephrite' was introduced by F. J. Turner of the University of Otago in 1935 to describe specimens with a structure that is not as well developed as nephrite – an intermediate stage between coarsely crystallised tremolite rocks and felted nephrite. Turner described five stages of the transition to nephrite, one of them being semi-nephrite. As these stages usually require microscopic analysis to differentiate between them, I have used semi-nephrite only in the broadest sense (see Chapter Nine).

GREENSTONE

This is a term that is popularly used in New Zealand to describe the stone – nephrite and, sometimes, bowenite (a type of serpentine discussed below) – used to make jade-like artefacts.

Geologically, greenstone is an old global term, seldom used, to describe fine-grained green igneous rocks which are not related to jade. The term 'New Zealand greenstone' is reluctantly accepted by gemmologists, but it applies to nephrite only. The term is occasionally used outside New Zealand to describe neolithic artefacts that look like jade but have not been

specifically identified.

Because I feel that the name 'greenstone' for nephrite is unsatisfactory and that the more correct and fitting term 'New Zealand jade' should be encouraged, I have avoided using 'greenstone' in this book.

In New Zealand the origin of the word greenstone is obscure but it probably arose from general descriptions by early European observers. Captain James Cook described Māori hei tiki and implements as being of a green, talc-like stone and stated, correctly, that they were 'of the nephritic species'. Other descriptions of jade-like Māori artefacts have been described as being a 'green stone', and this led to the word greenstone. The term greenstone was meaningless to overseas visitors and its use has declined steadily since 1970; it is gradually being replaced by 'jade' and 'pounamu'.

POUNAMU

Pounamu is a Māori term for nephrite and also, less commonly, bowenite. Māori named many varieties of pounamu. These can be roughly divided into four main types, with several diversifications: kawakawa, kahurangi, īnanga and tangiwai. The first three are nephrite and the fourth, tangiwai, is bowenite. Although Māori placed tangiwai as a variety of pounamu, they were well aware of its differences and its limitations, such as inferior hardness and toughness. The term pounamu is used generally throughout this book, and specifically where Māori culture is discussed.

BOWENITE – TANGIWAI

Bowenite was originally described by G. T. Bowen as nephrite. When this material was subsequently found to be a type of serpentine, it was named after him.

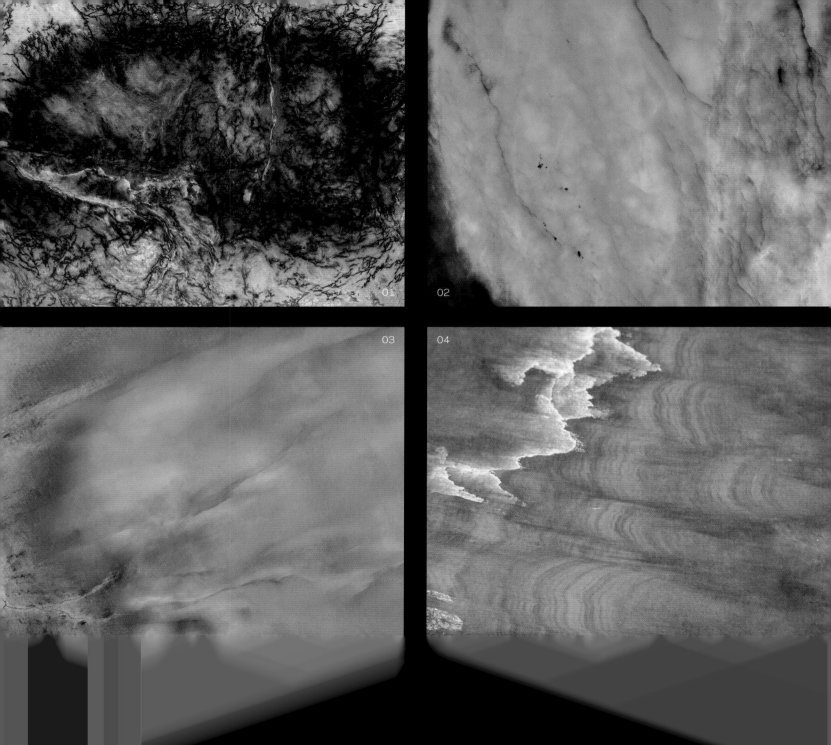

New Zealand bowenite, which is highly translucent, is found mainly at Anita Bay and Poison Bay near the entrance to Milford Sound/Piopiotahi.

The word tangiwai came from a Māori legend about a lamenting woman at Piopiotahi/Milford Sound whose tears turned to stone – hence 'tangiwai' or 'tear-water'. For this reason, some people think the term tangiwai should be used only if the stone is from the Milford source.

POUNAMU NAMES

New Zealand jade has a colour range similar to that of jade elsewhere, but it is particularly noted for its rich yellow-green shades and its high degree of translucency. Iron is the chief colouring agent in New Zealand nephrites, and is responsible for the wide range of green shades. The emerald green commonly found in jadeite owes its colour to the presence of chromium. A much less intense shade of emerald green can occur in New Zealand nephrite, but this is extremely rare; both nickel and chromium may be responsible. The numerous hues of green found in jade have been described by matching them to other things of a similar shade; for example, we have mutton fat, pearly green, apple or lettuce green, grass green, olive green and dark green.

In the 1880s Justice F. R. Chapman made enquiries from the early authorities and found that the Māori names for the main kinds of pounamu – īnanga, kahurangi, kawakawa and tangiwai – were widespread, but with many discrepancies in their use. New Zealand is a long and narrow country and the early Māori population was widely dispersed and had no written language, so it is easy to see how such variations might occur. Local names for particular shades, rare colours and general

01 / Olive green, weathered semi-nephrite with black moss-like dendrites. Mararoa field, Southland.

02 / Backlit kawakawa jade with black specks. Marsden, Westland.

03 / Backlit rare yellow jade. Marsden, Westland.

04 / Chatoyant īnanga jade. Olderog/Waitaiki Creek, Westland.

appearance had many variations; and there were sometimes several names for similar types. The shades blend into each other, which only adds to the difficulty in identifying different types. Several varieties can be present in one stone, or in an item made from it. For these reasons, it is not really possible to rely on a system based purely on colour comparison for naming pounamu.

It seems that events associated with the stone also played an important part in the origin of its name (see below).

ĪNANGA OR ĪNAKA

Īnanga is a pearly, pale grey-green colour and varies from strongly translucent to opaque. There is evidence that in the south this variety was the most highly prized pounamu and a desired material for making mere (a jabbing hand weapon).

One tradition credits Hineteuira, the daughter of the great Polynesian navigator Kupe, as the discoverer of pounamu in the Arahura riverbed. At the time of its discovery the women in Kupe's party were fishing for the native minnow, īnanga (*Galaxias matulatus*), more commonly known as whitebait. Hineteuira picked up a stone to anchor the net and noticed it was strikingly different from the other stones being used. They called the stone īnanga after the activity the women were engaged in at the time of its discovery. Other varieties of īnanga have been recorded, but without clear explanation.

Because īnanga was desirable and not always available, Māori developed a technique for artificially producing a silvery variation by heat-treating other varieties; this practice is covered more fully in Chapter Seven. With time, some īnanga specimens undergo a colour change to a light olive tint.

Note that the names 'īnaka', 'kahuraki' and so on reflect the dialect of southern Māori, who often use a 'k' instead of 'ng'.

KAHURANGI OR KAHURAKI

Kahurangi is the most highly translucent, flawless variety of pounamu, as well as the rarest. Most Māori esteemed it above all other varieties and fashioned from it some of their most treasured possessions, such as the ceremonial adze (toki poutangata). The word kahurangi derives from the clearness of the sky – it was likened to the range of colour observed in the sky, which varied in intensity according to the day and season, and not the specific colour. Hence we have a light apple green free of any dark spots. Small feather-like markings can give a cloud effect but without reducing the translucency.

KAWAKAWA

Kawakawa is a strong dark to rich green with varying intermediate shades, including grass green. Tradition suggests that the name was derived from the discovery of pounamu by a woman wearing a chaplet of kawakawa (*Macropiper excelsum*) leaves. These were worn by women who were grieving over the death of a loved one. Other accounts relate it to the colour of the kawakawa leaf. The kawakawa tree is found throughout New Zealand, except in the southern half of the South Island; an extract from its leaves was used by Māori for pain relief.

Kawakawa is commonly flecked with small dark inclusions which, rather than detracting from the stone's beauty, often add character and are seen as a desirable feature of New Zealand jade. Today, kawakawa is the most popular variety of pounamu used for carving.

TANGIWAI OR TAKIWAI

Tangiwai is a translucent to transparent, olive-green to bluish-green variety of serpentine known as bowenite, not to be confused with nephrite. The name tangiwai is a slight abbreviation of the word kōkōtangiwai: 'kōkō' means an incision or wound made into one's spirit by a deep sorrow that is never completely healed, and 'tangi' is the weeping associated with such grief, and 'wai' refers to the outpouring of tears. Traditional stories concerning the origin of the name are all associated with great sorrow. The nearly transparent teardrop-like appearance of the stone inspired the various tribal creation stories concerning kōkōtangiwai.

The following are other less well known varieties of pounamu.

AUHUNGA OR HAUHUNGA

A pale green, opaque variety, given as the intermediate shade between īnanga and kawakawa. This is a favoured stone of the Arahura people. The word auhunga or hauhunga, 'frosty', is generally associated with mountains and the colder regions. The dropping of the 'h' in auhunga is a dialectic variation of the Taranaki tribes. The origin of these words in association with pounamu is uncertain.

KAHOTEA

The name kahotea is an abbreviation of kākaho, meaning the white flowering seedhead of the toetoe (*Cortaderia richardii*). Tradition records that a daughter of Kupe found a white-skinned boulder high up the bank of the Arahura River close to a toetoe that was flowering at the time. The name commemorates the first discovery of a white-skinned pounamu boulder. Many boulders are completely white on the exterior and are called a 'kahotea'. Once sawn open, their true variety is revealed, hence there is some confusion with this name.

KŌKOPU

This is a variety of pounamu not originally recorded – the term seems to be of recent origin. Kōkopu is the Māori name for the adult of three species of native freshwater fish of the Galaxidae family. They occur New Zealand-wide in creeks and rivers and are of dark brown, olive green and

yellowish colourings. Nephrite with similar colour and markings, or with brown spots, is referred to as kōkopu or trout stone.

PĪPĪWHARAUROA

This variety – given by only one authority – takes its name from the shining cuckoo, whose green and white plumage matches the colour and markings of the stone.

RAUKARAKA

Raukaraka is a term for the kawakawa variety that is olive green. The name is used by Māori from the area known as Te Tauihu o te Waka a Māui, which includes Motueka, Nelson, Blenheim and the Marlborough Sounds. Raukaraka literally means the leaf of the karaka tree (*Corynocarpus laevigatus*). It may be descriptive of the leaf but, nonetheless, the origin of the name is uncertain.

TOTOWEKA

Totoweka is given as a green nephrite of the kawakawa variety, with small reddish spots and streaks. Recorded by only one authority, it is quite rare in the Westland field, but more common in the South Westland field. The reddish inclusions were likened to the blood (toto) of the weka (a native bush hen). Any traditional stories associated with the name are unknown.

No name has been preserved for the yellow-brown to yellowish-grey and reddish-brown varieties that have been found as artefacts in some Canterbury Māori sites, and to classify these under either totoweka or raukaraka would be misleading. Some specimens approach a definite rich, even yellow and others are quite patchy in colour.

Many other terms were used for describing the general appearance of pounamu, including tūāpaka, which is generally applied to any variety that is inferior in quality, and possibly to some heated nephrite.

These are the main recorded Māori varieties, and are only broad classifications. Māori had a complex naming ritual for individual boulders that was spiritual in origin and based on tribal tikanga (custom). The Māori mind moves easily between the physical and spiritual worlds, which created difficulties for many early European recorders. Local names must have existed especially for stone with mixed or unique colours and markings, but these details appear to be by and large lost.

It is good to see that, nowadays, people are increasingly using the Māori terms for the different kinds of pounamu.

TERMINOLOGY

Jade: A group term referring to the two different rocks, nephrite and jadeite

Greenstone: A word declining in general use in New Zealand which applies mainly to nephrite but also bowenite

New Zealand jade: This refers to nephrite

Semi-nephrite: A transition rock containing some nephrite

Pounamu: A Māori term used mainly for nephrite, but also for bowenite and, in some cases, for other species of the serpentine family

Bowenite/tangiwai: A variety of serpentine and therefore not jade

01 / Portion of a rare orange chatoyant pounamu Māori chisel. Canterbury Museum.

02 / 'Flower jade' in dark kawakawa variety. Marsden, Westland.

03 / Cloud-like mottled jade. Arahura River, Westland.

04 / Multi-coloured jade with the white skin of the kahotea variety. Arahura River, Westland.

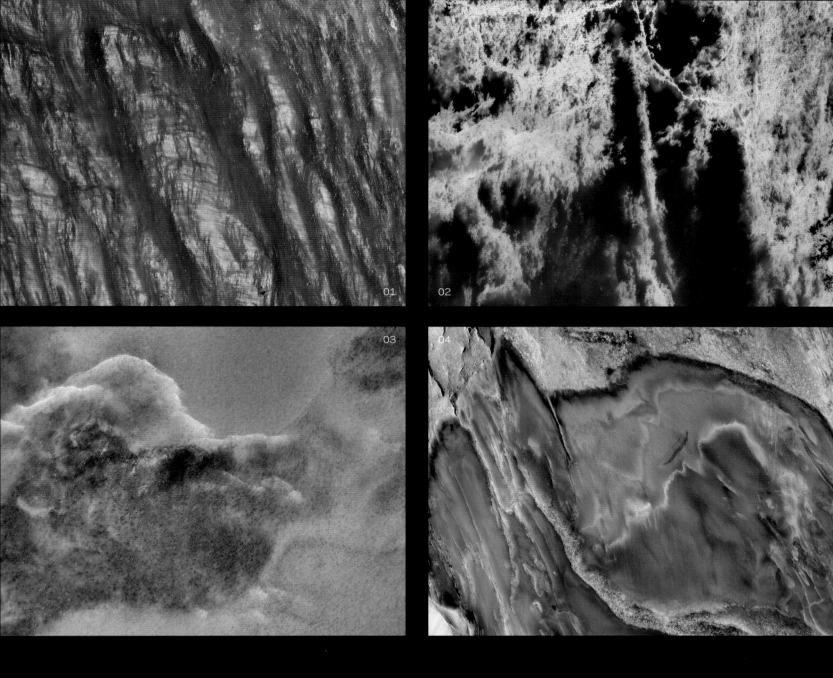

01

02

03

04

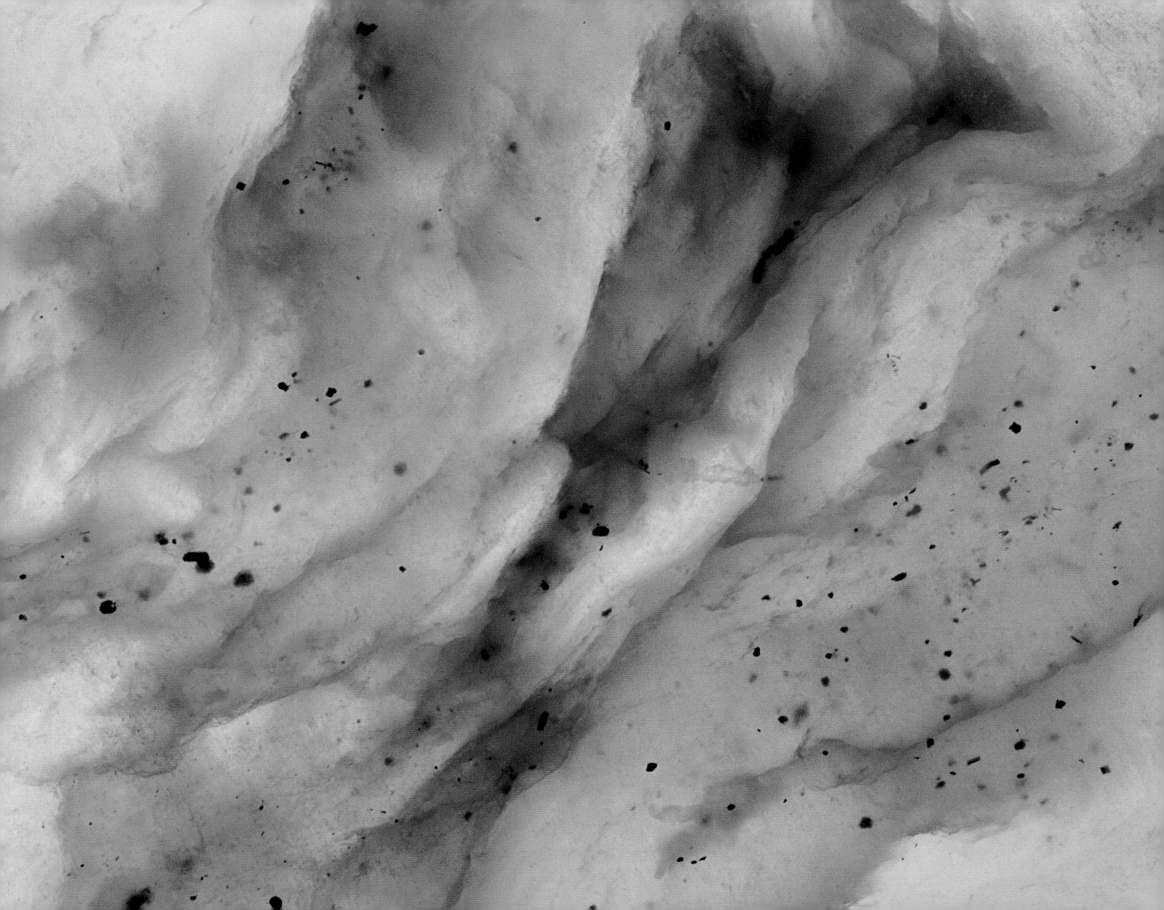

CHAPTER TWO/
NEPHRITE – THE WONDER STONE

HE POUNAMU
MANA MOTUHAKE

One stone, so precious and unique

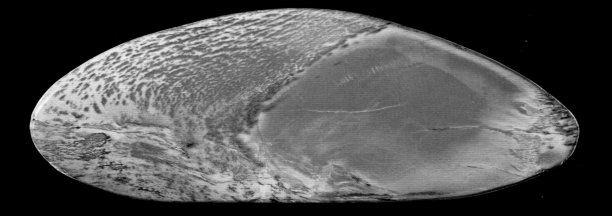

To gain an understanding of what makes nephrite so special, we must leap backwards in time to the earliest humans who made the turning-point discovery of using broken fragments of stones as tools. Beginning with brittle rocks such as obsidian or flint, they learned that these were easily flaked into implements with razor-sharp edges. The downside was that they kept on flaking when they were being used, either breaking or becoming blunt. Thousands of years later, more durable rock types were located and ground and sharpened to gain the most efficient cutting edges without flaking away. Although these took much longer to shape, they worked so much better and lasted longer.

The search was on to find the toughest rocks. The ideal stone should be hard, but not too hard, so that it could be ground to shape with quartz sandstone; as tough as possible so as not to break easily and keep a fine edge; and as heavy as possible for better kinetic energy values, or striking power, when wielded. Finding a stone with all these qualities is a tall order. The rocks dolerite and jadeite are reasonable choices; but

nephrite far exceeds them, meeting all of these conditions and more. The bonus features of nephrite are qualities such as translucency and colourful appearance, as well as tactile properties – in a nutshell, nephrite performs as well as metal and it looks attractive, too. A culture that had access to nephrite had huge advantages over others, especially in the speed of their technical development.

The use of nephrite spans at least 8000 years, and many cultures, including Māori, still valued its ornamental and spiritual qualities even after they began using metal for tools and weapons.

THE INHERENT QUALITIES OF NEPHRITE

TOUGHNESS

Nephrite belongs to the tremolite-ferroactinolite series of the amphibole group of minerals. It is a calcium magnesium silicate with varying small amounts of iron. Tremolite, named after the Tremola Valley in Switzerland, is a mineral that has a distinct habit of forming fan-like fibres radiating

from a point. When changed by heat, pressure and movement, these microscopic fibres become tangled among each other and form a dense interwoven matted texture, reinforced by the fibres. This is known as a nephritic or felted texture, and is what gives the stone its unique toughness or durability. It is frequently quoted as the toughest natural material. Toughness is sometimes a difficult property to visualise, and because nephrite was used for tools it is often referred to as being very hard but this is not correct. Glass is reasonably hard but very brittle; dense rubber is soft but extremely tough. Although it is one of the toughest natural materials, nephrite is only about mid range at 6–6.5 on the Mohs scale of hardness (see Chapter Nine) – harder than knife steel but softer than quartz.

Research on the toughness of nephrite has shown it can withstand forces of nearly 8 tonnes per cm² before fracturing. When you consider that a small nephrite boulder could theoretically withstand several thousand tonnes, you can begin to imagine just how valuable this material was to a stone-based culture. Its hardness was such that it could be ground to shape by other common rocks yet, as a tool, it performed as well as metal.

I put this to the test by duplicating modern metal tools in jade. A carpenter's spokeshave with a nephrite blade worked as well as one made of metal. Likewise, a carved replica of a twist drill bored holes in wood and aluminium effortlessly. A nephrite cold chisel sheared a 1-mm steel plate and even opened the end of an oil drum. Taking the test of toughness to the extreme, I fashioned nephrite nails which I then drove with a hammer into timber, and they certainly did not bend. With some lubrication, nephrite serves well as a bearing for steel shafting; and under certain conditions, it has a degree of flexibility. This is another property that is not found in most rocks (see page 149).

COLOUR AND TRANSLUCENCY

The general appearance of nephrite is dependent on the effects of light. Colour and translucency go hand in hand, each complementing the other. Nephrite can be every shade of green, as well as black, white, grey, blue, brown, orange and yellow. These colours, which can be measured by degrees of translucency from high to opaque, give life to the stone by allowing light to penetrate, reflect and glow, creating a waxy lustre. In addition, nephrite has an unlimited variation in markings, each contributing to the unique appearance – no two stones are the same.

SENSUAL QUALITIES

To gain the full appreciation of nephrite it must be handled, not just looked at. It has a pleasing, cool, slightly soapy feel that warms to the touch. This was deeply appreciated by Māori and they, like the Chinese and other cultures, fashioned their jade to enhance this attribute. Contemporary tactile pocket carvings make great 'worry stones', constantly fondled by their owners. In contrast, a mirror-like polish and fragile design will destroy the opportunity to appreciate this quality.

LEFT / Like the Southern Alps with a descending glacier is this sawn section of nephrite from Marsden, Westland.

Supporting the sense of feel is the inherent weight of nephrite. It is not as heavy as iron and bronze, but weighs more than most rocks, and has a density three times that of water in equal volume.

SOUND

The audio quality of nephrite has been appreciated for a long time, especially by the Chinese, who used it to make gongs and windchimes. Although no Māori artefacts are known to have been specifically designed for their ringing property, Māori were well aware of this attribute. A large pounamu slab was used as a gong in the pā of Kiwi Tamaki on Maungakiekie (One Tree Hill) in Auckland; and ear pendants were sometimes worn in a bunch so that they made a sound to attract attention. If you handle a large nephrite slab or, in particular, a group of long pendants, you are immediately aware of their pleasant metallic tinkling sound. The ringing ability is dependent on the quality of the stone and the shape of the item, so objects that are specifically designed to ring, and suitably suspended, can hold a note for a remarkably long time.

NOT JUST A PRETTY STONE!

You might ask why Māori, who possessed a stone with such attributes, would abandon it for European metal tools – especially as the metal available at that time was not very high quality. Perhaps the advantages of ease of manufacture, greater mass, the malleability of metal and, above all, the new technical designs such as toothed saws, twist drills and axes were the reasons pounamu was replaced. But it is still held in high esteem today.

Clearly, since its discovery, nephrite has provided an important link in the evolution of technology – bridging the stone age and the age of metal, while providing a durable medium with which humans may express their presence to this day.

CHAPTER THREE/A NEW LAND WITH THE GIFT OF POUNAMU

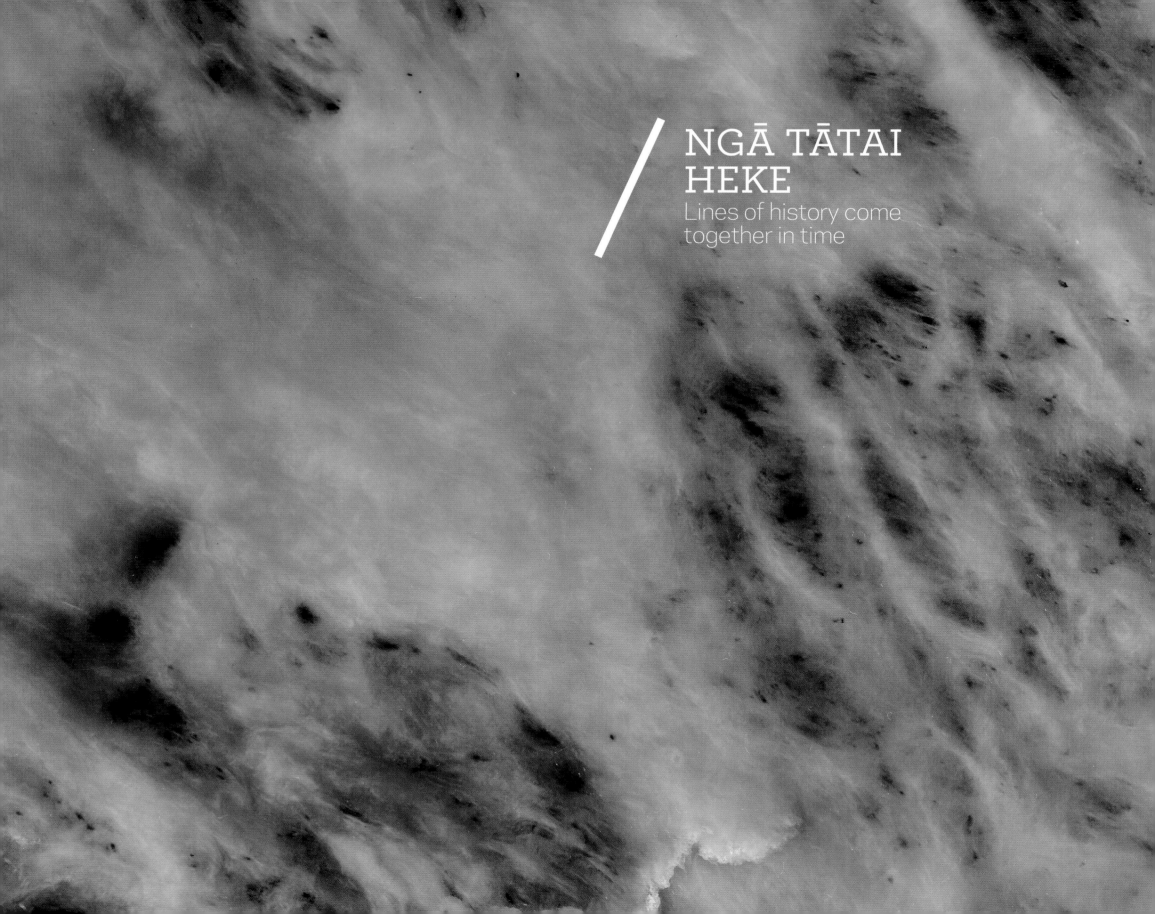

NGĀ TĀTAI HEKE

Lines of history come together in time

The New Zealand we know today is but a remnant of a much larger continental land mass referred to as Zealandia. Geological processes over many millions of years have produced a huge variety of rock types that were sometimes under water, caught up in mountain building, extruded from violent volcanoes, buried in ice and exposed to extreme climates.

During this whole process no human foot trod on this raft of unique flora and fauna. Indeed there were no land mammals at all until Polynesians arrived, probably around AD 1300, making it the last major habitable landmass to be populated.

Māori traditions tell of voyages of discovery and intentional migrations of settlement to New Zealand. The Polynesian people, believed to be of Southeast Asian origin, were natural wanderers who, by skilful navigation, migrated to and populated most islands of the Pacific. Permanent societies developed on these islands, each with its distinctive local culture, but the adventurous spirit remained. Many factors, including the passing of migratory birds and whales, population pressure on small islands, favourable climatic windows and the sheer excitement of exploration and discovery must have provided incentives for these Polynesian voyagers, who undertook well equipped expeditions, just as the Europeans did with their voyages of discovery several hundred years later.

The three main islands of New Zealand have been given several names connected with the great creation stories and myths, as well as names relating to the early settlement phase. The early naming of New Zealand relates to Māui, an early explorer, and shows that the shape of the country was already well understood. Māui's canoe was envisaged to be the South Island and his anchor, Stewart Island; the North Island was a fish he caught from his canoe. The general Māori name for New Zealand is now Aotearoa – loosely translated as 'Land of the Long White Cloud'.

The South Island is called Te Waipounamu, 'The Waters of Pounamu'; and Stewart Island is Rakiura, 'Land of Glowing Skies'.

These early Polynesian settlers found themselves in a world quite different from their tropical Polynesian homeland, but they soon adapted to the new environment. The opportunity to live by hunting seals and the plentiful moa (a now extinct giant flightless bird), especially in the South Island, enabled a rapid exploration of the land. They soon found types of stone that were suitable for tools. Toolmaking workshops were established in both the North and the South islands, where obsidian, silcrete, basalt, argillite and other brittle stones were fashioned into butchering knives and adzes for canoe building and general woodworking.

Recent archaeological evidence seems to show that pounamu was discovered not long after the first Polynesian settlers arrived; and several of these early sites contain pounamu artefacts with very weathered surfaces – a process that happens with aging. These examples are typical of pounamu from the main sources, which indicates that the stone was soon recognised for its properties and that the country was extensively explored in a relatively short time. The utilisation of pounamu was well established by the 1500s; and after that it accelerated and many new forms evolved.

The climate in the North Island and the northern half of the South Island was suitable for growing kūmara and other plants introduced from tropical Polynesia, and gradually a sedentary society emerged, based largely on fishing, birding and food cultivation. This later society, often referred to as the Classic Māori, became highly cultured and developed a unique art heritage. Pounamu fuelled this development, and as its use became widespread throughout the country, its far-reaching cultural significance deepened. With the accumulation of desirable resources, including

land, warfare developed between tribes, and by the time Captain Cook arrived in 1769, inter-tribal fighting was a prominent occupation. Their skill in warfare was demonstrated later when European settlement of several parts of the North Island met with long periods of resistance from Māori.

Because of the colder climate in the south of the South Island, nomadic tendencies prevailed there and the inhabitants preserved much of the early culture, specialising in stone toolmaking. Pounamu and other types of stone were manufactured into implements and traded and exchanged with the northern people for their prized possessions, such as finely woven garments and specialty food not available in the south.

The arrival of early European sealers in the far south in the 1790s launched the period of exploitation of New Zealand's resources that later led to permanent settlement and colonisation. Here, and in other parts of the country where mutual respect for each other prevailed, both Māori and Europeans integrated relatively smoothly. During these years Māori were quick to take advantage of the new European technology, and although it dismantled their stone-based culture and changed their way of life dramatically they survived colonisation better than most indigenous people at that time. Much of their history was recorded, but, likewise, much was lost.

The Chatham Islands, which lie some 860 km east of Banks Peninsula, are also part of New Zealand. They were inhabited by Polynesians known as Moriori, distant cousins of early Māori, who arrived on the Islands at a very early date probably via New Zealand. There they remained isolated from the rest of the world and unknown to Māori in New Zealand until after 1791, when Europeans discovered the Islands. A few pounamu artefacts have been found on the Chathams, but they were most likely taken there by New Zealand Māori who invaded the Islands in 1835 and settled.

PREVIOUS PAGE / The surreal Westland rainforest cloaked in fog.

LEFT / Totoweka variety of pounamu from Big Bay, South Westland.

FOLLOWING PAGE LEFT / A dramatic sunset in Milford Sound/Piopiotahi. The West Coast is famous for its sunsets, often enhanced by dust particles from bush fires in Australia.

FOLLOWING PAGE RIGHT / Jade can have dramatic features hidden within the stone only revealed by light, such as this example from South Westland.

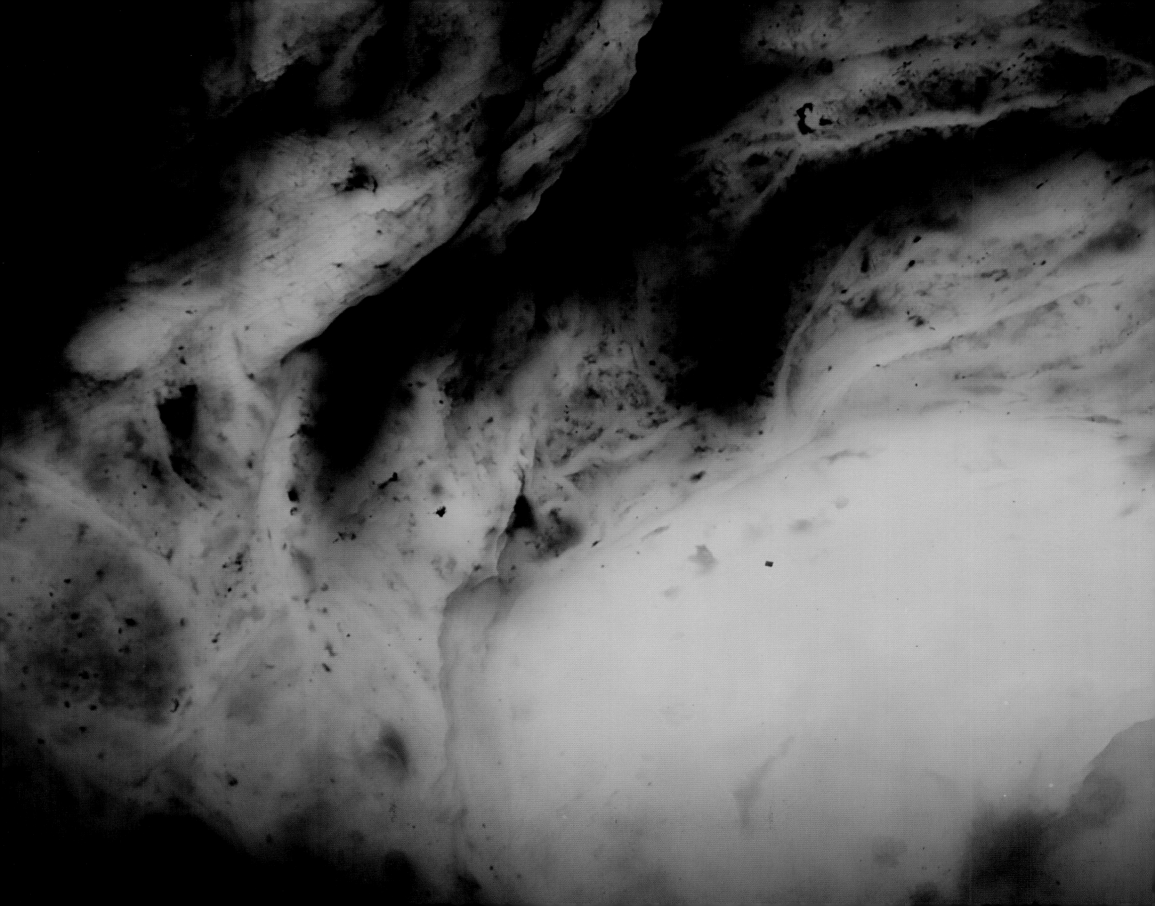

TANGIWAI – THE STONE OF TEARS

HE ROIMATA
TŪTURU

My sorrow has been
left in the stone

Tangiwai is a clear or translucent variety of one of the three serpentine minerals. Although tangiwai comes within the term pounamu, it is not jade, but is an important component in the story of pounamu. Māori were well aware of the difference and limitations of tangiwai and appreciated it mainly for its appearance. Early Europeans were amazed by its translucency – in some cases it is sufficiently transparent to read newsprint through. Worldwide, bowenite is not a plentiful mineral but does occur in other countries, especially China. From the specimens I have seen of bowenite from elsewhere in the world, they do not approach the degree of transparency achieved by the Milford Sound stone.

Māori probably discovered the existence of bowenite in the Milford Sound/Piopiotahi area at about the same time as they discovered nephrite. They made frequent canoe expeditions to obtain the stone at Anita Bay/Hupokeka over a long period of time, and there are some colourful stories on the origin of this beautiful stone. As noted earlier, the Māori translation of tangiwai is tear-water and the traditional stories speak of the petrification of the tears of mythical characters weeping for their lost loved ones.

It is my belief that the Milford tangiwai was an important early source of pounamu because of its inherent qualities: it is beautiful, it is easily split into a ripi (knife blade), and the resource can be readily accessed by canoe. There are many tangiwai ripi and adornments depicting early designs which are wholly or partly oxidised white – a process produced by ageing. In the later Classic Māori period, tangiwai appears to have been used almost exclusively for adornment, and some stunning examples such as long slender pendants were produced.

The resource was exploited by Europeans from the early 1840s, trading the stone to the North Island and further afield. Many people visited Anita Bay in search of bowenite, spurred on by their belief in the existence of a Māori quarry covered by a slip. William Bertram, a miner who had spent some time searching the area, announced in 1906 that he had found the original tangiwai deposit by mining through an old landslip. He formed the Milford Sound Greenstone Co. Ltd, and extracted the stone for his and other lapidary works in Dunedin; and he even sent samples to Germany – but the venture failed two years later. There were other announcements of mining ventures over the years, but none eventuated. Murray Gunn, a former resident of the Hollyford Valley, Fiordland, collected bowenite from his beach claim at Poison Bay for many years, until a slip covered the beach. He relinquished his claim about 1996. He recalls that fishermen would take him to and from the mine site, but on one occasion they forgot to pick him up and he was marooned on this rugged piece of isolated coastline for eleven days.

Milford bowenite occurs as small lenses contained in a narrow band of ultramafic rocks, the Anita Ultramafites, which extends southwest from Anita Bay to beyond Poison Bay (see map 03). Continuation of these rocks on the northern side of Milford Sound/Piopiotahi has been mapped as isolated pods. Bowenite occurs at the eastern end of Anita Bay and at Poison Bay, south of Milford. At Anita Bay, the reserves are now mainly confined to beach pebbles, although larger boulders have occasionally been found. Poison Bay is an inaccessible, deep bay, really a short fiord, facing the turbulent Tasman Sea some 14 km south of Milford Sound. Its isolation has protected its reserves of bowenite. The stone is found outcropping in a steep bank on the southern shore, but beach deposits are largely covered by debris from a slip. The Milford resource lies within the Fiordland National Park, under the control of

Department of Conservation and Ngāi Tahu.

The general appearance of Milford bowenite is schistose and occasionally fibrous, like asbestos. When these fibrous specimens are dense, a spectacular wavy chatoyancy brings the stone alive. The main colours are olive green through to dark green and occasionally a stunning bluish-green. On the whole the stone is semi-transparent, but often sprinkled with softer white inclusions; tiny pyrite crystals and numerous feather fractures dominate most stones. Polished pieces of bowenite are somewhat dark or dull and lack the rich colours of nephrite. This is counteracted by viewing the specimens against the light, which reveals tangiwai's true hidden beauty. Bowenite is a variety of antigorite serpentine and is relatively easy to distinguish from nephrite, as the values of the physical properties are lower; these are listed in the section on the identification of nephrite substitutes, pages 189–91.

Māori record a traditional source for tangiwai north of Milford Sound. Similarly, bowenite and serpentinite specimens found well north of Milford Sound may have been transported there by movement along the Alpine Fault. A bluish-green bowenite occurs as narrow veins in peridotite high on Red Mountain and in several rivers of South Westland.

Bowenite is also found on the Griffin Range, in the Arahura River in Westland, and the Cobb Valley in Nelson. The Westland bowenite ranges from very dark green to an olive shade with numerous black flecks and pyrite crystals; but although it is reasonably translucent it does not approach the clarity of the Milford stone.

Although tangiwai is not jade, such an attractive stone deserves more recognition, and under its own New Zealand name – tangiwai.

This traditional story was collected by Herries Beattie from members of an early southern subtribe.

PAGE 034/035 / Remote Lake Ronald, perched high in the hills between Anita Bay and Poison Bay, southwest of Milford Sound/ Piopiotahi. The rust-coloured ultramafic rocks are the host rocks for tangiwai.

PREVIOUS PAGE LEFT / Glass-like beach pebbles of tangiwai from Anita Bay, at the entrance to Milford Sound/Piopiotahi. The largest piece is 75 mm long.

PREVIOUS PAGE RIGHT / Polished fragment of tangiwai from Anita Bay, showing the easily split schistose structure.

RIGHT / Broken fragment of translucent tangiwai from Poison Bay. R. BECK

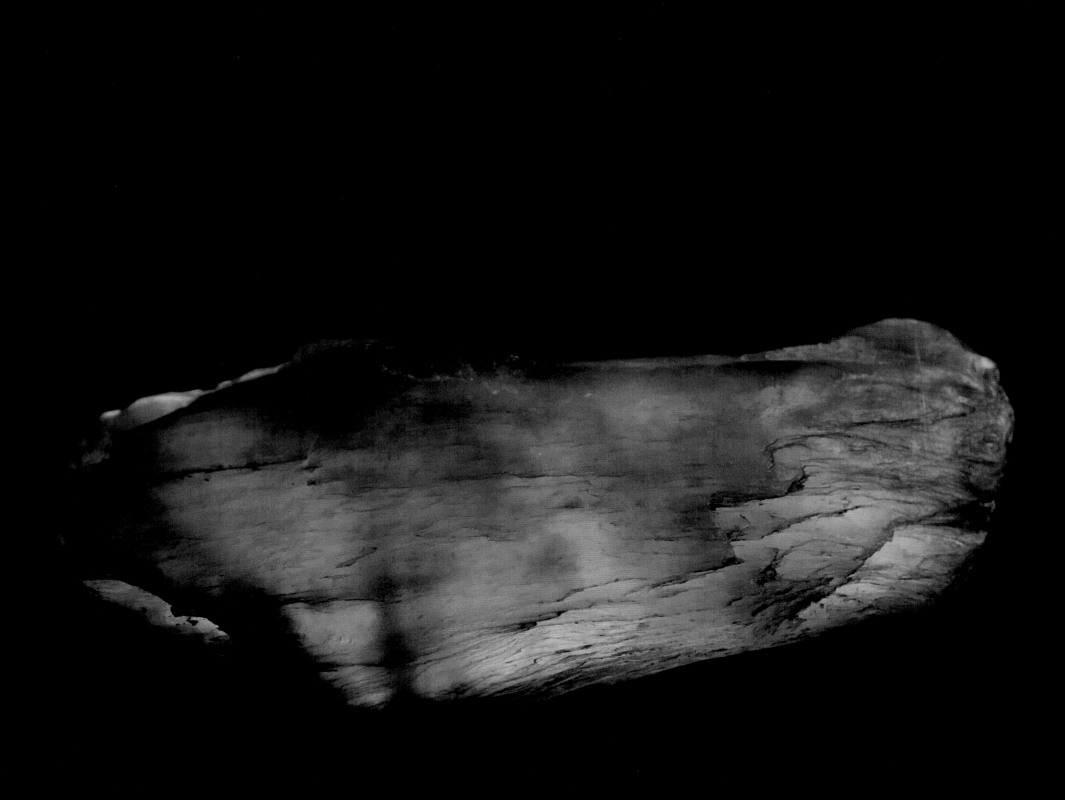

Milford Sound/Piopiotahi with the iconic Mitre Peak in the early morning light. The sound was carved out by ancient glaciers and is embodied in Māori legend in respect to tangiwai.

RIGHT INSET / Two long, elegant Māori ear pendants made from tangiwai, 01 / location unknown 02 / Greenhills, Southland. Canterbury Museum and Southland Museum and Art Gallery.

01   02

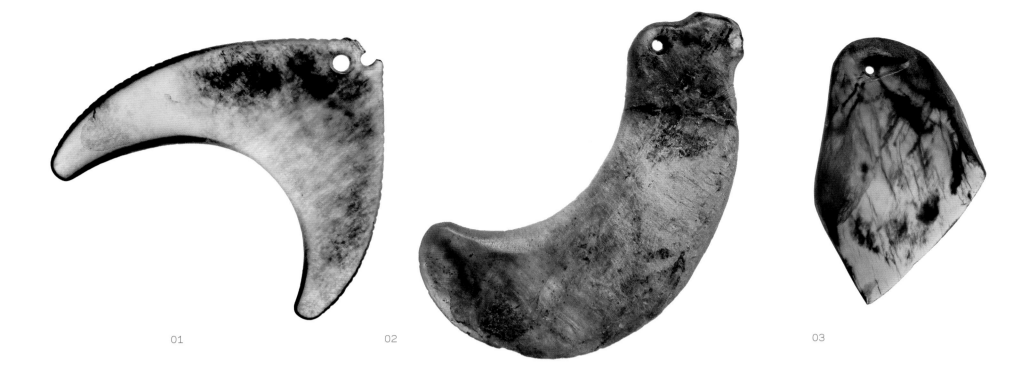

01   02   03

LEFT / Like in the depths of the ocean, this is a rare example of blue tangiwai from Anita Bay.

ABOVE 01 / A fish-like amulet from Ruapuke Island, Foveaux Strait. 02 / Pendant resembling a stylised whale tooth. The surface has signs of oxidisation, which suggests it is very old. 03 / A ripi or knife. A scarf has been made to enable easier drilling of the hole. Otago Museum.

These early people went to the sounds [Fiordland] and found a huge piece of pounamu in the sea, and set out to drive it round to Bluff. Three canoes followed it, one on each side, and one behind, and yet it nearly eluded them several times. They nearly got it ashore at Oraka [Colac Bay, 18 km west of Riverton], but it dodged on until it settled where it is, and it now forms Motupiu [Dog Island near Bluff]. His informant added that if you go down into its interior you would find it hollow inside and standing on three legs.

Māori, without a written language, narrated their histories and traditions through the generations by way of telling traditional stories called pūrākau. These creation and discovery stories of pounamu are colourful, with several variations. They provide an insight into the intimate knowledge Māori had of geology and the landscape.

The stories narrated to Captain Cook and other early explorers of how and where pounamu was found relate to it being a fish. It is said that when the fish is taken from the water it is so vexed that it turns into stone. Another version states that pounamu is found in the stomach of a large, shark-like fish; when the stone is first taken from the stomach it is soft, but it becomes hard on exposure.

Stories and myths centred around the fish perhaps arise on account of the colour of pounamu being green and found initially in rivers and coastal waters. The connection between the fish theme and pounamu is best explained by Māori whakapapa (genealogy). All things in the natural world of Māori have a genealogy that descends from Rangi, the Sky Father, and Papa, the Earth Mother. Pounamu is one of four descendant children regarded as a special kind of fish, their parents being Tangaroa (God of Fish) and Te Anu-mato (Chilly Cold).

THE STORY OF POUTINI AND POUNAMU
AS TOLD BY MAIKA MASON

To our Ngāi Tahu people, the great mountains of Te Wai Pounamu inspire not only fear and respect but also love and affection for the atua embodied in them. To us they are the physical presence of these beloved atua. When we look at them we hear in our minds the treasured stories handed down through the many generations of our people who have kept our fires burning on these lands.

From our homes at Arahura, we look at four such mountains that remind us of the long-standing rituals of these ancient lands. To the south stands Aoraki. He is the tapu son of Rakinui and Te Poharua o Te Pō, and rises supremely above all the other mountains of Ngāi Tahu. This most sacred ancestor glistens in the evening light like the pounamu that lies deep in the womb of this land. He stands before us, a link to time immemorial; we see him and know we are alive.

To the east, emerging with the first glimmer of the light of a new day, stand Tamaahua, Tūhua and Tumuaki. These are the mountains associated with the stories of creation of our taonga – pounamu, a treasure of great spiritual and economic value to our people, Ngāti Waewae, the hapū given the calling Poutini Ngāi Tahu. We take our name from the taniwha Poutini who first brought Waitaiki, the mother of pounamu, to our lands and waters. Our relationship to this guardian taniwha is an essential part of the identity, mauri and mana of our West Coast people.

I turn now to the story of Poutini, the kaitiaki or guardian of the mauri within the stone we call toka pounamu. Poutini is closely related to Takaroa, the atua of the ocean. The final resting place of pounamu is in the sea. Poutini is a taniwha, a giant water creature who in ancient times was a guardian for Ngāhue, the atua of the pounamu.

The only being Poutini feared was another taniwha named Whātipu, the protector of Hine Hōaka, the atua of the grinding sandstones our old people used to cut and saw the tough pounamu. Poutini and Whātipu alternatively pursued or avoided one another across the great ocean of Kiwa and around the bays and coastal waters of Aotearoa, the northern island. Poutini loved to cruise in the warm sparkling waters of Te Moana ā Toi te Huatahi (Bay of Plenty) between Tūhua (Mayor Island) and Whakaari (White Island). Being constantly pursued by Whātipu was tiring, and one evening he took refuge in the corner of a sheltered bay of Tūhua and rested. In the early morning, lying quietly in the still waters, Poutini watched a young woman come down to the water's edge to bathe. Her name was Waitaiki. As she removed her clothes, Poutini glimpsed her beautiful body and lusted for her. Overwhelmed by desire and forgetting his enemy Whātipu, he quickly and silently glided through the water, snatched Waitaiki without a sound and fled towards the mainland.

Back on Tūhua, Waitaiki's husband Tamaahua called for his wife to fetch his morning drink but there was no answer. He sent his slave Tumuaki to look for her but he could not find her. So Tamaahua started to look for her himself. He found her clothes on the beach and immediately realised that something had happened to her. As he was a powerful chief, skilled in the ritual of the spirit world, he sought by using his powers of karakia to discover her whereabouts. At his tūāhu, place of ritual, he hurled a tekateka, dart, into the air; it hung there quivering like his own rage and pointed in the direction Poutini had taken. Tamaahua and his slave leapt into his waka and paddled furiously in pursuit.

Meanwhile, Poutini had stopped to rest at Tāhanga, on the Coromandel Peninsula, and lit a big fire to warm Waitaiki. Hearing the approach of Tamaahua, he grabbed the woman and fled across the waters to Kaituna and up through the waterways of the Rotorua lake district to Whangamatā on the shores of Lake Taupō. There he lit another, much smaller, fire.

Tamaahua reached Tāhanga and discovered the blackened earth and cold ashes of Poutini's fire. Again he hurled his tekateka into the sky to divine the direction of his quarry. He resumed his pursuit and eventually arrived at Whangamatā, to find the remains of another fire.

Poutini had by then left and was fleeing down the Whanganui River. He continued to move downstream, out into Te Tai Hau-ā-Uru (the tides of the West Coast of Aotearoa) and across Te Moana o Raukawa (Cook Strait) to Onetahua (Farewell Spit) where he lit a large fire to warm the captive Waitaiki. He rested there because he knew Tamaahua was far behind and, perhaps, might give up the chase. Next he travelled to Whāngāmoa and thence to Rangitoto ki te Tonga (D'Urville Island) where he lit another fire and rested again.

In each place all that the now furious Tamaahua found were the cold ashes.

Poutini became aware that Tamaahua was closing in and turned down into the tides of the West Coast. He stopped first at Pāhautāne and hid for a while in a cave as heavy rain was falling and he felt the need to light another fire. At all of the places he stopped and lit his fires he blackened the earth. These places are the ancient stone quarries of our people. At Tāhanga they quarried the basalt and at Tūhua the grey obsidian. Whangamatā is the place of matā, black obsidian, and Whāngāmoa and Rakitoto-ki-te-Toka is where they quarried pakohe, the beautiful grey argillite.

Finally the weather cleared and he moved south to Piopiotahi (Milford Sound). There Waitaiki asked him to stop as she was becoming increasingly cold in the numbing waters of the great southern ocean of Te Moana Tāpokopoko a Tāwhaki. She begged him to turn back and wept, and wept, and wept. Her tears are still found today in tangiwai, the stone of that place. Reluctantly, Poutini turned back until he reached the Arahura River. Up the river he went, seeking a place to hide.

While crossing the Arahura, Tamaahua noticed that its waters were noticeably warmer than the other rivers he had come across, but he was in too much of a hurry to stop and check why. His tekateka was calling him southwards. On he paddled to Piopiotahi, his paddles flashing like lightning. When he got there the tekateka hovered in the sky and pointed back along the route he had just taken. At that instant he knew that the warmth he had felt was that of his wife Waitaiki. Tamaahua was furious with himself. Once he reached the Arahura he could still feel the lingering warmth of its waters. He knew his beloved wife was in distress up the river but the light was fading and he bade his slave to prepare food. Tumuaki spoilt the food, a single kōkā, and the angry Tamaahua kicked it and the remains of the fire into the river. They remain there to his day, embedded in the stone we call tūtaekōkā.

After this incident, Tamaahua said to his slave, 'Tonight I will sleep alone and dream of my beautiful wife. Her spirit will come to me and early tomorrow morning I will find my iti kahurangi'.

He rose before dawn and prepared for battle with the trapped taniwha. As the mist was lifting from the valley he stretched his hand into the water, but it felt strangely cold.

Poutini knew that he was confronted by a powerful atua who would surely kill him. With little chance of escape with this beautiful captive, Poutini decided that if he could not have her, neither would anyone else. He transformed her into his own likeness and essence – pounamu – and laid her in the bed of the river near the stream that today bears her name. Then he slipped quietly away, past the sleeping Tamaahua.

Tamaahua found his beautiful young wife lying in her eternal resting place, all grey and green and smooth – īnanga, kahurangi, kawakawa, auhunga, kahotea and so on, which are all names for different kinds of greenstone. His long and painful takiaue for her resounded throughout the mountains. Our old people say that you can hear it even today, if you are in harmony with the ebb and flow of Te Ao Māori, the natural world.

When his takiaue was over he looked around and named two of the mountains that overlooked the river. One he named Tūhua, so Waitaiki and those who followed would forever remember from whence she had come. The other he named after himself so she would not feel lonely and would always have her husband nearby. His slave Tumuaki he turned into a third mountain for breaking the tapu with the preparation of his food. Tumuaki remains a reminder of the importance of rituals to our people. Tamaahua returned to his northern home and is known in the traditions of several northern tribes.

Poutini is destined to swim up and down the waters of the West Coast as the kaitiaki of the land, the people and the sacred stone. These waters are known as Te Tai o Poutini and their moods are likened to those of the taniwha, sometimes at peace, sometimes stormy.

The high peaks of the Southern Alps catching the last of the sun before it sets into the Tasman Sea. Mt Tasman and Aoraki/Mt Cook in centre.

LEGEND OF LAKE WAKATIPU

A fearsome giant Matau once lived in the mountains of the interior of the southern South Island. He was so large that he could step from one mountain to the next. This monster troubled the people of the coast by carrying their maidens off to his mountain home. Once he carried off a great chief's daughter, Manata, who was about to be married to a young warrior, Matakauri. This young man went in search of his betrothed and found her tied by a thong made of the skin of a two-headed dog to the ogre, who was fast asleep on the ground. He tried to cut the thong but nothing could sever it. To escape together was therefore impossible and Manata, with tears in her eyes, begged her lover to leave her because if the monster awoke he would be killed. He refused and Manata cried on until her tears fell upon the thong at her waist. Surprisingly the tears dissolved the thong that not even the sharpest pounamu would cut. The couple fled together and the monster awoke in a raging temper and was just about to chase them when the east wind sprang up and took away his strength. He fell upon the land, asleep.

Manata and Matakauri returned home and asked the tohunga to marry them, but he refused. Instead he told Matakauri to go and pile up wood around the sleeping giant and set fire to it to burn him up before

The mid section of Lake Wakatipu at the end of a clear winter's day with the lights of Queenstown like stars upon the land.

CHAPTER FOUR/WĀHI POUNAMU — PLACES WHERE JADE IS FOUND

NGĀ TAMARIKI
O WAITAIKI

From the pounamu source
comes many treasures

The widespread distribution of Māori artefacts found from the top of the North Island to Stewart Island is testimony to the high value placed on pounamu, for the sources of the stone are confined to a few specific areas of the South Island (see map 01).

The districts surrounding the Taramakau and Arahura rivers in Westland, coastal South Westland and the Lake Wakatipu area in Otago provided Māori with their principal deposits of pounamu. Several other minor deposits also exist, some of which have been found in recent years, and there are undoubtedly more yet to be discovered.

It never ceases to intrigue me that all the world jade sources I have visited are invariably situated in spectacular environments. Little wonder, as the same tectonic forces necessary to create mountains are responsible for the creation of nephrite. New Zealand is no exception – pounamu deposits are set in some of the most scenic parts of the country.

WESTLAND – TE TAI POUTINI

The rivers between Hokitika and Greymouth were the main pounamu collection grounds for Māori, and are still important sources. The region is known as the Westland – or sometimes the North Westland – jade field. The origin of the jade lies in the foothills of the western slopes of the Southern Alps, within a discontinuous belt of rocks which extends approximately 80 km south from Jacksons (on the Taramakau River) to the Cropp River, with an isolated extension further south in the Waitaha River watershed. These rocks were suitably named in 1906 by the geologists James Bell and Colin Fraser as the Pounamu Formation. This has since been renamed the Pounamu Ultramafics, which are within a wider zone of associated rocks defined as the Pounamu Ultramafic Belt (see map 02).

Contained in this belt are parallel lenses, or pods, of ultramafic rocks, up to 100 m in width and 4 km in length. (Ultramafic rocks are of igneous origin and are rich in iron and magnesium silicates.) Numerous streams and rivers, assisted by erosion and past glaciers, have cut into or completely eroded these nephrite-bearing lenses, freeing the tough jade and distributing it through the gravels over a large area to the west. The subsequent harsh action of the rivers over a long period of time has tumbled the jade, giving it the characteristic water-worn or polished surface, and at the same time producing concentrations of pounamu, as well as gold. Hence almost every river and stream west of the source rocks, and as far north as Greymouth, potentially contains alluvial nephrite. Many fine specimens are also found in unexpected localities as well as on sea beaches from Hokitika to as far north as Punakaiki, transported there by the northerly flow of the Westland current.

Westland nephrite deposits can be grouped into four general regions: Arahura, Taramakau, Marsden and Hokitika districts. Jade from each of these regions can have visually distinguishable characteristics, and some experienced prospectors are able to localise specimens quite accurately.

Charles Heaphy was the first European to record the occurrence of jade in 1846 in Westland when he and Thomas Brunner and a dog were guided by Kehu and other Māori from Nelson to the Taramakau River. At the mouth of this river they visited a Māori settlement where the inhabitants were busy collecting and working pounamu. Edward Shortland, doctor and administrator, who travelled the eastern South Island, mentioned in 1851 that Māori sought pounamu from the Arahura and Hōhonu rivers. And as early as 1864 the German geologist Professor Ferdinand von Hochstetter published a very detailed paper on the chemistry and other

physical properties of Westland nephrite – the first scientific study of New Zealand jade.

Many alluvial boulders of nephrite have an oxidised brownish or grey rind covering the surface, making them very difficult to distinguish from the surrounding weathered rocks; jade prospectors the world over agree that it can be the most difficult stone for the untrained eye to detect. Māori, though, developed a skilful eye for recognising pounamu.

With the introduction of sluicing and dredging during the Westland goldrush era, vast areas of jade- and gold-bearing fluvioglacial gravels that would otherwise have remained hidden were exposed. During the early part of this period of dredging, sluicing and prospecting, miners placed relatively little value on the then plentiful jade, and in many cases the boulders were reburied as quickly as they were uncovered. All they wanted was the gold. This occurred for many reasons: the early miners' inability to recognise nephrite; an underdeveloped market for the material; the difficulties of transporting heavy boulders from the field to the few buyers; and most importantly, there was no easy method of sectioning boulders for an appraisal of quality to justify the effort. In spite of this, many tonnes were taken for both New Zealand and German lapidaries.

ARAHURA

The Arahura jade field has, in the past, supplied both Māori and European with many hundreds of tonnes of quality stone. It is still producing, but is no longer the main source for the industry. The field is principally the Arahura River and its tributaries from the sea to the source at Olderog/ Waitaiki Creek in the headwaters.

In 1997 the Crown returned ownership of all pounamu within the catchment of the Arahura River to Ngāi Tahu, who, in turn, returned it to the Mawhera Incorporation. Authority to gather

PREVIOUS PAGE / Boulder Beach near the mouth of the Spoon River, north of Big Bay, South Westland.

LEFT / The legendary Arahura River emerging from the foothills of the Southern Alps. In times of flood, the river swells to a raging torrent, stirring the gravels and exposing pounamu.

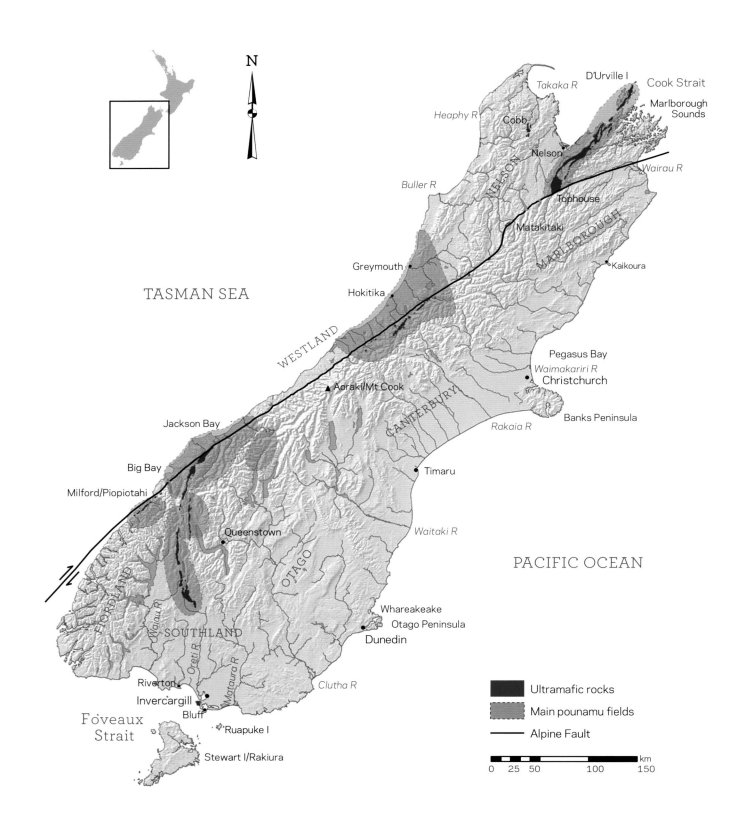

N

TASMAN SEA

Takaka R
D'Urville I
Cook Strait
Heaphy R
Cobb
Marlborough
Sounds
Nelson
NELSON
Buller R
Wairau R
Tophouse
Matakitaki
MARLBOROUGH
Greymouth
Kaikoura
Hokitika
WESTLAND
Pegasus Bay
Waimakariri R
Aoraki/Mt Cook
Christchurch
CANTERBURY
Banks Peninsula
Jackson Bay
Rakaia R
Big Bay
Timaru
Milford/Piopiotahi
Waitaki R
Queenstown
PACIFIC OCEAN
OTAGO
Waiau R
Whareakeake
FIORDLAND
Otago Peninsula
SOUTHLAND
Dunedin
Oreti R
Mataura R
Riverton
Clutha R
Invercargill
Bluff
Foveaux
Strait
Ruapuke I

Stewart I/Rakiura

Ultramafic rocks

Main pounamu fields

Alpine Fault

km
0 25 50   100   150

LEFT, MAP 01 / South Island, New Zealand, showing main pounamu fields. COURTESY GNS SCIENCE

RIGHT, MAP 02 / Westland pounamu field. COURTESY GNS SCIENCE

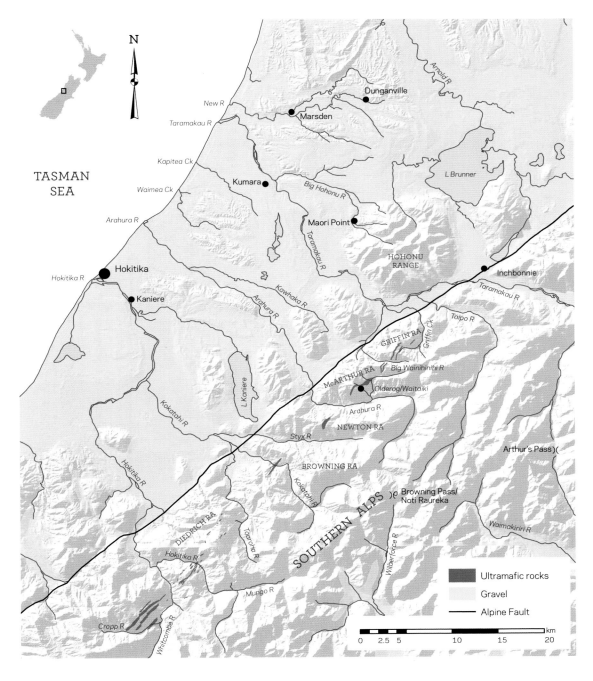

N

TASMAN
SEA

New R
Taramakau R
Marsden
Dunganville
Arnold R

Kapitea Ck
Kumara
Big Hohonu R
L Brunner

Waimea Ck

Arahura R
Maori Point
Taramakau R
HOHONU
RANGE
Inchbonnie

Hokitika R
Hokitika
Taramakau R

Kaniere
Kawhaka R

Arahura R
Taipo R

L Kaniere
GRIFFIN RA
Griffin Ck

Kokatahi R
McARTHUR RA
Big Wainihinihi R
Olderog/Waitaiki
Arahura R

NEWTON RA
Arthur's Pass

Styx R
BROWNING RA

Kokatahi R
Browning Pass/
Noti Raureka

Hokitika R
DIEDRICH RA
Toaroha R
Wilberforce R
Waimakiriri R

Hokitika R
SOUTHERN ALPS

Mungo R

Cropp R
Whitcombe R

Ultramafic rocks
Gravel
Alpine Fault

km
0   2.5   5   10   15   20

pounamu is now restricted on the Arahura riverbed to shareholders of the Incorporation or its invitees.

Arahura jade is generally quite distinctive and offers the widest selection of types and colours. Very dark greens through to the silver-green of īnanga, as well as the yellowish-brown shades of the kōkopu variety are represented. Some pieces are water-polished while others possess a greenish to almost white rind that can sometimes be quite thick. This makes it difficult to differentiate between many of the plentiful weathered serpentinite boulders. Another important contributor to the Arahura field is Kawhaka Creek. This stream joins the Arahura and is particularly noted for the fine specimens of the kōkopu variety.

ARAHURA SOURCE

During their geological survey of the Hokitika district in 1906, Bell and Fraser published in their bulletin that large boulders of good quality nephrite were found in the Olderog/Waitaiki Creek bed; but possibly because of its isolation this deposit was not exploited until half a century later. Over subsequent years several Westland people were aware of or had visited the site, including members of the Ngāti Waewae hapū (subtribe) of Ngāi Tahu, who were seeking the return of the river, including the pounamu source. In 1962 three Westland men, Murray Allan, Walter Tainui and Bernie Radomski, pegged out their mining licence area over this deposit of alluvial nephrite boulders. The publicity created much interest and sparked a rush of mining claims by several syndicates.

In January of the following year two jade prospectors, Andrew Dalziel and Alan Robins, who had been searching for some time for the source of Arahura jade, reported a find of what appeared to be an in situ occurrence high up in the bed of a tributary of Olderog/Waitaiki Creek. Because nephrite frequently originates in association with very soft, easily decomposed rocks such as serpentinite and talc, the nephrite can be exposed without any sign of the host rocks. Such was probably the case with the find in Jade Creek, as it was subsequently named. In the late 1970s Cyril Win and associates mined several tonnes of dark green jade from an in situ outcrop on a spur immediately beside the creek, and later Cliff Dalziel found nephrite in the ultramafic rocks that were exposed higher up in his licence area. Further in situ finds have since been made.

The Olderog/Waitaiki Creek deposit occupies the creek bed, reaching steeply up the slopes of the McArthur Range to an altitude of 1000 m and more in some of Westland's most difficult country. During the 1960s and '70s, commercial mining operations were very active and many tonnes of good quality stone was removed. The size of the boulders (many estimated to be 5 tonnes and at least one was 20 tonnes) and the mountainous nature of the region made transporting the boulders difficult. Portable diamond saws, core drills, crowbars, hammers and wedges were used to reduce the boulders to pieces of manageable size, which were then airlifted by helicopter to the nearest road. Explosives were no help, as they shatter the stone into myriad fractures.

In short, jade mining boils down to just plain hard work, often in wet or icy conditions. The creeks become roaring torrents when it rains, and the heavy jade boulders are either buried, with only a small portion of their true size showing, or tightly wedged under fallen trees in precarious positions. These problems presented a real challenge to the miners who, with their enthusiasm and determination, enjoyed solving them. Seldom were they beaten.

The only remaining licence in this area rests with Mawhera Incorporation, which in recent years has recovered several large boulders for 'touchstones' (see Chapter Five).

ABOVE / Barrytown/Pikiroa, north of Greymouth, where jade pebbles carried north by the ocean current can be found on the beach.
COURTESY TE RŪNANGA O NGĀI TAHU

LEFT / The Kokatahi River (centre) with its tributaries, Styx and Toaroha rivers, which reach deep into the Southern Alps. The Kokatahi intersects an ultramafic pod near its headwaters.
COURTESY TE RŪNANGA O NGĀI TAHU

Dark green and kawakawa varieties are well represented, but the locality is more noted for the paler shades of green, especially the īnanga variety. Some īnanga boulders are of truly magnificent quality – highly translucent and pale green with a definite bluish tinge. These stones are keenly sought after by carvers and command high prices. Silky chatoyant bands and streaks (the reflection of a silky band of light if correctly orientated) are frequently found here, along with the kōkopu variety with its mottled markings.

There have been reports of finds of Māori pounamu workings and artefacts at high altitude in the area. This is not unexpected, as parties travelling from the east coast across the mountain passes, especially Browning Pass, would follow down the Arahura River from its headwaters until they reached Olderog/Waitaiki Creek, the source of pounamu. Another possibility may have been to navigate around the ridge tops, maintaining altitude. Perhaps there is a connection with the pounamu variety auhunga, which relates to mountains; and H. D. Skinner, former director of Otago Museum and lecturer in anthropology at Otago University, records a comment from a Māori informant, collected by G. J. Roberts, that 'hine auhuka' related to 'highest up greenstone'. Certainly Māori would have collected pounamu from the source as well as the lower reaches of the Arahura River. It is not hard to imagine the awe and frustration of those Māori explorers when they encountered these huge pounamu boulders. Because of their size, caressing and admiring them was the only option.

Olderog/Waitaiki Creek is a very special place. Over the years I have visited the area several times as a guest of licence holders and Mawhera Incorporation. I am always deeply moved with the experience, for it is a most spectacular place charged with a rich history.

North of the Arahura River is the Taramakau

pounamu resource well known to Poutini Ngāi Tahu, who, as Charles Heaphy found in 1846, maintained a permanent pounamu workshop on the south bank near the river mouth. In the years that followed this village ceased to exist as the sea encroached on it, and its inhabitants moved to Mawhera (Greymouth) and later to Arahura.

When the early European explorers walked from Canterbury across the Southern Alps to the Taramakau, it is said that their Māori guides took them along the still definable trails made by east coast Ngāi Tahu in their seasonal quest for pounamu.

TARAMAKAU

The Taramakau River is some 72 km from source to mouth, but nephrite is confined to approximately the lower half. During past ages the river or glacier may have taken other possible courses and it is probable that during some period it flowed between the two granite masses of the Hōhonu Range at Inchbonnie, forming Lake Brunner (Moana) and depositing gravels over the plains westwards to the sea. Taramakau jade may have originated in the ultramafic pods of the Griffin Range area.

In 1906, the geologists Bell and Fraser recorded nephrite in situ at the headwaters of Griffin Creek. They added that although the nephrite was often impure, there was some of a fine, dark, translucent quality; they estimated that many tonnes could be obtained at this locality. Despite this tantalising appraisal, little attention was paid to the deposit until 1974, when T. Sweetman and D. F. Cole began mining operations and removed several tonnes of nephrite. A dark variety of serpentinite/bowenite also occurs there.

There are several scenarios for the source of Taramakau jade. One proposes that before the Taramakau glacier gouged out its present valley, a large nephrite-bearing pod, similar to

the other pods within the Pounamu Ultramafic Belt, was situated near Inchbonnie. The glacier gradually cut into the pod, freeing the nephrite and spreading it westwards. This could account for nephrite in the Big Hōhonu and possibly Marsden districts. We will never know as any trace of the pod would have been completely removed by the glacier. Another possibility is that glacial drift from the Arahura has been carried northwards by movement along the Alpine Fault, which would account for some nephrite being in the Taramakau region.

Around 1911 an ambitious venture began near the summit of Mt Griffin, where an outcrop of serpentinite was quarried by a German-based company for ornamental building stone. An aerial cableway was used to transport the blocks of stone down the mountain for sawing and polishing. But the venture was shortlived and ceased during the First World War. A stairway in the Otago Museum and other buildings in Dunedin and Wellington are faced with this material.

KUMARA

The largest contributor to the Taramakau jade field was the Kumara district. The township of Kumara is situated on the south bank of the Taramakau River near the mouth of the Big Hōhonu River (also known as the Greenstone). Like most West Coast towns, Kumara was an active goldmining settlement. The gold was recovered from the surrounding dry gravels by hydraulic sluicing and the riverbed and streams were worked by several dredges. Because the gold-bearing gravels deposited by the ancient glaciers carried numerous boulders of nephrite, these boulders were seen by gold prospectors as indicators of possible concentrations of alluvial gold.

Hydraulic sluicing was the invention of the Californian miners and was introduced to New Zealand for use extensively in the Westland

and Otago goldfields. The principle of sluicing entailed a supply of water with sufficient head, or pressure, being carried to the workings from artificial lakes by means of water races, fluming and pipes, and then being directed from a nozzle to the working face. The nozzle was manoeuvrable and the jet of water was directed in such a way as to keep the gravel face even to avoid collapses. The sluiced gravels flowed across the riffles in the bed of the tailrace to catch the heavy gold, while the pebbles and small boulders rolled on with the water to the tailings. This was dangerous back-breaking work in all weathers and seasons.

The high terraces south of the township of Kumara, and to a lesser extent the terraces of the Big Hōhonu River, have been the scene of such extensive hydraulic sluicing that whole hills have been washed away to low levels. Tunnels were driven from the Kumara terraces down through the gravel to the Taramakau River where the unwanted tailings were deposited. During sluicing the miners encountered numerous large boulders and these were either stacked neatly into piles in the worked areas of the claim or used as walls to guide the water and gravel down the tailrace. When a hefty boulder of nephrite was found it was often placed at the entrance of the tailrace so that it would not be reburied. Its sheer weight kept it in place, and should a buyer at any time wish to inspect the stone it was always easily found and removed.

The gold and, of course, nephrite-bearing gravels extended several kilometres to the south and east of Kumara township and included the hilly block of the Waimea State Forest. The region is drained by numerous streams, all of which were worked for gold.

Westland gold dredges carefully turned over many square kilometres of gravels stone by stone, and during this process a great number of nephrite boulders, from giants of several tonnes to small pebbles, were hoisted on board. If these were recognised by the workmen they were saved and sold, but the undetected ones were passed on to the tailings and reburied.

The gold dredge is a New Zealand invention and the credit for this goes to the resourceful miners working on the Central Otago rivers. Many prototypes were made before the well known, efficient bucket-type dredge was built at Alexandra in 1881 by Charles McQueen. The gold dredge comprises a large, flat-bottomed, barge-like floating hull, a boom with an endless chain of buckets that dig deep into the river bed, gold-saving machinery, and a stern boom to carry out the unwanted tailings.

In the early 1900s there was a dredging boom in Otago, with 187 dredges working the waterways; and by 1906 Southland had 85 and Westland 40. They turned over a vast amount of ground in search of the precious metal. With the diminishing workable gravels, the number of dredges gradually decreased until only a few remained. The last of these giants, the *Kaniere* dredge at Kaniere, was dismantled and moved to the Taramakau River near Kumara, where for many years it produced some fine jade; then it was finally shifted to the Grey River. Smaller dredges of a new design without a bucket boom now operate on several goldmining licences.

HŌHONU

Another important contributor to the Taramakau jade field is the area surrounding the Big Hōhonu or Greenstone River. In 1864 Albert Hunt, a track cutter and prospector employed by the Canterbury Provincial Government, reported a payable goldfield on the Greenstone River and was awarded £200. Māori knew of the existence of gold and pounamu at this locality, and it is believed that Hunt attached himself to a Māori prospecting party. A goldrush followed this discovery and miners flocked in overnight. They encountered nephrite throughout a large section of the river, and the small mining settlement that sprang up was named Greenstone. As a large part of the river was eventually dredged and the surrounding creeks and terraces worked over, a considerable amount of jade was found, especially in the vicinity of Māori Point (see Chapter Five).

The Taramakau field holds all types and qualities of nephrite and has produced many examples of gem-quality stone of the kawakawa variety. Generally the colour is rich green to dark green; the paler shades are rare. Sometimes the outer weathered rind is a greyish white to brown, but several have no rind at all, being smooth, river-polished boulders and pebbles of great beauty. Unfortunately, few of these have survived – most were sacrificed to the lapidary's saw. Many stones at the Taramakau field are particularly hard and fine grained. They show the effects of severe treatment by swift rivers which cause surface bruising in the form of distinctive small crescent-shaped fractures known as 'moons'. These stones are invariably of high quality and are known locally as 'glacial stones'.

The extensive mining activities in the Taramakau area, with the focus on Kumara, once earned it the title of the biggest jade producer in New Zealand. Now, however, with the decline in goldmining activities, nephrite recovery has been drastically reduced to stones that escaped earlier detection.

MARSDEN

North of the Taramakau River is the New River/ Kaimata, and its numerous tributaries constitute a large goldmining area referred to as the Marsden district. Sluicing and dredging of the ancient glacial gravels extracted the gold from this district, and also produced nephrite. The creeks and rivers in this area would have been an easily accessible source of high-quality pounamu for Māori.

RIGHT / Sunrise on the Big Hōhonu or Greenstone River above its junction with the Taramakau River. The tops of the Hōhonu Range emerge from the cloud. This river was once rich in gold and pounamu.

There is not much left of the mining township of Marsden, or the nearby settlement of Dunganville, which was a centre for the extensive sluicing and dredging claims. Considerable ground was turned over during the gold era and many specimens of nephrite, from pebbles to large boulders, were exposed. Poor roads and the bush-clad, hilly terrain added to the difficulties of transporting any jade that was found, and consequently few sizeable pieces were saved. However, a fine example recovered in the 1980s is preserved as a touchstone in the Museum of New Zealand Te Papa Tongarewa in Wellington (see Chapter Five).

Nephrite stones from this field usually have a very thick, rusty-buff-coloured rind, making them distinctive to this district but difficult to distinguish from the surrounding stones of a similar colour.

Several of the early claims were operated by Chinese miners who, in their spare time, experimented with fragments of jade, polishing one or two faces by hand. Interesting examples of their work have been found by present-day prospectors in the old deserted mining camps. Nephrite was used as fireplace hobs and one large specimen was found to have served as a blacksmith's forge. Nephrite can withstand heating without breaking and for this reason several pieces, usually oxidised red, have been discovered in the old abandoned fireplaces.

Boulders of all sizes, but seldom exceeding a tonne, have been found in this area. The colour and texture of many Marsden specimens is magnificent – the shade is intense rich greens (kawakawa to kahurangi varieties) and the structure dense and free of fractures. Occasionally, partly or wholly rindless river-polished specimens of this quality are found, and these are among New Zealand's finest examples of jade. Several specimens, when they are sawn in half, display a colour range from brownish yellow directly beneath the rind to olive-green toning then a beautiful rich green centre. Others are oxidised brown right to the core of the boulder and some still retain a dense texture and hardness. These multicoloured examples are most attractive and have great potential for carving. Distinctive in many Marsden stones are the contrasting cream-coloured markings known as 'flower jade'. These are usually found on the outer edges of the boulders but sometimes throughout or in the vicinity of fractures. They are produced as part of the weathering process and thus reveal the hidden structure of the specimen.

For obvious reasons jade from the Marsden field is in strong demand for carving, museum specimens and investment. In more recent times old tailing heaps were reworked by bulldozer in the search for the occasional boulder that the miners reburied.

The nephrite in the Marsden field has been subjected to a long period of severe weathering and oxidisation. The fact that these specimens are more oxidised than the boulders found to the south at Taramakau and Arahura may provide a clue to their origin. The most likely explanation is that they were transported north by lateral movement along the Alpine Fault. From a brief glance at a geological map or a satellite image of the South Island, the Alpine Fault is a dominant feature as it runs almost in a straight line from Milford Sound to east of the Marlborough Sounds and beyond (see map 01). The abrupt ending of the ultramafic rocks against

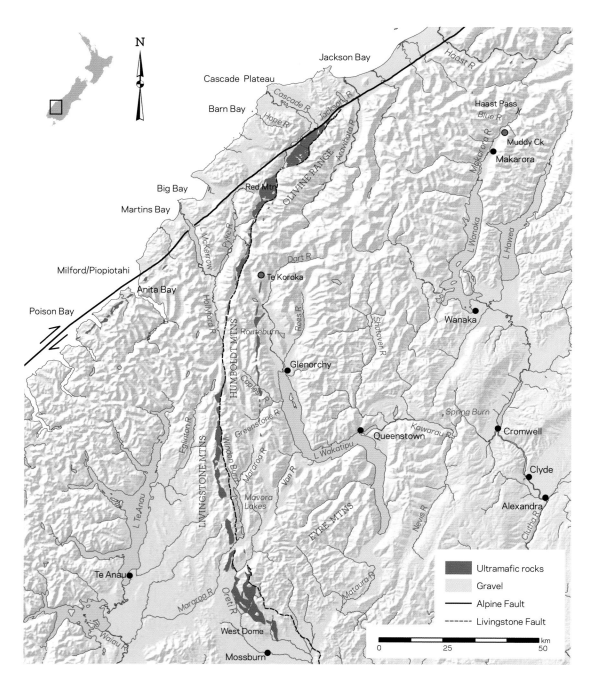

the fault near Jackson Bay in South Westland and their equally abrupt reappearance some 460 km to the north on the opposite or western side at Tophouse in Nelson is obvious evidence of this lateral movement. It has taken many millions of years of progressive movements for the two blocks of land to slide apart, and the fault is still very active with an average movement of 36 mm per year. This is caused by the Australian Plate colliding with the Pacific Plate, resulting in the creation of the Southern Alps.

We find that the jade-producing rocks of the Pounamu Ultramafics are east of the Alpine Fault and south of the Taramakau River, whereas the glacial gravels that contain the nephrite boulders lie west of the fault. The land and gravels on the western side have been gradually carried northwards during or since deposition, and thus the oldest and most deeply weathered nephrite specimens would be to the north of the ultramafic lenses. This is so in the Marsden area. The same situation exists further south in the South Westland jade field.

HOKITIKA

The southernmost section of the Westland jade field is the Hokitika River field. Many rivers with their sources deep in the Southern Alps flow into the Hokitika River. Pods of the Pounamu Ultramafics occur within this watershed and are cut by the Cropp River, the main Hokitika Branch, Diedrich Creek, Toaroha River, Kokatahi River and a branch of the Styx River. These are obvious sources for the nephrite found in the Hokitika field, and although they are not prolific jade producers, these rivers and glacial deposits have, in the past, yielded many fine specimens, particularly in dark green shades. At the mouth of the Hokitika River lies the town of Hokitika, the former centre of the Westland goldfields and now an important hub of the New Zealand jade industry.

MAP 03 / Lower South Island showing South Westland, Wakatipu, Mararoa and Milford pounamu fields.
COURTESY GNS SCIENCE

The alluvial gravels surrounding the settlements of Kaniere and Rimu, southeast of Hokitika, were worked for gold by sluicing and dredging, and the bulk of Hokitika jade was recovered during the course of these operations. In the 1920s, several large dredges were built, and some carried on working for 30 years or more.

Many square kilometres of ground were worked, leaving vast hills of gravel tailings that are now smoothed over and planted with forest. During bulldozing, several nephrite boulders were found. Both the Kaniere and Rimu goldfields, apart from containing the odd boulder of nephrite, are famed for 'ruby rock'. Goodletite, as it was named, is a most attractive rare rock composed of small deep-red to purple corundum crystals (rubies) in a matrix of emerald-green massive fuchsite mica. The goodletite source has not been located, but probably originates in the ultramafic rocks of the Hokitika River watershed.

These are the main known jade areas of the Westland field. Other small isolated regions have produced nephrite, and there may be others yet to be discovered. Westland's high rainfall (about 3000 mm annually) produces numerous flash floods in the rivers, and these in turn reshuffle the gravels and expose fresh alluvium. Finds of good quality nephrite are, however, becoming rarer, and the outlook for future reserves is uncertain. Unless the glacial gravels are worked again for gold by large-scale operations, Westland jade seems likely remain in its present short supply. This has placed a higher value on Westland stone, and has generated a desire to preserve rather than cut up attractive pounamu.

The ownership and management of Westland pounamu resources is now held by Ngāi Tahu, managed by Mawhera Incorporation and local rūnanga. Prospecting and collecting without their consent is prohibited (see Chapter Seven).

SOUTH WESTLAND – TE TAI POUTINI KI TE TONGA

This field is from the south side of the Haast River to Martins Bay in the south and inland to the Main Divide, enclosing many thousands of hectares of what is some of New Zealand's most rugged country. Also within this region is a large portion of the Mount Aspiring National Park.

Geologically, the field contains a massive body of ultramafic and associated altered rocks, known as the Dun Mountain Ophiolite Belt. These nephrite-bearing rocks emerge abruptly on the Alpine Fault in the Jackson River valley and extend southwards for some 80 km before narrowing, thinning out completely, then reappearing near Cascade Creek in the Eglinton Valley, Southland. Ophiolites occur elsewhere in the world, but are not common. They are separated sections of the earth's mantle (peridotite), oceanic crust (basalts) and sea-floor sediments which have suffered some alteration from the process of being manoeuvred to the surface by plate tectonics.

The South Westland field is bisected by the Alpine Fault, which – as previously mentioned – is a major feature of the South Island and one of the most active faults in the world. Over a long period glaciers and rivers have carved into the South Westland hinterland, releasing the jade and distributing it in the gravels to the west. The sliding effect of the Alpine Fault has carried whole valleys and their cargo of gravels containing jade far from their original sources. Wave action of the turbulent Tasman Sea and changing sea levels have eroded into ancient glacial moraines and concentrated the nephrite on boulder beaches. Not surprisingly, nearly all the rivers and creeks in the field from the Jackson River to Big Bay have produced jade.

The knowledge of South Westland as a nephrite source has undergone a history of

rediscovery, at least twice. The many Māori artefacts recovered from archaeological workshop sites along the coast in the region are testimony that early Māori knew of this resource. The style and method of manufacture by flaking rather than sawing, and the presence of many examples with surfaces that have oxidised since manufacture, suggest that the area was visited and exploited for its pounamu at a very early date, and was probably visited subsequently only spasmodically over a long period.

It is tempting to propose that South Westland was the first nephrite source to be discovered, but we will have to wait for controlled excavations and dating to confirm this. It is also interesting that, although numerous examples that match South Westland stone show up throughout New Zealand, the Westland source by far overshadowed South Westland. Its remoteness was certainly a factor in this. Archaeological and historical evidence shows that later Māori resided in South Westland before and after the arrival of European sealers and whalers in the early 1800s. These people were entrepreneurial opportunists and, with the help of Māori from the south, they collected jade on several occasions from the beaches and rivers to trade with the north and further afield.

The existence of nephrite in this important field was first recorded in 1845 by the writer J. Brodie, who mentioned Barn Bay as a site for 'Maori greenstone workings'. Ferdinand von Hochstetter quoted the neighbourhood of Jackson Bay, and later Arthur Dieseldorff, a German geologist, listed Barn Bay and the Hope River as sources. In 1920, historian Herries Beattie, who was informed by southern Māori, stated that good pounamu could be obtained at Barn Bay. A later mention is from F. J. Turner who, in the early 1930s, carried out geological exploration of the region and collected specimens of nephrite and semi-nephrite in

Red Mountain, South Westland. A huge body of ultramafic rocks rich in magnesium and other minerals, which are toxic to most plants. Nephrite, bowenite and asbestos have been found associated with these and other adjacent rocks.

white, eyes, ribbons and veins. Occasionally it is a brilliant green with a hint of the emerald shade, and in a few cases, the quality equals that of the best Westland jade. The water-polished boulders often have reddish brown staining on part or all of their exterior surface, which makes them exceptionally colourful. These bear a striking resemblance to the nephrite boulders found at Kobuk in northwest Alaska.

The features that make South Westland jade so different and recognisable from other sources are the included minerals. These show as numerous black specks, commonly surrounded with a soft dark green or purplish-brown matrix. The local people interpret this as the totoweka variety. In addition, there are usually abundant inclusions of tiny brassy sulphide crystals and occasionally clusters of radiating albite crystals that look like snowflakes.

The glacial moraines in the region are spectacular – particularly the Cascade Plateau, where huge blocks of ultramafic and other rocks have been dumped by great ice monsters. Among these giant erratics are a few jade examples, which have a distinctive weathered rind that make them easily identifiable; but sadly, some of these have been illegally cut up.

Further south, very large boulders of semi-nephrite and nephrite are exposed between the tidal zones at Awarua Point and along the rocky northern shore of Big Bay. This glacial deposit, which was discovered in the 1980s, was commercially mined, but some boulders of more than 15 tonnes remain. Big Bay nephrite often has a rough outer surface, while the undersides show interesting polished dimples that are produced by the grinding action of these heavy boulders resting on pebbles and being pounded by rough seas.

Other occurrences in the South Westland field are in the rivers and on passes to the south, in association with the ultramafic rocks where

LEFT / The Cascade River drains the rugged jade-producing mountains of South Westland as a series of wild rapids and waterfalls. Seen here in its subdued final meander before meeting the Tasman Sea. The terraces to the right form part of the Cascade Plateau.

ABOVE / Jackson River, South Westland. The straightness of this river is because it flows along the Alpine Fault, an active fracture in the Earth's crust and a dominant feature of the South Island.

the Jackson River area. With the Westland source turning up considerable quantities from goldmining operations, the general knowledge of South Westland as a source of jade seems to have been largely overlooked.

A find of Māori pounamu artefacts in the late 1960s apparently prompted a search for the source of the stone. The occurrence was confirmed a few years later when local farmers Mr and Mrs C. Eggeling found waterworn gem-grade specimens in the Cascade area. This discovery, and finds by E. Buchanan and others about that time, soon sparked a jade rush and the beaches and rivers of the whole region from seashore to mountain top were combed by prospectors. The intensive search and mining

used helicopters and bulldozers; and divers even scoured the sea bottom. Many fine stones were found, including some exceptionally large boulders estimated to exceed 30 tonnes.

Guessing boulder weights can be speculative and estimates tend to be on the heavy side. The hardest part is getting an accurate assessment of the cubic capacity, especially when the shapes are quite irregular. Convert the measurements to regular shapes (cylinders, cubes etc) to get the volume in cubic metres, then multiply by three, as one cubic metre of water is one tonne and jade is about three times the weight of water.

The colour of South Westland stone ranges from very rich to paler green, including olive green; and sometimes it has distinctive, almost

geological mapping survey. The pod is composed of tremolite, semi-nephrite and gem-grade green nephrite nodules and veins. Because of its importance, Te Rūnanga o Makaawhio, the council representing local Ngāi Tahu people, has placed a wāhi tapu (reserved ground status) over the site.

Tracing the sources of South Westland jade is perplexing, and although several smallish outcrops occur on both sides of the ultramafic contacts, no one mother lode has been located. Multiple sources are more likely. Certainly active fault displacement and extensive glaciation is responsible for spreading the jade. Nephrite has a habit of being associated with soft host rocks that are prone to erosion, so it is probable that ancient glaciers have completely carved away some of the sources. Detailed geological investigation of potential areas will no doubt reveal more sources.

Access to the field without helicopter transport is arduous and, with the exception of the ultramafic zone, the region is heavily bush-clad, with a dramatic climate and prolific sandflies. The region yields its secrets slowly – but probably no other area in New Zealand has such potential for further jade discoveries. This task is now entrusted to the Makaawhio people, who have, in the interim, taken the positive steps of implementing a management plan with strategies to evaluate and care for the resource.

OTAGO – ŌTĀKOU

WAKATIPU AND TE KOROKA

Wakatipu or Whakatipu pounamu is a fascinating story of discovery, utilisation, obscurity, then multiple rediscovery. It is a classic case of just how easy detailed knowledge of a once vitally important resource can be forgotten within a relatively short period of time, simply because of changing values.

they have been squeezed by the enclosing rocks. In the mountains on the south side of the Haast River there are some isolated outcrops of tremolite and serpentinite, and it's possible that nephrite is present there too.

To the east of the Livingstone Fault lies the Olivine Range. Within these spectacular mountains are narrow bands of green schists and pods of serpentinite. One of these contains nephrite and has been named Te Raukura o Papatūānuku by the local Ngāi Tahu people, in recognition of its special relationship to

Papatūānuku, the Earth Mother. This is a pod of great interest as well as great beauty, especially when wet. It was a privilege for me to briefly see this occurrence while on a recent wānanga (seminar) and hīkoi (a walk, or field trip). It is truly one of the most beautiful jade spectacles I have seen – a unique taonga and a national treasure.

The reef is exposed in a classic setting beside a waterfall on the steep rocky side of an alpine creek which has cut deeply into an old fault. The pod was reported by geologists Ian Turnbull and Simon Cox in 1990 while they were undertaking a

LEFT / Simon Cox, GNS Science geologist, inspects a rare in situ pod of nephrite deep in the mountains of South Westland.
S. HINERANGI BARR

RIGHT / The glacier-fed Dart River, on its journey to Lake Wakatipu, viewed from Mt Alfred near the head of the lake. The Route Burn flat on the far left, and behind Lake Sylvan lies the Rock Burn, then the Beans Burn. Cosmos Peaks/Te Koroka (cloud) and the Bride Peaks in the distance. Southern Māori made long journeys to this beautiful region to gather pounamu.

Towards the head of Lake
Wakatipu, with the Humboldt
Mountains dominating the skyline.
One of the trails for southern
Māori to access this region was
via the Greenstone River, which
flows into the lake
on the left.

The early European explorers, beginning with Captain James Cook in 1773, who were in contact with north- and east-coast South Island Māori recorded that the source of pounamu was said to be at a place called Te Wai Pounamu, which was described as 'near an inland lake or river in the South Island'. Most placed it somewhere in Otago, and others gave more definite directions such as 'the head of Lake Wakatipu' (see maps 01 and 02).

It is puzzling, however, that there was no specific mention of the Westland occurrence, which at that time must have been well known to Māori. This may be because Māori favoured the pale, light-green īnanga variety common in the Wakatipu field. Although the Arahura resource was without doubt also a major source for īnanga, the Wakatipu field supplied a large proportion of this variety, especially to Southland and Otago Māori. It was not until the epic journey made by Charles Heaphy and Thomas Brunner, with Kehu and others, from Nelson to the West Coast in 1846 that we learn of a major Māori source of pounamu in Westland. Later, when West Coast miners unearthed considerable quantities of nephrite during the goldrush era, the general belief arose that Westland was the sole supplier of pounamu for Māori, and Wakatipu as a source was more or less forgotten. In fact, some researchers questioned whether it had ever been a source.

As Europeans settled the Wakatipu region, small slivers of nephrite were occasionally found in the Dart River, the main contributor at the head of the lake. Local runholders and goldminers apparently knew of its presence in the Wakatipu area, but considered it of low quality. Charles Haines, a resident of Glenorchy (originally a small farming and mining settlement at the head of the lake), spent considerable time and effort prospecting during the early 1900s; he found many

LEFT / The clear cold water of the Route Burn at the confluence with Sugar Loaf Creek/Waiaio – a traditional source of pounamu for Māori.

RIGHT / Geologist Alan Cooper of University of Otago beside an outcrop of semi-nephrite within the altered rocks in the Greenstone Melange in the Humboldt Mountains, near Lake Wakatipu. T. POPHAM

outcrops in a belt, but showed that it truncated just north of the Route Burn. We now know that this is not the case; the belt extends several kilometres north.

Norrie Groves, a Kinloch farmer and miner, and Dr Geoffrey Orbell of Invercargill announced in 1965 that they had discovered nephrite and semi-nephrite boulders of all sizes in the Route Burn and in a tributary, Sugarloaf Stream/Waiaio. With this 'discovery' and the subsequent mining activity, the belief was widespread that this was the 'lost' Māori source, and any further searching was effectively curtailed, especially when the current geological maps showed no northern extension of nephrite-producing rocks. Fifty years passed before the information Herries Beattie received from Māori was proven correct in every detail.

Nephrite in the Wakatipu field is derived from a narrow belt of ultramafic rocks. In recent years, these rocks have been studied by Yosuke Kawachi, D. G. Bishop and other geologists, who have established that they are part of a structural belt containing blocks of several rock types – pillow lava, serpentinite, metagabbro and sedimentary rocks, to name a few. The belt is sandwiched between altered sedimentary rock (schist) and extends for many kilometres. Known as the Greenstone Mélange, it was named after the Greenstone River and not because it contains 'greenstone'. In fact, a very small proportion of the belt contains nephrite. General erosion since the last ice age has formed many creeks and rivers, severing this belt in numerous places, eroding the harder nephrite masses from the softer rocks and depositing them as boulders deep in the beds of the rivers.

A reasonably high proportion of the stone can be described as semi-nephrite, which differs from nephrite in one respect only – its fibrous structure is coarser and not as densely felted, making it a softer more fissile (easily split) stone. The chemical composition of both semi-nephrite and nephrite is the same.

pounamu artefacts and located the remains of several Māori encampments. Further evidence for the Wakatipu source came to light in 1920 when Herries Beattie published important information from old Māori informants on the source of their pounamu. They indicated the general area was up the Dart River at the head of the lake, and mentioned that pounamu of the īnanga variety was obtained in a slip on a mountain called Te Koroka, rather than in a river, but that the exact location was lost. The head of Lake Wakatipu is all mountains, so which one was Te Koroka?

In the mid 1930s, two geologists, F. J. Turner and C. O. Hutton, discovered outcrops of serpentinite containing nephrite in the Caples Valley and in the Route Burn. They published their finds in scientific journals, but this knowledge largely went unnoticed. When the artefacts collected by Haines were compared with the specimens from the Route Burn they showed similar characteristics, and this established that they were of local origin. There was finally reasonable proof that Wakatipu was a pounamu source for Māori, but for some reason it was not well known.

Later, in the 1950s, more detailed geological mapping confirmed these nephrite-producing

CAPLES TO ROUTE BURN

The southern boundary for the Wakatipu field lies approximately 10 km south of Kinloch in the Greenstone and Caples rivers. The name Greenstone River is believed to have originated from the knowledge that it was part of an old Māori trail from the east coast to the pounamu source at the head of the lake. Although the river cuts the mélange about 6 km upstream from the confluence of the Caples River, any nephrite there is rare and of poor quality.

In the Caples Valley, by a small knob a little beyond the old deserted homestead, is an outcrop of semi-nephrite that was first described in 1936 by Hutton. Some 35 years later, Alf Poole and I relocated the site and found that the stone was somewhat opaque and quite different in appearance to any Māori artefacts. We concluded that this occurrence was not the 'lost Māori source'. It was, however, an interesting occurrence for, in places, it had developed a botryoidal form; that is, bubbly or resembling a bunch of grapes.

About halfway between the Caples River and the Route Burn lies the Scott Basin, a spectacular hanging glacial valley drained by Scott Creek. Ultramafic rocks are exposed for the whole length of the basin, with associated nephrite and semi-nephrite. In recent years Scott Basin has been intensively studied and evaluated by Ngāi Tahu, University of Otago and GNS Science geologists.

Directly below Scott Basin on the banks of the Dart River near the bridge are the remains of an interesting Māori campsite. Haines collected many artefacts from here and it has since been archaeologically excavated. The site seems to have been repeatedly visited throughout the Archaic period and contains evidence of cooking tī (cabbage tree; *Cardyline australis*) root, moa hunting, pounamu working and some unusual stone paving. The recovered pounamu artefacts suggest the inhabitants were collecting their pounamu locally probably at the Route Burn or nearby Scott Creek. Cooked tī root produces an energy-giving caramel, an ideal food for travelling. The site was more likely to have been a stage camp for travellers venturing further afield or to the West Coast via the Route Burn, rather than a pounamu workshop. On the other side of Mt Alfred near the Rees River is Camp Hill, another Māori campsite where pounamu artefacts have been recovered.

The Route Burn flows east from high in the Humboldt Mountains to join the Dart River. In the past, the valley served Māori and early European explorers as a route over the Harris Saddle to the West Coast via Hollyford Valley and then to Martins Bay or Big Bay. Likewise, today, the Route Burn is a popular walking trail, known as the Routeburn.

THE SEARCH FOR TE KOROKA

It was generally accepted that the Route Burn was the primary Wakatipu source for Māori; however, in my privileged position of working in a museum I pondered that, although most artefacts in museum collections attributed to Wakatipu were somewhat similar in appearance to the Route Burn stone, they were also markedly different. Their colour has a vibrancy and the quality of the stone is superior. This suggested to me that they originated from a source formed under similar circumstances to the Route Burn, but at a different, unknown locality. Searches were made in the Dart River above the Route Burn, but only serpentinite was found. This, in itself, was encouraging as it indicated that ultramafic rocks did occur somewhere further upstream.

Such was the position until late in 1970. What was about to happen in the following years has since proved to be of national and international importance. In the summer of that year a commercial venison hunter, Tom Trevor, was shooting near a small tributary of the upper Dart River when a fragment of a greenish scaly rock caught his eye. Realising that it was quite different from the surrounding rocks and resembled nephrite, he took a small sample in to the Southland Museum for examination. I identified it as semi-nephrite with characteristics similar in many respects to Māori artefacts in the museum's collection. The find immediately rang bells suggesting that the occurrence could be of archaeological significance and that the pounamu-bearing rocks previously mapped as terminating near the Route Burn might extend further north.

I immediately contacted Tom and outlined the potential of the find. He generously offered to take a small party in his jetboat to the location, and on 9 January 1971 Arthur Mackenzie (then Director of Southland Museum) and I met Tom near the road-end at Paradise by the Dart River. The 15-km jetboat journey up the treacherous, glacier-fed river between lofty mountains was spectacular, and a little scary, because of the low level of the icy water – it was a small craft and this was my first jetboat experience.

In the lower reaches the Dart River is braided and up to 1.5 km wide, but there is a section between the Beans Burn and Slip Stream that is narrow with huge boulders and rapids. Tom had pioneered jetboat access to the upper Dart River by clearing all the timber obstacles, and we were grateful for his navigation of this formidable river. We arrived at Slip Stream and climbed to where Tom had found the original sample in recent avalanche debris. We soon found a whole range of specimens of serpentinite, talc, semi-nephrite and, sparingly, nephrite of the īnanga variety. We collected only a few small hand specimens, conscious that we were already on the limit for weight for the journey back in the boat. This was an important find – and it got better, as when we clambered down the steep stream to the boat, Tom discovered a huge boulder of nephrite with one end buried in rubble. We stepped it out and estimated

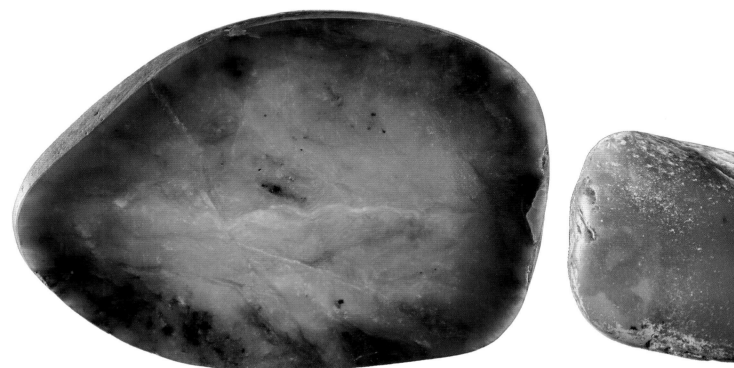
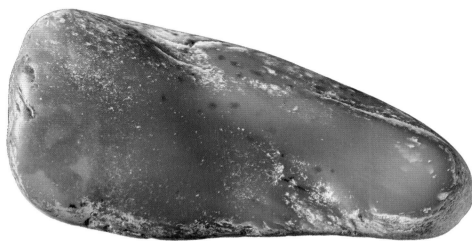

ABOVE / A brilliant green jade cobble from Barn Bay, South Westland. Like most of the nephrite in this region, it has travelled far from its source by glaciers and earth movement. The yellowish nephrite cobble of the kōkopu variety from the Arahura River has been carried downstream by the swift water.

the weight to be in excess of 20 tonnes. What a find! The surface was pale green, water-polished, and without the white rind often present with nephrite. Because of its size, beauty and cultural significance, we unanimously decided that this unique boulder should be preserved and protected. We could hardly contain ourselves when we returned to Glenorchy late that afternoon and informed the Mount Aspiring National Park authorities of the find (see Chapter Five).

From detailed examination of the samples that we collected in 1971, it became clear that they were identical in every way to the artefacts in museum collections and that the area was of immense archaeological significance. For this reason, it was decided not to make any public announcement of the rediscovery until further work had been carried out. A small, dedicated team of park staff, geologists, archaeologists and museum staff in collaboration with Ngāi Tahu kaumātua began an intensive investigation into the many aspects of the site. This was spread over several years. These were exciting times, especially as the facts were pieced together and it became apparent that the Te Koroka site was indeed unique in that it was undisturbed with little change since Māori had last visited it.

Now that the obvious importance of the find to New Zealand's heritage had been established, positive steps were taken to preserve the area for all time. Consequently, 1618 hectares were set apart as a 'Special Area', gazetted under the National Parks Act 1952. This means that entry is by written permit only. The site is also protected under the Historic Places Act 1954.

The pounamu rediscovery was finally made public on 4 December 1976 and immediately aroused much attention – and respect for the action taken.

The general appearance of the pounamu is distinctive and easily distinguished from other New Zealand and Wakatipu sources. The colour is from a vibrant light lettuce green to milky green, through to olive shades, often with spectacular pearly, pale grey bands. The stone tends to have a strong grain and many examples display an internal scaly sheen, not unlike the skin of a fish. It also has chatoyant streaks and high translucency. It is easy to understand why Māori placed so much value on this beautiful stone known as īnanga (see pages 122 and 151).

The large boulder found by Tom Trevor is of the īnanga variety with some talc inclusions and is now completely buried in gravel following a recent flash flood of the stream. Large surviving boulders are rare. I say 'surviving' because, although much larger ones have been found, especially in South Westland and overseas, they hold a high commercial value and are soon cut up and gone forever. In this respect the boulder in the Special Area grows more significant every day.

The in situ nephrite source lies some distance away from the boulder within the Special Area and is quite small in extent; in fact, the large boulder may have represented a considerable portion of the original deposit. Natural erosion of the whole Slip Stream region is extremely rapid and unstable because of the easily decomposed nature of the surrounding rocks.

Te Koroka pounamu is commonly found as slabs or angular lumps requiring much less work to shape into implements than waterworn boulders – another feature that would have made this source a favourite. Such unworked pieces from Māori archaeological sites are identical in appearance to the loose pieces found near the source, and this, supported by archaeological field evidence, indicates that Māori collected pounamu from the source area as well as the stream bed.

When we look closely at the early directions given to Herries Beattie and others we begin to see just how accurate Maori oral records were. All mentioned that īnanga was obtained at the head of Lake Wakatipu; some said 'under a mountain'. Several named it Te Koroka, a bold peak at the head of the lake. Some also mentioned that pounamu occurred in a great cliff or slip named Te Horo. All of these descriptions fit perfectly with the Special Area, and the combined weight of geological and archaeological evidence clearly shows that this was a major pounamu source for southern Māori. The 'lost' source had finally been rediscovered. Te Koroka is the mountain known as Cosmos Peaks.

As expected, worked and unworked pieces of typical Route Burn and Te Koroka pounamu have been found in archaeological sites on the east coast of the South Island, but with higher concentrations in workshops north of the entrance to Otago Harbour and particularly in the Foveaux Strait area, where nearly all the material appears to have originated from the Special Area. Finished artefacts of Te Koroka stone have been found as far away as the top of the North Island, indicating such preference for the stone that it was a valued item of trade. One can appreciate the immense effort it took for Māori living on the east coast to travel inland some 200 km over extremely rough terrain, raging rivers, lakes and passes to reach Te Koroka. This is only half the journey. It has been recorded that pounamu was loaded onto flotillas of mōkihi or rafts made from New Zealand flax (harakeke; *Phormium tenax*) flower stems and paddled down the lakes and rivers. These collecting trips would have been major events involving whole families and requiring a detailed knowledge of the routes and food resources. One such route from permanent settlements in Foveaux Strait was up the Waiau then the Mararoa River, Mavora Lakes, on to the Pass Burn and into the Greenstone Valley, which led to Lake Wakatipu. The Otago people had further to go and followed the rivers and overland trails into inhospitable Central Otago to reach Lake Wakatipu.

While we were analysing photographs we had taken on an early expedition, we recognised a most astounding feature: the profile of the rocky skyline was like a human face. We pursued this, and by matching adjoining photographs found, to our amazement, the convincingly realistic image of an enormous person lying down. On a subsequent visit we were able to see the 'giant' in the flesh, so to speak. It was awe-inspiring; so much so that we were immediately aware of its powerful presence in more ways than one. Before long we made an even more remarkable discovery.

Because of the difficult access and rough terrain, exploratory expeditions to the area were spread over several years. Our efforts to locate the source proved elusive, but eventually it was found in a narrow band at high altitude. To our astonishment, it gave the appearance of coming from the mouth of the 'giant'. I am sure Māori would have recognised this feature, and just what interpretation resulted, we will probably never know. It has been suggested that this could well be the basis for the Māori legend of the 'Ogre of Lake Wakatipu', a story relating to a sleeping giant in the shape of the lake (see pages 046–047). It is tempting to connect it to the story surrounding the origin of pounamu, in which Tumuaki was turned into a mountain when, on wounding his finger, he committed the forbidden act of putting it in his mouth – but this is unlikely, as the event is firmly attributed to the Westland source. Wishful thinking or not, the giant certainly contributes to the importance of Te Koroka, and contemporary respect among Ngāi Tahu for it. Furthermore, the translation of Koroka can mean old man. Research on this is pending, but complicated, as the early spelling of southern Māori placenames vary, which can alter the meaning.

Since pounamu resources were handed back to Ngāi Tahu in 1997, an active programme of exploration and evaluation has continued at Te Koroka and the other Wakatipu sources. Probably

no other New Zealand nephrite source has received such intensive recording and study. This valuable work is being managed and carried out by the combined Otago and Southland Ngāi Tahu rūnanga, geologists from GNS Science and the University of Otago, Department of Conservation archaeologists, Historic Places Trust staff and myself. To date, a vast amount of new knowledge has been assembled using GPS technology to fix positions of every piece of pounamu and quantative surveys undertaken. Studies of the surrounding geology and archaeology are ongoing along with several educational hīkoi to the mountain which will provide a comprehensive resource to assist Ngāi Tahu in the management and interpretation of the site.

Contemporary collecting from the site has been restricted to carefully selected pieces for research and touchstones for special Ngāi Tahu purposes.

For me, the rediscovery of Te Koroka has fulfilled a long quest to understand the achievements that early southern Māori made in exploration and stone technology. I feel privileged to have been involved. I am not aware of any other nephrite deposit in the world that was utilised by a stone-based culture and which has not subsequently been exploited. The continued protection of the Te Koroka source is, in many ways, dependent on public appreciation and respect for a unique cultural site of national and world importance.

MAKARORA

Pounamu at Makarora would have been known to Māori, but the resource is relatively minor. It is, however, an interesting occurrence because of its geological aspects.

The main contributor at the head of Lake Wānaka is the Makarora River, which has its origin on the eastern side of the Haast Pass. Near the old sawmilling settlement of Makarora is a small, steep stream with the uninspiring name Muddy Creek, which crosses the Haast Highway before joining the Makarora River.

Since the early 1960s nephrite has been found in the lower reaches of the creek and the Makarora River downstream for a few kilometres. Geoffrey Orbell and I visited the area in the mid 1960s and saw numerous examples of semi-nephrite and the occasional small nephrite specimen. The general appearance of the stone is very schistose (slab-like), often with coarse sparkly tremolite crystals, numerous patches of soft talc and small pockets of the bright green mineral, fuchsite. On the whole, the fissile structure renders most of the slab-like boulders unsuitable for lapidary purposes. Within some specimens there are small, dense nodules of gem-grade nephrite of a strong grass-green colour. These are rare, and good examples that demonstrate the formation of nephrite even though on a small scale (see page 190).

My interest at that time was tracing the source and this proved quite elusive as, the further we climbed up the Muddy Creek fan, the lower the incidence of semi-nephrite. I discussed the problem with Professor Alan Cooper, a University of Otago geologist who had done extensive studies of the geology of the region. He suggested several scenarios: the source had eroded away completely, or was now very small and in a stable location not affected by erosion; or the fan contained glacial deposits with semi-nephrite from further afield and the creek was cutting into them in the lower reaches. Additional prospecting over several years established the absence of nephrite in the Makarora River above Muddy Creek and in the nearby Blue River, so the source had to be in the Muddy Creek catchment. It was with some satisfaction that I learnt that, when Alan was on a subsequent visit, he discovered the source in the headwaters of Muddy Creek – some twenty years after the first find of nephrite at Makarora.

It occurs within a small lenticular pod sandwiched in the schist. Geologically this is interesting because it is well outside the other nephrite-producing areas at Wakatipu and South Westland, and may be related to the lone occurrences of ultramafic rocks much further south near Queenstown, Springburn and Clyde (see map 03). Also, it is one of the few in situ occurrences and provides a good understanding of a two-phase mechanism for the origin of nephrite. In this case the original ultramafic and mafic (gabbro) body, which had been intruded or tectonically emplaced into sedimentary rocks, was subsequently altered by heat and pressure, forming a margin of tremolite and talc. The sediments were converted to schist.

The Makarora River in late afternoon, near the mouth of Muddy Creek, a minor source of nephrite. The Makarora River originates near Haast Pass and flows south to the head of Lake Wānaka.

Later intense movement and shearing with recrystallisation formed thin veins and nodules of nephrite from the tremolite.

The emerald-green fuchsite inclusions are useful markers, as these rarely occur in nephrite from other localities. Examination of a few Māori artefacts in museum collections shows these and other characteristics, so it is almost certain that Māori would have procured some pounamu from this resource. Furthermore, the nearby Haast Pass and other passes were well known by Māori as east–west routes, and this is supported by ample evidence of Māori occupation in the general Hawea and Wānaka lakes area.

The directions for obtaining pounamu 'at the head of an inland lake', as related by Māori to the early Europeans, could apply to Lake Wānaka as well as to Lake Wakatipu. However, there is overwhelming evidence in favour of Wakatipu as the lake referred to. The scarcity and limitations of the Makarora stone for implements could explain the small number of artefacts attributed to this source.

North and west of Makarora there are further isolated outcrops of tremolite rocks and serpentinite; and nephrite may occur there too.

SOUTHLAND – MURIHIKU

LIVINGSTONE MOUNTAINS OR MARAROA

The Livingstone Mountains are a long, high chain running approximately north to south and rising midway between Lakes Te Anau and Wakatipu. The Mararoa River lies to the east of these mountains and feeds into and from the Mavora Lakes, which were originally known as Lake Hikuraki and Manawapouri at the north end. The Livingstone Fault bounding the ultramafic rocks on the eastern side is a major inactive fault that can be traced from the Pacific coast right across the lower South Island to the West Coast. This boundary probably continues northwards beyond New Zealand. The Mararoa field is occupied by the southern portion of the jade-bearing South Westland section of the Dun Mountain Ophiolite Belt, so it is not surprising that nephrite has been found here as well (see map 03).

The first suggestion of nephrite in the Mararoa field was given in 1958 when George Grindley, in his geological survey of the Eglinton Valley and surrounding area, described grey to greyish-white felted tremolite rocks. A few years later I found alluvial specimens of semi-nephrite and rodingite in Cascade Creek, Eglinton Valley; and a Southland prospector, Bill Gray, located similar specimens in the East Branch Eglinton River. Associated with this belt are rocks that have interested me primarily as possible sources for some of the many rock types used by Southland Māori for toolmaking. In the course of investigations spread over several years and a lot of country covered, occasional semi-nephrite specimens were encountered, although they were generally of low grade. In 1971, while with a small party at the head of North Mavora Lake, I found an unusual example of a semi-nephrite boulder that aroused my interest because it was completely different from known varieties. Much of the region has since received close examination from prospectors and geologists, and more recently surveys conducted by Ngāi Tahu.

There are three distinct varieties of Mararoa nephrite, each quite different from the others. The most unusual type is white or milky green with folded veins of dark olive green to vivid green. The stone, which could be described as an impure semi-nephrite, is unusually hard and contains fibrous diopside – a member of the pyroxene group of minerals – in varying proportions; some are composed almost completely of diopside. A similar-looking rock occurs in South Westland, New Caledonia and California. Selected pieces containing the bright green colour resemble jadeite from Myanmar, and to begin with we thought it might be that material; but, of course, the physical properties of jadeite are quite different. Examples of this variety are not plentiful, and only a small number of good stones have been found. Although some quite large boulders of varying quality occur as float in the rivers and creeks at the head of the lake, the source is as yet uncertain. Again, the region has been glaciated and the boulders could

ABOVE / A water-polished nephrite boulder in a mountain stream in the Mararoa field, Southland. The 1.5-tonne specimen is being evaluated by Ngāi Tahu representative Dean Whaanga and myself, and observed by GNS Science geologist Chris Adams.
C. SAND

RIGHT / Rare examples of pounamu from the Mararoa field. A sawn section of bluish nephrite with characteristic inclusions and a sawn fragment of green and white semi-nephrite containing diopside.

The Mararoa River between the two Mavora Lakes, with the Livingstone Mountains on the left where ultramafic rocks occur in a band. This glaciated valley was a direct route for Māori to reach Lake Wakatipu, who would then return on rafts.

have been transported for some distance.

The second variety is even rarer, but is found over a wider area. The general colour is an olive green outer with a bluish grey centre often with small light green veils and black fern-like dendrites, making it an attractive stone. Some beach pebbles from D'Urville Island are very similar.

The third group is more plentiful and not unlike some semi-nephrites found in the South Westland and Wakatipu fields. This variety is usually more opaque, softer and without the strong greens often associated with nephrite. As well as stream boulders, it forms small isolated outcrops within the Livingstone Mountains and the southwestern Eyre Mountains.

The Mararoa resource does not appear to have been utilised by Māori, as the obvious hallmarks – especially of the two former varieties – that are so distinctive of this field have not been so far observed in any artefacts. In saying this, there are a few very dark green pounamu adzes in museum collections around the country, labelled 'found in Southland', that arouse suspicion. These have been manufactured by hammering, and I had tentatively ascribed them to a South Westland source. Recent finds in the Mararoa field suggest a closer comparison, but more research is needed.

Archaeological evidence shows that Māori visited the general area to quarry metasomatised (baked) argillite for toolmaking, and particularly as a walking and rafting trail to and from Lake Wakatipu for pounamu. It is inconceivable that they would not have noticed the Mararoa pounamu, so why ignore this deposit in preference to Wakatipu? In some ways this is not surprising as most of the Mararoa pounamu occurs as quite large, rounded boulders which would have been nearly impossible to work. The Wakatipu pounamu was of the highly sought-after īnanga variety; and furthermore, it could be gathered at Te Koroka as convenient flattish pieces, some almost the right size and shape, thus saving many hours of hard labour working it into the various taonga.

The Mararoa area offered a relatively open route from Foveaux Strait to Lake Wakatipu. Two alternative routes are possible – one following the Waiau and Mararoa rivers via the Greenstone River; the other following the upper Oreti Valley and Von River to the lake. On the former route there was more streambed, so rafts could be used. Getting the stone at Te Koroka was hard enough, but the journey home to the Riverton area loaded with stone would not have been easy and would

be fraught with obstacles. An example of how challenging these expeditions could be is told by Ro. Carrick in an account, published in 1900, of a pounamu-gathering expedition he learned of from southern Māori. Although the source of the pounamu was not mentioned, Carrick assumed that it was the tangiwai at Anita Bay, Milford Sound. I feel sure it would have been Te Koroka, as it was their primary source. A journey overland across Fiordland to obtain tangiwai from Anita Bay would have been a major undertaking and the bay was easier approached by canoe or boat around the coast, especially as Māori at that time were working closely with European whalers.

The story tells of a flotilla of 20 mōkihi loaded with pounamu that had negotiated the rivers, reaching their destination at Ōraka (Colac Bay), 10 km southwest of Riverton. As they were coming through the surf to the beach, one raft was carried out to sea in a rip. It was crewed by four women with infants, and as they had no paddles, they were helpless. Three days elapsed, and two Māori who attempted to save them lost their lives. Help was sought from the whaling base at Riverton, but the mōkihi had drifted out to sea with only one surviving occupant. The Riverton whaling base was established around

1838, so this tragic event must be after this date and may have been one of the last expeditions to the interior for pounamu.

The other ultramafic rocks exposed in Southland are at Milford Sound and Greenhills near Bluff. Bowenite is from the Milford area – although this material is not jade, it is part of the New Zealand pounamu story and is covered separately. The old quarry for dunite (a rock composed of olivine) at Greenhills occasionally turned up narrow veins of fibrous masses that were akin to semi-nephrite.

NELSON

From a glance at a geological map of the Nelson district you would suspect there were considerable deposits of nephrite, since its geology is an extension of the jade-productive South Westland rocks that have been separated by movement along the Alpine Fault. The Dun Mountain Ophiolite Belt extends some 145 km from the northern end of D'Urville Island south to the Red Hills near Tophouse. Here it is truncated by the Alpine Fault to re-emerge in South Westland, although a small fragment lies at Matakitaki (see map 01). Known locations of pounamu in the Nelson region are the Dun Mountain complex, Matakitaki, D'Urville Island and Cobb River area; but to date, the pounamu that has been found there does not compare in quality or quantity with its cousin, from South Westland.

DUN MOUNTAIN

Within the Dun Mountain area along the contacts between the ultramafic and adjacent country rocks, especially in the areas where the serpentinite has undergone intense shearing, there are numerous lens-shaped pods of altered rocks. Thin greenish semi-nephrite has developed around the margins and has been found at several localities, according to R. G. Coleman (a petrologist who pioneered jade petrogenesis) and others. Also, within the mélanges, thin veins and nodules of semi-nephrite can be found contacting the serpentinite in some road cuttings and at numerous other places. The earliest report of nephrite in the area is in 1864 by Ferdinand von Hochstetter, who picked up a cobble beside a large serpentinite vein on a beach at Current Basin opposite the southern end of D'Urville Island.

As expected, the many rivers that drain the whole region are potential sites of jade deposits, and most have, from time to time, produced reasonable examples of semi-nephrite and nephrite. Generally the colour is dull greyish green to olive, often with a chalky or rust-coloured rind. However, a few specimens found in the Roding River are an attractive light green with chatoyant ribbons. Many examples from this region also contain diopside in varying proportions, like the material in the Livingstone Mountains in Southland.

Further south along the Alpine Fault is the Matakitaki ultramafic body, an isolated occurrence of Dun Mountain Ophiolite rocks. Here contact rocks have been altered, and Coleman reports that some have been reconstituted to a fine-grained semi-nephrite.

D'URVILLE ISLAND

The geology of D'Urville Island is an extension of the Dun Mountain Ophiolite Belt and, likewise, has an assemblage of a wide variety of rock types capable of producing nephrite, so it is no surprise that in a number of places, nephrite beach pebbles and in situ nephrite occur sparingly.

D'Urville Island is renowned for its deposits of metasomatised argillite rocks, which were quarried and worked extensively by early Māori for toolmaking. Before they discovered nephrite, early Māori also used serpentinite from the Nelson region for fishing lures and other purposes, and to create some exceptionally beautiful items of adornment. Because serpentinite, argillite and nephrite often occur in close association, Māori would have soon discovered the properties of nephrite, and this may explain the origin of semi-nephrite fragments and artefacts recovered from early archaeological sites at the Heaphy River and in the general Nelson area. Whether they used D'Urville Island pounamu or not is unclear. Further research using the techniques mentioned at the end of this chapter may resolve this.

Arthur Dieseldorff analysed a selection of rocks from D'Urville Island, collected by the director of the Bremen Museum, Germany while on a zoological expedition to New Zealand in 1901. Dieseldorff described three nephrite beach pebbles in great detail, and the small inclusions of nephrite occurring in the in situ serpentinite that was found nearby. It is interesting that his findings, published in German, appear to be the first account of an in situ nephrite occurrence in New Zealand.

The few D'Urville Island in situ veins that I have been able to inspect on both sides of the upper half of the island are frequently botryoidal, forming sculptural nodules of convoluted bubbly-looking masses. When they are unweathered, the curved surfaces are naturally polished from earth movement and make very appealing specimens. The colour is opaque olive to light green.

OTHER SOURCES

Between the Cobb and Takaka rivers in northwest Nelson there exists a large mass of ultramafic rocks, and an attractive dark green translucent bowenite has been found in the vicinity. Many years ago an isolated boulder of light green nephrite was recovered in the Cobb River. There are also claims of other boulders being found in the Takaka River, which suggests that the area may have nephrite deposits.

To the east of Nelson lie the Marlborough Sounds. Captain James Cook visited the sounds, and while in Queen Charlotte Sound recorded from Māori that their pounamu source was from a large lake to the south, which we presume was Lake Wakatipu. Interestingly, he also later understood from Māori that pounamu could be found at the head of the sound. J. R. Forster, who was Cook's scientific officer, described a 5-cm-wide vein of nephrite in talc schist on a tiny islet near Motuara Island in Queen Charlotte Sound. This is geologically possible, but the occurrence has never been relocated. Some 200 years later I managed a brief visit to the island with the Department of Conservation. We did not see any nephrite; instead, there were conspicuous greenish veins protruding from the schist in the cliffs surrounding the island. These green quartz-rich veins, being harder than the enclosing soft schist, were weather-proud, and about the same width as Forster describes (i.e. about 5 cm). I feel sure Forster mistook these

for nephrite. Dieseldorff attempted to locate Forster's samples in England for analysis, but they seem to have disappeared.

Further prospecting of the ultramafic rocks in the Nelson area and the Marlborough schists may yield new occurrences and suggests that the potential for substantial further discoveries may lie more with in situ occurrences rather than alluvial deposits.

It is fascinating that the Dun Mountain Ophiolite Belt, an ancient slice of Earth's mantle and oceanic crust, continues northwards beyond D'Urville Island beneath Cook Strait and under the western North Island. Using geomagnetic measurements the data suggests that the belt is a continuous arc under the sea beyond New Zealand heading for New Caledonia. Certainly, serpentinite has been dredged from the sea floor many kilometres north of New Zealand. Apart from a brief resurface at Piopio near Hamilton, the belt is buried under billions of tonnes of more recent rocks. One can only imagine what jade treasures might exist concealed deep within, but 1.6 km down – untouchable as it will always be!

SOURCING JADE

Knowing the source of jade artefacts is valuable for archaeologists and anthropologists. Sourcing is also important for forensic purposes; an example of this is the recent prosecution for illegal mining of jade in the South Westland area. In recent years there has been a flood of raw nephrite imported from Russia, Canada and Australia to New Zealand to supply the jade industry. In most cases, the origin is declared, but there is a growing need to be able to accurately establish the source. Experienced jade workers can spot the differences and this relies heavily on recognising the various

distinctive characteristics. In my own case, fifty years of accumulated knowledge from studying specimens, artefacts and characteristics has provided me with the confidence to identify the source in most cases. Proving it beyond any doubt is another story.

There are several scientifically based methods for sourcing. These generally involve developing a large database from known sources, using an analytical method to highlight distinctive characteristics for each source, then applying this same method to analyse material from an unknown source and comparing results with the reference database. To prove a particular source conclusively requires there to be no overlap of the characteristics from source to source. In practice, each source contains variability, so scientists are more comfortable defining the statistical probability that a particular sample has come from one source or another.

Analysing the chemical composition of jade, either major or trace elements, and the tiny included minerals has not been straightforward. It was pioneered by N. Richie in 1978 for a MA thesis at the University of Otago. He attempted a method which did not destroy the sample. Results were inconclusive due to a lack of sensitivity of the equipment. With advances in technology a number of other researchers have since trialled chemical analysis with some success.

More recently, Dr G. Campbell re-examined the use of chemical analysis for sourcing in a PhD study in forensic science at the University of Auckland. His study, completed in 2009, trialled micro-analytical techniques using a laser to vaporise tiny amounts of the jade. This method allows detection of much smaller amounts of trace elements than methods used in any previous work. Campbell's own use of data in combination with the latest statistical methods showed that it is possible to discriminate between

LEFT / The southern end of D'Urville Island, Marlborough Sounds. The island was an early traditional Māori source of argillite for toolmaking. Several small veins of pounamu occur in the ultramafic rocks.

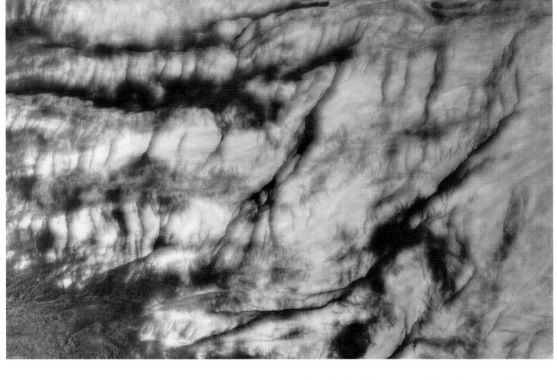

LEFT / Moss-laden trees in the Wild Natives Valley at the head of Bligh Sound, Fiordland.

ABOVE / Moss patterns veining a backlit slab of nephrite from Marsden.

sources of jade, both within fields and between fields in New Zealand. The scientific method of sourcing requires a large set of analyses to be developed from samples whose origin is known, for reference against samples of unknown origin. With further database development it should also be possible to distinguish between imported and New Zealand jade.

A different technique was recently developed by GNS Science geochronologist Dr C. Adams, who established a fingerprint method for sourcing nephrite by measuring the isotopic composition of the element strontium. When nephrite is formed it acquires a strontium isotopic signature identical to that of its meta-sedimentary component host rocks. Precise measurements of the strontium isotopic compositions from tiny pieces of nephrite can then be matched to the known data from the host rock terrane.

Preliminary data from other Pacific Rim jade occurrences has shown that they are distinctive. With only a small amount of overlap with New Zealand jade, this process should prove to be a valuable additional tool for sourcing nephrite and other materials.

It is interesting and convenient that the known New Zealand jade sources are from several different geological terranes, and the strontium isotope data also indicates that nephrite has formed at different time periods. For example, a specimen from the Dun Mountain Ophiolite Belt in the Livingstone Mountains was formed 236 million years ago, while a Wakatipu sample is 170 million years old and the youngest from Westland 6 million years old.

Sourcing jade artefacts and works of art is more difficult, as most methods require a small sample to be destroyed. However, researchers at the Institute of Earth Sciences, Academia Sinica, Taiwan, have confidently sourced Taiwanese nephrite artefacts using non-destructive processes. Sourcing is an important field of research that may in the future be able to solve the many ethnic jade distribution mysteries.

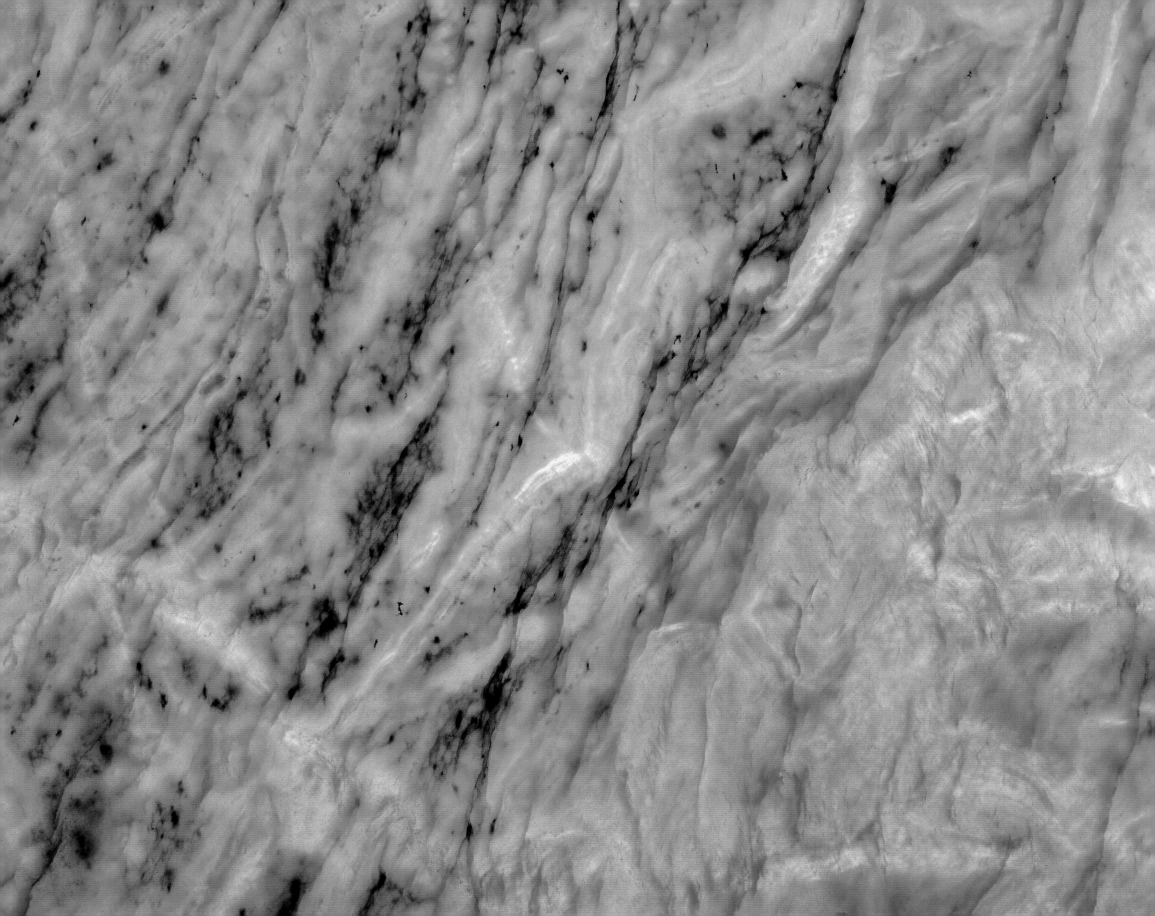

CHAPTER FIVE/STONES WITH STORIES

TŌNA AKE
MAURI KŌRERO
Everything possesses its own
life force

Jade is a stone with intrinsic value which has involved people the world over for a long time, so it is inevitable that stories of discovery, appreciation, utilisation, greed and conflict surround it.

In New Zealand there are many such stories. Most, of course, have never been recorded – just imagine the histories that bygone Māori could tell, with their several hundred years of association with the stone. In more recent times, after the 1860s, some remarkable stones were found; and stones found even more recently have been named after their finders. Alas, now all of them are cut up, mostly into little pieces that are widely distributed as jewellery throughout the world. Ironically, about half of each boulder is reduced to stone dust during processing and has now gone back to the land.

In New Zealand, it has become popular to have a pounamu touchstone at the entrance to public or corporate buildings, and there are many throughout the country. These pounamu are normally water-polished naturals of great beauty and value with thought-provoking names. Some of these are rather more than a touchstone and have become mauri (life force) pounamu.

At the entranceway to the National Army Museum at Waiouru in the North Island is a spectacular memorial wall composed of 437 polished jade tiles from South Westland. It commemorates all New Zealanders lost in conflict. 'Tears on Greenstone' has water flowing over it, symbolising mourning and renewed life.

Numerous stories of well known stones are recorded in other publications. The following are some that either came the way of Maika and me, or that we were somehow involved in.

ANGLEM STONE

This is a fascinating story of a 10-tonne pounamu boulder. It involves speculation, secrecy, disaster and intrigue.

Beginning in 1841 a Stewart Island settler and whaler, William Anglem, and others are reputed to have collected pounamu at Milford Sound and successfully traded it with North Island Māori for flax fibre. In turn, Anglem took the cargo of flax to Sydney where he sold it to ropemaking merchants.

In 1842, Anglem and others attempted to sell the stone direct to the Chinese market. The origin of this ambitious scheme began much earlier, in 1830, when a Captain Dacre acquired a Māori mere and, during his travels, exhibited it to jade merchants in Manila. They are said to have offered him the fantastic price of £1500 per ton for the rough stone and would accept all he could supply. Dacre has been credited with the fitting out of the sailing ship, the *Royal Mail*, at Sydney for the mining venture. Captain Anglem, who was visiting Sydney at the time, is reported to have sailed the *Royal Mail* via Nelson to Bluff in 1842, where he gathered some local Māori as extra hands. He then sailed around the coast to Milford Sound where he met the ship *Anita* at a bay now called Anita Bay. It is presumed that the crew of the *Anita* were also searching for pounamu.

During blasting operations of a large pounamu boulder, Anglem and two of his crew were badly injured from a premature gunpowder explosion. The *Royal Mail* dashed to Nelson with the injured for medical treatment, taking 10 days to get there. Anglem suffered serious injuries to his face, arms and hands – he lost an eye and finger; and the others were more or less blind. While at Nelson, Anglem was questioned about where the event took place, but he was reluctant to say other than that he and his crew ascended a large river in a boat somewhere on the West Coast.

The *Royal Mail* departed Nelson a month later, on 14 February 1843, bound for the West Coast. Presumably Anglem went back to pick up the cargo of pounamu, which is reputed to have then been taken to China. There is some doubt as to whether Anglem accompanied the cargo, however. The story goes that the Asian lapidaries rejected it because of numerous black specks throughout the stone. Other accounts of the same ill-fated enterprise give us a little more information.

Edward Shortland visited Otago and Southland in 1843 and adds to the tale. He mentions a 10-tonne boulder sitting in the middle of a stream at Piopiotahi/Milford Sound, and a party of miners who intended to blow it up into manageable chunks. They diverted the river by digging a new channel to access the boulder. After several months' work the extreme toughness of the stone had ruined their tools, but they managed to obtain sufficient stone to send a few tonnes to Manila. Apparently the workmen stayed on at the site, but eventually, with no sign of payment, they buried the product of their work and returned to the Foveaux Strait settlements. He adds that the following year a small quantity of this stone was taken to Wellington and sold to Māori for one shilling per pound weight.

Another version of events is recorded by Ro. Carrick. It refers to a man named Escott who was involved with Anglem and the pounamu venture. Escott apparently wrote a favourable account of the stone, which Anglem showed to an ex sugar planter, Long, who became enthusiastic about trading the stone with China. He arranged for the *Royal Mail* to collect a cargo of stone and take it to China. A second ship, the *Anita*, also with pounamu, went to Manila with Escott in charge. At Manila Escott became very drunk and deluded, thinking he had an antipapal crusade, which resulted in a falling out with the authorities. Apparently the cargo was to be used for crucifixes for the Catholic Church. The result was that he was

forced to sail away without unloading the cargo.

The stone that went to China on the *Royal Mail* was rejected. Carrick mentions a letter to the governor of Tasmania in 1843 petitioning to have a fine reduced for a New Zealand trader who had aided a convict prisoner to escape. Evidently the prisoner was involved in getting pounamu from New Zealand and a cargo of jade was landed at London and subsequently sold to the lapidary industry. The petition was based on the fact that the convict would be able to identify the place where the stone was obtained and thus assist in the colony's export potential. Carrick suggests that the prisoner was Escott.

Another possible twist on these stories is given by Dr Leonard Kinnicutt. He mentions that an officer of a small vessel that was sheltering in a bay off the south coast of Australia found a vein of a green stone and took a sample to China, where he discovered it was jade. A ship was taken to the site, and returned to China with the stone. The local jade merchants, fearful that so much jade would flood the market, refused to purchase – they commented that the stone was 'too young'. The cargo was abandoned and stored in 50 boxes and placed in a receiving-ship owned by Russell & Co., near Macau. They were given a receipt for the stone. Amazingly, about twenty years later, in 1851,

somebody produced the receipt, demurrage of $7000 was paid and the cargo was released.

At that time, New Zealand was often confused with Australia and the comment that the stone was 'too young' suggests that it may have been bowenite from Poison Bay, where there is an outcrop.

According to Anglem's daughter, who was interviewed by Herries Beattie, both vessels, the *Anita* and *Royal Mail*, took cargoes of pounamu from Piopiotahi (Milford Sound) to China. Although Piopiotahi is generally attributed as the source, I am not convinced. Another possibility is Poison Bay, a little further to the south. Here, pounamu is more plentiful and occurs as larger

ABOVE / The mouth of the Hope River near Barn Bay, South Westland. A source of pounamu for Māori and possibly early European entrepreneurs during the 1840s. COURTESY TE RŪNANGA O NGĀI TAHU

pieces. The pounamu found at Anita Bay and Poison Bay is bowenite. It has formed as narrow veins and casings around peridotite and is most unlikely to be in the form of a solid bowenite boulder of several tonnes. Milford Sound appears to have been often confused with the bays further north. There are no rivers in the area, only small creeks – and certainly not a torrent or a stream with a volume of water necessary to divert, as is described in the story.

Anglem never disclosed where he mined the pounamu. Others later mentioned that pounamu was obtained by whalers at Barn Bay. Of course, in this case the stone would be nephrite, rather than bowenite. Anglem knew the West Coast well from his sealing days, and had Māori companions and crew who we know had knowledge of pounamu at Barn Bay and several other bays on this part of the coast.

Large jade boulders on the South Westland beaches are not uncommon and in 1977 a 10-tonne semi-nephrite boulder from near Barn Bay was taken to Hokitika to be cut up. There were several boulders at Big Bay also that would exceed this weight. If Anglem's 10-tonne boulder was sitting in a river – which I suspect was the Hope River – it would have been water-polished and very obvious. The black specks peppered throughout the stone, which made it not acceptable to the Asian lapidaries, are rare in Milford bowenite but are distinctive hallmarks of South Westland stone. Furthermore, there is a large number of pounamu artefacts, particularly in the North Island, that were produced about that time from South Westland nephrite. I have recorded over 70 mere and other items, that appear to have been cut out of one stone, for they all have the same general appearance and identifiable inclusions. Are these pieces made from Anglem's rejected stone, or are they from other entrepreneurs at that time?

In 1845 another Stewart Islander, Captain James Joss, is reputed to have collected a shipload of stone from the same source as Anglem, and called at Wellington before sailing for the Pacific Islands. At about this time it was reported that a load of stone was sold to Māori at Wellington. Maybe this was either Joss's cargo or Anglem's rejected stone.

An interesting specimen was found at Barn Bay in the 1960s that may give some validity to early mining in this area. It is a nephrite fragment with a handmade hole for explosives.

TUANGAU AND HIS POUNAMU

This is a noteworthy story of a pounamu boulder weighing nearly 2 tonnes which was found by Māori in a branch of the Hōhonu River in 1864. A European miner claimed and removed it and this resulted in a legal wrangle – probably the first court case over the ownership of pounamu in New Zealand. Such was the complexity of the matter that it required three court hearings to sort it out. Despite the frenetic activity in the Westland goldfields at that time, court cases occurred in 1866 which demonstrated that pounamu was still highly valued by Māori.

Below is a summarised version extracted from the detailed court reports published by the *West Coast Times* and the *Daily Southern Cross*.

The first case began on 28 March 1866 with James Reynolds, defendant and Simon Tuangau, plaintiff.

On 19 March 1866 Tuangau handed Reynolds a summons to attend the Warden's Court on 28 March. The summons stated that Reynolds 'had taken possession of a block of greenstone awarded to Tuangau by the Warden'. No such award had ever been made. Reynolds was committed for trial by the magistrate, but the Grand Jury ignored the bill and he was discharged.

The second case began on 7 August 1866, but this time Reynolds was the plaintiff and Tuangau the defendant.

Evidence given was that in February 1864 a large pounamu boulder was found by a Māori, Simon Tuangau, while he was searching for gold at the Hōhonu River. He was accompanied by his wife and a Māori friend. Recognising the significance of their find, they spent three days digging the stones away from the sides of the boulder and levering it out of the river, now known as Greenstone Creek. By using two skids under it they got the boulder to the side of the bank, covered it over with wood and left with plans to come back after they had gone to Christchurch to buy tools to break up the stone, as Tuangau believed that he could not get permission to buy blasting powder.

They returned in June or July and broke two pieces off the stone and then later another piece, which was estimated to be 300 kg. It was well known to Māori in Greymouth that Tuangau had discovered the stone, and according to their custom, it was his. He then left the stone in charge of a group of miners. On returning he found that the people who had been caring for the stone had moved it to another place where it should have been safe from being buried by flash floods. In all, he had visited the boulder about five times, and after December 1865, he left it in charge of another miner, thought to have been Bill Chappell.

James Reynolds, who had left a position with the Southland Provincial Government, moved to the West Coast for 'the purpose of bettering himself'. In December 1865 he went to Greenstone Creek looking for pounamu and discovered a large block. He proceeded to peg out a claim under his miner's right. He then went to Greymouth and hired a skilled man who understood boring and blasting and they returned to the creek with drills, erected a forge for sharpening them and commenced working on the stone.

After a few hours of work they were stopped by Bill Chappell, who was working a gold claim immediately above the spot. He informed them that they must stop work because the stone belonged to a Māori and he was minding it on his behalf. Reynolds refused. Chappell continued to badger them and Reynolds threatened to jump his claim. Chappell retorted that he would inform Māori, which he did.

A few days later Tuangau and Mr Revell, the warden from Greymouth, met Reynolds near Māori Point, where Revell told him that he had taken possession of that which belonged to Tuangau and that he had better not touch it. Reynolds replied that the claim was abandoned and that he had taken it up under his miner's right. Revell said that it was not a mining question, but one of property and that the stone had been discovered by Tuangau before the area was proclaimed a goldfield.

Reynolds' circumstances did not allow him to pursue the matter to enter an action in the Supreme Court, so he discharged his man and returned to Greymouth, having lost £20 in wages and materials.

Believing that the stone was under the protection of a miner, Reynolds met with Tuangau at the end of February and offered to break up the stone and share it, with half going to Tuangau. After consulting with his partner, Tuangau decided that half was not enough. Reynolds then increased the offer to a three-quarter share, but no agreement was reached.

A few days after this discussion, Reynolds was told that there had been nobody in possession since about the beginning of January and that Tuangau had not been up the creek since the middle of December. This information prompted Reynolds to return to the creek, where he found the stone, still in the riverbed and now covered by boulders with water flowing over it from subsequent flooding.

Again he took possession of the stone, engaged a man, purchased more tools, and worked from the first week in March until 17 March without interruption. They broke up the stone from some six heavy blasts and packed the broken pieces in 16 bags, sending them to the junction of the Taramakau River and Greenstone Creek, 20 km over a rough road, to be ferried by boatman, Brodie, to the mouth of the Taramakau. The total weight was 843 kg. Ten bags were delivered to Robert Robb, hotelkeeper, for transporting to Hokitika. The remaining six bags were taken on 20 March by Brodie, but when landed they were seized by a constable under a warrant issued by the resident magistrate at Greymouth. The 10 bags had been seized some days previously.

In his address to the jury, Tuangau's solicitor said that the evidence might be divided under four headings: the evidence of detention; as to Reynolds' right to the property; as to the abandonment by Tuangau; and the stone's value, which was estimated to be between £2500 and £5000. Considering values at that time, this stone was a precious commodity.

Reynolds' solicitor added a fifth heading: wrongful detention. The stone had been seized by the police and had never been returned to him.

In his lengthy summing up of this second case, among all the other considerations, the judge said that the case was of the greatest importance, not for the amount of property in litigation, but as between a Māori and European, for it was of great consequence that a kindly feeling between the two races should be maintained, and impartial justice should be accorded to both. The case needed to be considered the same as if it were between two Europeans, or two Māori. After guiding the jury on the various issues he finished his remarks by telling the jury that they were to judge all the different issues and give their decision.

By midnight the jury had not come to a

decision. The judge explained that if, during the night, they should come to a decision, they were to let him know, but if not, he would be in attendance at 8 a.m. the next day. After being locked up all night, the jury did not arrive at a verdict.

On Saturday morning, 11 August, the jury was recalled and this time returned a verdict. Although they said that they felt Tuangau did not show an intention of abandoning the stone, they stated that they would leave it for the court to determine whether a verdict should be entered for Reynolds or Tuangau. The judge said that he would have a discussion with both solicitors and give his decision on the following Monday.

Both solicitors agreed that the case should be laid before the Court of Appeal by forwarding a statement of the case in writing to the court. That concluded the second sitting of this case at the Supreme Court in Westland.

On 15 October 1866, the Court of Appeal met at Wellington with five judges, and no solicitors appearing on either side; then in November 1866 Mr Justice Johnston gave judgement saying that the court was unanimous that Reynolds' case was not proven. The claim was that he had a quantity of pounamu which he thought was his and that Tuangau took it from him. Reynolds admitted that Tuangau found the stone first and started to break it up, but he thought that Tuangau had lost interest and abandoned it. The judges found to the contrary, that he did not abandon it, and the opinion of the court was that a verdict should be entered in favour of Tuangau.

It is not known what happened to the stone, but, at that time, there was a ready market with Māori in the North Island for pieces large enough to make mere.

Another example of explosives used at an early date is from von Hochstetter, who records that

Dr J. von Haast informed him of a story about a big boulder in the Arahura River. Tamati Freeman was a Māori chief from Aorere, Nelson, who visited the Arahura River in 1860 with four of his tribe, and while there, purchased a pounamu block weighing 35 kg. Apparently the piece was part of a big boulder that had been broken up using explosives. Considering the values at that time, the £60 that Tamati paid to the locals was quite high, but he estimated four mere could be made from it.

NGĀ ROIMATA O NGĀTI RAUKAWA – THE TEARS OF NGĀTI RAUKAWA

In 1894, William Colenso, printer, botanist and explorer, related an interesting story tracing the history of a big piece of nephrite. The stone weighed some 150 kg and was purchased by the Ngāti Raukawa tribe from a European in the Cook Strait area. The boulder remained in the tribe's possession until the death of Chief Moses Tarapuhi. The Ngāti Kahungunu tribe of Hawke's Bay on the East Coast of the North Island, learned of the death and assembled a large group, which travelled to Foxton on the west coast for the funeral. The big boulder was exhibited at the ceremony and given the name 'The Tears of Ngāti Raukawa'. It was then presented to the visitors.

Its long journey began. It was first taken by canoe up the Manawatu River to the village of Moutoa, then to another village, Te Hautotara, by members of the Ngāti Pakapaka hapū and rested there for a long time, attracting a lot of admiration. Eventually it was carried on a stretcher overland by Ngāti Pakapaka bearers and placed in the care of Henare Matua at Porangahau, who later handed it over to Te Harawira Te Tatere, who had it carried further to his village, Waimarama, south of Cape Kidnappers on the East Coast. Here it remained

in his possession for several years until eventually, in 1878, he took it to Napier to be sawn into slabs suitable for making mere. Te Harawira arranged for this work to be done by a European, James Rolfe, of Emerson Street. Colenso visited Rolfe's workshop and described the operation as underpowered and 'makeshift' with 'three small saws in brisk movement worked by steam', and remarked that as the speed of cutting was very slow, it would take a long time. Rolfe eventually had 11 saws operating at one time, and took nine months at 10–15 hours a day to cut the boulder into 12 slabs.

From this description it sounds like Rolfe was operating a reciprocating drag saw with several parallel steel blades. This type of saw, using abrasive grit and water, was common for cutting granite but is slow for working on nephrite.

Te Harawira had apparently agreed for the boulder to be cut into 12 pieces for the sum of £200, to be paid in installments. After an initial payment of £10, no more money was forthcoming. After some bargaining, Te Harawira later agreed to pay £100 for six slabs, with Rolfe keeping the remainder. The dispute dragged on for some years with still no payment, so the matter finally reached court in 1881. The case was dismissed because of insufficient evidence and Te Harawira said that there was no agreement and considered that the charge was too high. Two years later, back in court, Rolfe won his case with Te Harawira to pay £150 for the 12 slabs. Again, no payment was made, so the bailiff took possession of the pounamu slabs and advertised them for sale by auction. Colenso attended the auction and purchased five slabs, the whole 12 bringing only £20.10 shillings.

Colenso later made a present of one of his slabs to the Māori King, Tawhiao, at a public meeting and banquet in his honour. The king subsequently ate the meal from the pounamu slab and after the dinner proudly exited carrying the pounamu slab across his chest.

The stone was canoed and carried by Māori from the west coast to the east, some 280 km, which at that time was no mean feat; and they were then deprived of their treasure. The name given to the stone, 'The Tears of Ngāti Raukawa', was indeed apt.

VEEK BOULDER

The story begins in Germany in the picturesque forested highlands west of the Rhine River at a small place, Idar-Oberstein, a major gem-cutting centre of the world. Here an extensive stone-processing industry was well established by the early 1600s, using local semi-precious stones. By 1800, stone was being imported from all over the world and cut and shaped into jewellery and other items on huge water-powered sandstone grinding wheels.

Back in New Zealand, around 1900, the Westland goldfields were producing a steady source of nephrite. This was at the time probably the world's largest supplier, with much of its stone finding its way to Idar-Oberstein.

While Alf Poole and I were visiting Germany in 1980 we met the descendants of the Veek and Dalheimer families, who, among others, worked with New Zealand jade in Idar-Oberstein. Rudolf Veek was born in 1883 and represented the family business of August Veek (established 1842) as a diamond and gemstone dealer. Between 1904 and 1909 he maintained an office in Sydney and spent quite a bit of time in New Zealand, especially at Kumara. There he purchased nephrite from the miners and agents dispatching it back to Germany, where the family business processed it into various items. One such agent was his fellow countryman Louis Seebeck, a butcher at Kumara. Much of it went back to New Zealand in the form of jewellery and, in particular, souvenir hei tiki.

A memorable story is recalled by Rudolf Veek's wife, Mia. While on one of his visits to the West Coast Veek purchased a very large jade boulder, but because he had to return to Germany urgently he left it behind and paid a person to arrange for its transport home. The boulder did not arrive. A year later Veek returned to New Zealand. He could not locate the man who had agreed to send the stone, which was still lying where he had left it, so he personally organised the shipping to ensure its departure. After nearly a year the giant boulder arrived in Idar-Oberstein, where it caused quite a sensation. It was so big that no saw was capable of cutting it, and much professional and amateur advice was offered in an attempt to overcome the problem. Finally a decision was made to blast it with explosives, and this event attracted considerable attention. The result was disastrous because the quality of the stone was poor and the blasting rendered it useless, so that it did not even cover the cost of the gunpowder. The reward for all Veek's trouble was laughter from his peers.

During this period there was no easy way of proving the potential of large boulders with thick rinds, and they were very much a gamble. Heavy sledgehammers just bounced off unless there was a fracture or sharp corner. The desperate practice of using explosives on nephrite was quite common, but required just the right technique to reduce it into manageable chunks and avoid spoiling the stone with fractures.

DEVLIN BOULDER

At the entrance to the Tangata Whenua Gallery in the Otago Museum, Dunedin, is displayed a big Westland pounamu boulder with a story.

The Devlin brothers, Andrew and Thomas, operated a lapidary business in South Dunedin for around fifty years. When it closed down in 1941,

LEFT / German lapidary Rudolf Veek (right) atop his purchase of a large Westland jade boulder awaiting shipment to Germany at the Sydney dockyards, c. 1905. COURTESY M. VEEK

RIGHT / My wife Ann beside the Devlin jade boulder with the sawn groove in a drill hole. It is displayed at the entrance to the Tangata Whenua Gallery, Otago Museum, Dunedin. R. BECK

the boulder was donated to the museum.

The stone is dark green with reddish streaks, and the typical rusty, chalky rind covering half of it. The rest is jagged, and it is obvious that the piece has been broken off an even larger water-worn boulder. Near the midsection is a worked, smooth groove running vertically, occupying the remains of a drilled hole. This half hole explains much for, at some time in the past, it has been made laboriously by hand using a punch drill and hammer. An

explosive charge had been inserted and blown the boulder apart, explaining the jagged side.

Some thirty years ago when I was researching the history of the Devlin brothers, I spoke with Andrew's family, who told me how the smooth groove came about. Apparently this piece of pounamu languished in the factory yard for a long time, as it was too big to do anything with. One family member said that as a young girl she worked in the factory making jewellery after

school, and Andrew, in all seriousness, told her that if she could cut this stone in two he would grant her any wish. In her spare time she worked away at the groove, rubbing with an old piece of grindstone in the remains of the drilled hole as a starting point. A smooth groove developed, but progress was incredibly slow and she soon realised that this task was virtually impossible, and it was all a practical joke! It's a lovely story, and her efforts and aspirations are now preserved.

LEFT / Tom Trevor beside the nephrite boulder he discovered at Slip Stream in the Dart River Valley, 1971. Weighing some 20 tonnes, it is now completely buried under gravel from recent flash floods. The whole Te Koroka site is protected within a special area of the Mt Aspiring National Park, with entry by permit only.
R. BECK

ABOVE RIGHT / Michael Skerrett, Waihopai Ngāi Tahu kaumātua, acknowledges Te Koroka with a karakia to uplift pounamu. He is accompanied by A. Chapman, Ngāi Tahu Dart River Jet Safaris, and Puketeraki Ngāi Tahu kaumātua Matapura Ellison.
R. BECK

BELOW RIGHT / Ōraka/Aparima Ngāi Tahu kaumātua Muriel Johnstone, Stewart Bull and Jane Davis preparing the touchstone 'Manatu', recovered from Te Koroka for the Ngāi Tahu exhibition, 'Mō Tātou'.
R. BECK

TE KOROKA BOULDER AND TOUCHSTONES

The 20-tonne jade boulder discovered at Te Koroka, mentioned in Chapter Four, is one that has been studied possibly more than any other. The stone has been regularly visited and reported on since its discovery in 1971, and data relating to its condition and other details have been documented for nearly forty years.

I can vividly recall the day it was found – Tom Trevor, Arthur Mackenzie and I were returning down Slip Stream to the Dart River, scrambling over slippery boulders, when the creek diverted off to one side exposing a deep dry channel ahead of us. We dropped into this and lowered ourselves down between huge boulders and then came the cry from Tom, who was leading: 'What do you make of this?' We caught up and were astounded to see the big boulder partly buried – and to realise it was jade! The stone was dry, so we scooped water with our hands from the nearby waterfall and splashed it over to bring out the colour. We drooled over it for some time and made a rough measurement with our boots: approximately 4 m × 2.1 m × 1.2 m.

Taking the relative density of nephrite at 3, this gave a theoretical weight of 30 tonnes; however, it is not a perfect rectangle and it contains a little talc, so a reduction of 25% may be in order, resulting in a weight of some 22 tonnes – to be safe, we have reckoned 20 tonnes. The īnanga boulder is pale green to silvery green with chatoyant areas, and there are inclusions of soft talc and purplish chlorite. The quality varies from hard compact nephrite to schistose semi-nephrite. When wet, it looks magnificent.

Since 1976 when the find was publicly announced, the stone has been visited by many people from New Zealand and overseas, including Māori kaumātua, professional scientists and researchers. In recent years there have been several

Ngāi Tahu hīkoi pounamu to the area arranged by Otago and Southland iwi. Every time the boulder has been visited it has been noticed that its immediate environment and the fan below were changing rapidly. Slip Stream is actually part of a huge landslide, regarded as one of the most active in Otago. A recent geological study of the slide shows that the sediment and debris movement is hazardous, especially with storm events, when debris flows with the consistency of wet concrete and can travel at high speed. Little wonder the big pounamu boulder was being progressively buried until 2007, when it was completely covered by shingle. The huge gravel fan far below has engulfed large areas of mature beech trees, leaving just dead upright shafts of timber.

That the area is dramatic is an understatement. The surrounding towering peaks at the head of Lake Wakatipu make it one of the most scenic parts of New Zealand, a favoured tramping route and location for the film industry. Because of this unique setting, an investigation by Ngāi Tahu of the feasibility of uncovering the boulder and possibly moving it to a safe site nearby, but out of reach from the landslide, is underway. If this can be achieved, it would be an added attraction and a wonderful opportunity to interpret the Te Koroka story.

In 2009 the Southern Kaitiaki Rūnanga Pounamu Committee resolved to visit Te Koroka and gather some pounamu for each of the rūnanga, plus extra stones for special requests for touchstones.

Two teams of iwi, Department of Conservation staff and I were helicoptered to the site and spent the whole day searching for suitable pounamu. It was a historic occasion as this was the first time that an expedition to collect pounamu had taken place since the iwi forebears last visited the site back in the early 1800s. The ceremony, which involved a karanga (call) that echoed around the mountains and appropriate karakia (prayers) under the gaze

of the 'resting giant', was a moving experience. By the end of the day enough suitable stones had been found and taken to Glenorchy at the head of Lake Wakatipu, where they were photographed and checked against the GPS register.

The committee named the stones:

Manatunga: The name reminds us that it is no ordinary pounamu, it is a memento which comes from a very special place, a wāhi tapu, a koha from our tupuna Koroka who lies resting there. It commands respect. This 120-kg piece is mounted on a plinth in the courtyard of the Ngāi Tahu precinct buildings, Queenstown.

Manawawera: Reminds us that the natural world can become very excited and angry if it is not looked after properly. Manawawera is here to support and encourage ngā tamariki a Tāne and must be touched from time to time to be kept calm; touching it will clear the mind for the mahi (work) at hand. It now rests in the Department of Conservation Visitor Centre, Queenstown.

Manatu: Tells us to bear in mind the very special place the pounamu comes from, the wāhi tapu. It comes from the very throat of our tupuna Koroka. We must touch it, stroke it, otherwise it will become anxious and homesick and want to go back. The mana endures, we must appreciate it. This stone was brought back to the Ōraka/Aparima marae at Colac Bay where the sharp edges were smoothed by descendants of the original people who collected from Te Koroka so long ago.

After a special ceremony Manatu travelled to Wellington for temporary display in the Kura Pounamu Exhibition at Te Papa, to later return to Glenorchy at the head of Lake Wakatipu to be the focus in the Ngāi Tahu Dart River Jet Safari visitor centre.

TE MĀORI MAURI STONE

This story has its beginning in April 1984 when I joined rangers Brian Ahern and Paul Chapman of Mount Aspiring National Park on a survey expedition to a remote mountainous area that we had wanted to visit for some time. It involved crossing several passes and rivers in a huge loop covering a distance of some 45 km in seven days. I am a keen tramper, but these boys were much fitter, so for me the trip was both exhilarating and a struggle. The bonus was exploring new country in perfect weather with crystal-clear starry nights, and camping out at high altitude.

We were about to cross a river known to Māori as Kaoreore, a name associated with pounamu, when I spotted a boulder of nephrite partly immersed in water. The others shared in the moment, then waded across the river. Meanwhile I rolled it towards the bank and, after a closer inspection, took a photograph and proceeded to catch up with the others. We were on a tight schedule with a long way to go and I was disappointed that we could not spend longer in this place.

Some two years later I received a phone call from Piri Sciascia, who was involved with the Te Māori Exhibition of Māori Art and was entrusted with the task of initially obtaining a pounamu for the American end-of-tour arrangements. Te Māori was at that time touring four American museums and, on its return, would be shown in four New Zealand venues. Piri was keen on a special expedition to search for such a stone, rather than use an existing boulder from somebody's collection.

Jade boulders are not just lying around, and instantly my mind flashed back to the one spotted in 1984. This was a long shot, as floods in the interim would have surely washed it away – but perhaps there were others. Piri duly organised a team consisting of Brian Ahern, Alf

The pounamu boulder Te Māori, safely wrapped in a bush shirt and bound to a carrying branch with flax/harakeke for the downstream trek. R. BECK

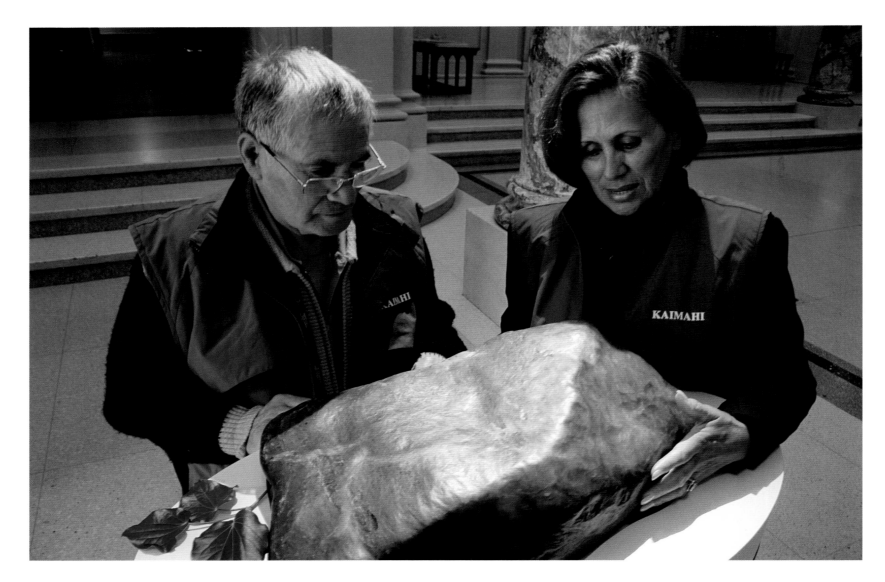

Poole and me, representing Southland Museum, plus Piri and his friend Chris Porteners. In May 1986 we all met at Queenstown in the late afternoon at Alf's holiday home and discussed plans for the next day. Weather was a big consideration and the long-range forecast was not good, so before retiring to bed we checked the night sky. The moon was shining brightly, surrounded by a huge halo – usually this phenomenon indicates an impending weather change for the worse. Piri pointed out that the lunar halo or kurahaupō was associated in Māori literature with 'successful findings'. Likewise, next morning, a kūkupa or kererū (wood pigeon) flew into a kōwhai tree beside the house, something that was quite remarkable as Alf had never seen these birds in Queenstown before. Piri and Chris assured us that this was also a good sign as the bird's plumage was speaking pounamu to our willing eyes.

The morning was clear, but the helicopter pilot was reluctant to fly as rain was forecast where we were heading – thick clouds and mountains are not a good combination. We were about to postpone the trip when Brian radioed one of his staff who was stationed deep in the mountains, who reported that it was clear. So the trip was on!

The helicopter flight was spectacular, passing over jagged mountains dusted with their first snow of the season. It was difficult to contain our excitement – this expedition was important and we had high expectations for a successful outcome. I warned the others that we would need all the luck

Ngāi Tahu exhibition guides, Wilfred Tekoeti and Marie Mahuika-Forsyth of Makaawhio, caress Te Māori at the entrance to Te Hokinga Mai, featuring 'Mō Tātou', the Ngāi Tahu whānui exhibition in Christchurch, 2010. The leaves beside the stone are an offering to the taonga. R. BECK

we could get, and there was a strong possibility of returning empty-handed.

We had some difficulty actually pinpointing the area, but finally set down in a small clearing close to the river. The cold water was crystal clear and we headed upstream searching for any sign of pounamu. The river was a series of gravel bars, rapids, deep holes and bluffs, so we were all soon quite wet. After about two hours, a pounamu boulder was discovered sitting half out of the water, but glowing among the other grey stones. There was little mistaking what it was. It was the right size and, from memory, looked like the one I found in 1984 – but I could not be sure. We were confident that we had our stone, and wondered what else the river offered. Many Māori believe that pounamu is not found: it reveals itself to you. We continued further upstream and there was an even larger pounamu boulder, half buried, too big to move. We caressed it and turned back as time was running out. During our journey back down the river, the light was from another quarter, which allowed us to see the stones on the bottom more clearly. Suddenly, in a waist-deep torrent, was a portion of pounamu partly obscured by other stones. It was wedged tightly; nevertheless, with rock picks and fingers we were able to prise it out, getting very wet in the process. This one was quite different from the first boulder, being ovoid and strongly foliated, with birdlike characteristics. It seemed fitting to name it Te Kererū after the bird we saw that morning.

We now had two boulders to get back to the helicopter, which was quite a distance away. Te Kererū, about 50 kg, just fitted into a pack. Chris and Brian took turns to get it well down the river, stumbling over slippery boulders and often taking short rests. The other boulder was much heavier, and Piri and I elected to carry it. First we wrapped it in Piri's heavy bush shirt, suspended on a long branch, but it kept slipping out. None of us had

any rope. Our luck continued with the discovery of a wharariki (small mountain flax bush; *Phormium cookianum*) on the river bank. Just as early Māori would have done, we bound it with the flax until secure. Progress downstream was now much faster, with each of us carrying one end of the pole and the boulder slung between, sometimes in the water and other times being slid over the stones.

We arrived at a high bluff with a very deep pool below. There was only one way, and that was to climb and sidle around the rocky face. Halfway around, catastrophe struck – the boulder slid out of the shirt and was heading for the pool. I desperately blocked it with my knee. I called to Piri to help, but he was couldn't, because he was above me and totally exhausted. We caught our breath, then together clawed the boulder back to a safe position and repacked it in its sling. The journey from there on was relatively straightforward. We were soon flying high towards home with our precious cargo, passing over the mountains now pink in the setting sun.

Back at Queenstown we compared the photograph that I took in 1984, and, yes, it was the same stone. The angular shape reminded us of an adze, so it was named Te Toki.

Both stones were taken to Invercargill to the home of Naina Russell for her blessing. Naina was a highly respected kaumātua and great-great-granddaughter of Tuhawaiki, the famous paramount southern chief. Te Toki and Te Kererū, which were their initial or finding names, then journeyed to Wellington to be received at a ceremony with the Arts Council and Te Māori Management Committee. Mawhera Incorporation gifted a piece of pounamu from Waitaiki Creek, Arahura River, with one end cut off and taken back to the creek, the concept being that each part would think of the other.

The committee now had three pounamu at their disposal, so three were blessed by tohunga

Henare Tuwhangai and given official names: Te Waipounamu (South Island) was the name for the Arahura piece, and it was given to the first venue of *Te Māori* – The Metropolitan Museum of Art in New York. Te Kererū became Aotearoa (New Zealand), and it now rests where the exhibition finished, at the Field Museum in Chicago. Te Toki was renamed Te Māori – keeper of the spiritual force of *Te Māori* exhibition, and it toured four New Zealand cities, where it greeted visitors and was touched by hundreds of thousands of people. At the completion of the tour, it was agreed that the mauri touchstone, Te Māori, should return to Murihiku, and a special group of trustees was appointed as caretakers. It is now displayed in the Māori Gallery at Southland Museum and Art Gallery in Invercargill, but from time to time it travels to be present at important Māori occasions and special exhibitions.

Te Māori was brought from Te Papa, where it was part of the Ngāi Tahu *Mo Tatou* exhibition, for the 25th Celebration of *Te Māori* Exhibition on 10 September 2009. The celebration was held at the Te Māori Centre on Waiwhetu marae, home of Kara Puketapu, who was chair of the *Te Māori* Committee during its American tour. The stone Te Māori continued touring the South Island in the *Mo Tatou* exhibition where once again it greeted visitors.

For nearly 10 years before retirement I had the privilege of touching Te Māori every day, each time generating such wonderful memories.

TE PAPA STONE

Alf Poole and I often travelled to the West Coast to purchase jade specimens, which was always exciting as we had our contacts to call on and see what they had to offer. I was looking for a particular small boulder with a thick rind so that I could carve an emerging green centre. As was always the case, our contacts would say, 'You should call on so and so. He found a nice piece the other day.' I was referred to Peter Haddock, who operated a goldmine in the Dunganville area near Marsden. He had a depot in Greymouth and we met him and looked over a few small boulders and cobbles. We made some purchases, then he took us to another room where there was a huge water-worn boulder under a tarpaulin. The lighting was poor, but I could see immediately that it was a gem. Peter had discovered it while digging in his gold claim and felt strongly that he did not want to see it sacrificed to a diamond saw. He asked if Southland Museum would like to purchase it, and he generously offered it at half price. This was tempting, but we were planning a big redevelopment and needed every cent for bricks and mortar, so I agreed to find a suitable home for it.

I contacted the National Museum in Wellington and convinced them that this stone was a 'must have'. Museum personnel eventually visited Peter and viewed the stone, but before finalising the deal, they asked me for a professional opinion. Alf and I were again on the Coast in the following year and we spent two days closely inspecting and testing the stone, this time under better conditions. This work had to be done very carefully so that it did not spoil the appearance. The stone was quite rectangular in shape with a thick, weathered rind on the base, a mid section of solid green with water-polished sides and ends, grading upwards to a more granular textured top. Viewed from above the overall shape resembled the South Island; even the Alpine Fault was represented by a natural crack, so we tentatively named it Te Waipounamu. From our discreet testing, we concluded that the stone was an exceptional example of New Zealand nephrite and worthy to be preserved as a national treasure. The weight was a little over 1.3 tonnes and it

measured approximately 150 cm × 60 cm × 60 cm. The museum duly made the purchase and, after a special ceremony in 1990, it was displayed in the foyer of the old National Museum in Buckle Street. The boulder was eventually placed at the entrance to the marae in the new building, Te Papa, which was opened in 1998.

We recommended that the boulder's appearance could be improved if some of the thin oxidised surface could be carefully removed. The idea of having small pieces of sandstone available

for the public to do this with was not practical, so instead coarse quartz sand was substituted. The boulder now rests in a shallow pool of water with the sand, and the public have been rubbing the stone with the grit for many years . This alone will not remove the rind, but it has put a fine polish on the stone, thus enhancing it.

This boulder has become a very popular hands-on exhibit in the museum, and since installation it has been touched and appreciated by millions of hands.

ABOVE / Children enjoying Te Papa's mauri stone. MUSEUM OF NEW ZEALAND TE PAPA TONGAREWA

RIGHT / The two 1990 symposium jade boulders representing the North and South islands, linked by a woven flax cord. Nine carvers worked on the stones, which are permanently displayed in the pounamu section of the Left Bank Art Gallery, Greymouth.

THE 1990 SYMPOSIUM STONES

In 1990 the New Zealand Government encouraged the country to celebrate 150 years since the signing of the Treaty of Waitangi.

The West Coast Society of Arts in Greymouth, which had held jade carving exhibitions since 1984, took up the challenge and received funding from the 1990 Commission to purchase two beautiful nephrite boulders for a jade carving symposium project. The larger boulder (60 kg) came from the Kaniere area; the other (30 kg) was found in the Arahura River.

Governor-General Sir Paul Reeves was welcomed by local iwi and he blessed the stones at a special ceremony in Greymouth.

Nine carvers – Russell Beck, Robyn Barclay, Ian Boustridge, Brian Robinson, Peter Tennant from the South Island; and Paul Annear, John Edgar, Hepi Maxwell and Donn Salt from the North Island – were invited to a meeting at Greymouth to decide what to do with these significant boulders. The day was very wet and we all sat in a circle in a small room with the stones in the centre. Our host explained the project, then left us to brainstorm on possible ways to collectively create a work of art. Discussion varied from quite elaborate ideas to doing nothing at all, or working one stone only. As a general rule, when boulders are smooth and water-worn, most carvers are reluctant to carve them as they are too precious, but this was not an option for us. We began discussing what the minimum was that we could do, while still creating something worthy of the project.

After much deliberation, which took nearly three days, we all agreed to link the boulders together with a plaited tether symbolic of the two main islands of New Zealand – the larger stone being the South Island, the smaller the North Island. Discussion then switched to how to achieve

this. Believe me, there are many different ways to attach a rope or make a hole!

With our concept finally approved, the large boulder journeyed to Invercargill for work to commence; then it travelled back to Greymouth for the other South Island carvers. The smaller stone went as far north as Whangarei for its hole; then both were returned to Greymouth two years later, where they were linked with a specially woven flax-fibre rope made by Dante Bonica.

At the official opening of the Left Bank Art Gallery, Greymouth in 1992, the stones were welcomed and placed on display in a special pounamu gallery.

TE HUARAHI TŌMAIRANGI AOTAETAEATA – THE PATHWAY OF THE DEW BEFORE THE CLOUD OF THE EARLY MORNING RAIN

In 2002 a Westland man, Tony Maitland, who had a deep appreciation of pounamu, discovered a 600 kg nephrite boulder in the rugged country north of the Taramakau River. The ownership of all pounamu in its natural state was handed back to the Ngāi Tahu tribe in 1997, so Tony took a photograph and informed Te Rūnanga o Ngāi Tahu authorities. They, in conjunction with Te Rūnanga o Ngāti Waewae, organised a small party

which visited the site and extracted the boulder.

This pounamu is in its natural water-worn condition with the typical yellowish weathered rind, but with tantalising small windows of green showing through in several places. This was an important find, and it was embraced by Te Rūnanga o Ngāi Tahu and Ngāti Waewae as a symbolic relationship-building process between the Maitland family and the local community.

After the boulder was named, it was displayed at Ngāi Tahu Head Office in Christchurch for some time. It is now a feature exhibit at their recently established pounamu shop in Hokitika. It is the wish that this pounamu will eventually rest as a mauri stone in the planned marae at Arahura.

EXPO BOULDER 'MATAWAI'

In 2004 a small group of Mawhera people, accompanied by Maika Mason, were seeking pounamu high in Waitaiki Creek, a tributary of the upper Arahura River. A young woman, Te Koha Raki Mason, discovered a large pounamu at the base of a low waterfall. It had been recently exposed after heavy rain and was embedded between large rocks with a portion showing above the gravels. There was no indication of its size but it did have a tantalising water-polished window that was a deep rich green. This was obviously an important find – but it was going to be a challenge to remove it.

Pounamu boulders in steep mountain creeks are usually tightly wedged and can be difficult to extract without dislodging the huge surrounding rocks. Another factor was that the stone could easily be buried again in another flood, so its removal was urgent. Maika contacted Ian Boustridge, a Greymouth jade carver with considerable experience in extracting heavy boulders, and he accepted the project.

The find created great excitement within Mawhera, and the young woman's grandmother Auntie Lady Mason told Ian she would like to see the stone before her eightieth birthday. Ian and a small team of helpers helicoptered in to the creek, armed with all the necessary gear, and began digging it out. Adjacent boulders were first secured so they could not fall back on the workers. Then, with the aid of hand-operated winches and wire ropes, the pounamu was slowly hoisted out of its bed to the edge of the waterfall. The boulder, encapsulated in a heavy net, was now ready to be lifted out by the helicopter. So far, so good – but nothing is ever straightforward.

The helicopter, a heavy lifting model used for logging, carefully manoeuvred into position with strop attached and everyone scrambled back to a safe position to watch the spectacle. Lifting stones can be quite dramatic, with the air blasting down from the rotors swirling spray everywhere, and a deafening noise from the jet engine. The machine took up the slack and the boulder nudged only slightly. The weight indicator on the helicopter read about 1.8 tonnes which was right on the lifting limit, especially at high altitude. More attempts were made, but the helicopter could not lift it clear and kept dragging it back into the waterfall. A final attempt only managed to slide it down the creek about 20 m, so reluctantly they had to leave it perched precariously on top of a huge rock.

The disheartened group returned to civilisation and discussed their strategy. Sawing off a piece to reduce the weight was not an option as it was a beautiful stone and its value was in its wholeness. There was a larger helicopter in New Zealand capable of lifting heavy loads, and it was the best – but expensive – solution. Several weeks later, while waiting for this machine to arrive, the pilot of the original helicopter said he was confident that it was worth another try, as he felt that his machine at the time was down on power. His challenge was: 'If I

can't get it out, there is no charge; if I do, you pay.' The team returned to Waitaiki and the boulder was still there, waiting. The helicopter hooked on the net. At first it struggled, but ever so slowly the pounamu rose amid cheers and both disappeared down the valley to lower altitude, then to a waiting trailer at the road end.

The stone created a lot of attention and many people came to see it and, yes, Ian delivered the stone before the eightieth birthday. Parts of the boulder's surface were enhanced by light polishing and the pounamu was named Matawai, meaning 'look closely'.

The Ministry of Trade and Enterprise required a centrepiece feature for the New Zealand display at the International Expo, to be held in Japan. They contacted Maika about finding a suitable touchstone. A special display was designed, with Matawai resting in a pool of water with a low waterfall cascading over it – just as it was found high in Waitaiki Creek.

Matawai was shipped to Japan and installed in a dramatic display in the New Zealand Pavilion, where it was a show-stopper, touched and appreciated by huge numbers of visitors. Matawai duly returned and rested at Rotorua for a while before travelling again to another International Expo, this time in Shanghai, China.

Matawai, like other touchstones, grows in mana, becoming more precious every day.

TE HERENGA A PITO – THE JOINING TOGETHER OF TWO ENDS

The city of Christchurch has a Chinese sister city, Wuhan, and the city council asked Ngāi Tahu if a suitable pounamu boulder could be obtained for a gift to Wuhan as a symbol of their close relationship.

The Murihiku people of Southland in association with Te Rūnanga o Ngāi Tahu offered to carry out the request, and suggested a special trip to find a piece of tangiwai from their traditional collecting place.

After an appropriate karakia, a small team consisting of Michael Skerrett, Dean Whaanga, Ricky Topi and Raiha Bull set out early one morning in February 2008 by motor vehicle to Te Anau, then by helicopter to Anita Bay at the entrance to Milford Sound/Piopiotahi in perfect weather. Big specimens of tangiwai are rare and several hours were spent searching among the huge peridotite boulders for just the right piece. Several were considered, but for various reasons they were not suitable. Finally, just as they were about to leave, a piece was spotted almost buried in shingle, and they dug it out with their hands. This piece had definite potential, and a prayer of thanks was made before the long journey back to Invercargill.

I was not able to accompany the team at the time, but was pleased to be involved with the subsequent work on the stone to enhance it. Tangiwai is often found as thinnish casings around altered peridotite, and this was the case with this stone. It was decided to smooth one side to reveal the beautiful bluish green colour and translucency of the stone just underneath the weathered surface. Dean and I worked on it, mostly in the traditional manner, until we were happy with the result.

The stone was placed in a special kete woven from harakeke (flax) by the Awarua whānau, who also made other smaller gifts from harakeke and pounamu. It was named, blessed and farewelled at a special ceremony held at the Waihōpai marae before its long journey to China commenced.

Dean and Ann Johnstone, from the Ōraka/Aparima Rūnaka accompanied the Christchurch City Council delegation to China and Air New Zealand, as a mark of respect, offered to transport the stone in the cabin locker instead of the baggage hold. This caused an unwarranted and ill-informed headline in the media.

The tangiwai was duly handed over by the Christchurch Mayor to the Mayor of Wuhan and was placed on permanent display in a special museum in the Civic Building where it can be touched and appreciated by the Chinese people of Wuhan City.

For thousands of years Chinese culture has appreciated a number of stone types for their carvings – nephrite, jadeite and bowenite, so the choice of a piece of New Zealand bowenite (tangiwai) was fitting.

This project was a joint effort with Te Rūnanga o Ngāi Tahu, Christchurch City Council and Southland Rūnanga.

The name, Te Herenga a Pito, was given by a Ngāi Tahu elder and can be translated as 'the joining together of two ends' – the rationale being that the stone is still connected like an umbilical cord to its source and people in Murihiku, even though it resides far away in China.

LEFT / Matawai after it was enhanced by careful polishing beside Aunty Lady Mason (seated) and Hilda Tainui before the stone was shipped to Japan for the International Expo Exhibition. COURTESY H. TOOTELL

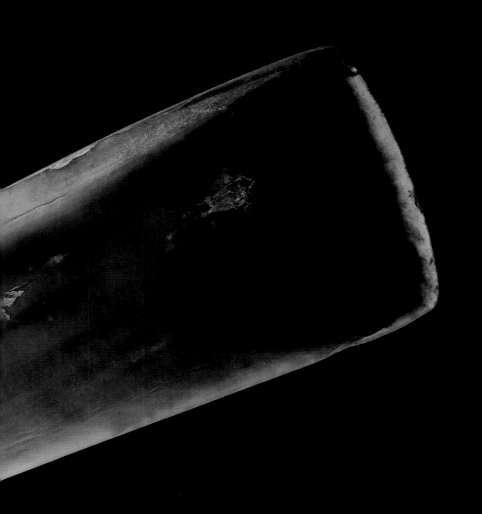

CHAPTER
SIX/TAONGA
MĀORI

TŪ TE
MANA

My prestige stands
before you

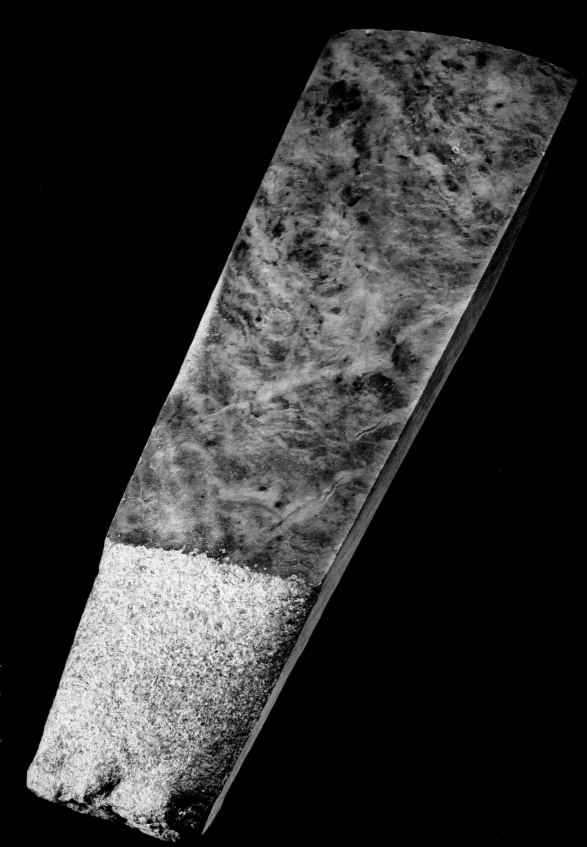

PREVIOUS PAGE / Toki poutangata. These important ceremonial adzes have blades of the finest kahurangi pounamu secured to elaborately carved wooden handles. Otago Museum.

LEFT / Chatoyant īnanga pounamu from Olderog/Waitaiki Creek, Westland.

RIGHT / Toki pounamu (adze) from Barn Bay, South Westland. The green nephrite has changed colour due to weathering and the bruised poll (handle end) suggests that the adze was made by the hammering process. Canterbury Museum.

New Zealand is a very museum-conscious nation, with one of the highest number of museums per capita in the world.

Small regional museums and large institutions alike hold collections of pounamu treasures (taonga), some of them quite extensive, and museum staff often have a close association with Māori communities. These storehouses of taonga are assisted by legislation prohibiting the export of New Zealand's cultural heritage, and the sale of all artefacts found after 1976. Although New Zealand museums have a wealth of pounamu taonga, there is still a reasonable amount of material in foreign countries, taken there before the end of the nineteenth century. It is the policy of several New Zealand museums – in particular Te Papa – to repatriate these artefacts, sometimes at considerable cost. Māori today retain ownership of many family heirloom taonga that have been faithfully passed down with their history.

Over the years I have had the privilege of studying the collections of pounamu in most New Zealand museums. In 2001–02 Maika Mason and I undertook an extensive survey of Ngāi Tahu taonga pounamu in five major New Zealand collections. We researched some 3700 Ngāi Tahu pounamu artefacts and discovered some interesting trends and made new observations, which are included in this chapter.

IMPLEMENTS

TOKI – ADZES

The first and most consistent use of pounamu by Māori was for tools, and the majority of artefacts preserved today are toki (adzes) and whao (chisels). Throughout much of Polynesia adzes were the predominant woodworking tool, and in New Zealand their efficiency was put to use in the

01

02

03

04

felling of large trees for conversion into canoes of all sizes. Toki were necessary for the shaping and dressing of timber in the construction of buildings and, occasionally, for working whalebone. The toki head, which was made from a variety of other stone types as well as pounamu, was always attached to a wooden handle and used in a similar fashion to the present-day adze.

The toki was an important tool that was wreathed in ritual. Many celebrated toki were accorded spiritual power to clear a pathway across the ocean in times of storms. This stemmed from the relationship with Tangaroa (spiritual guardian of the seas).

Toki were made in different sizes and shapes to suit the task. Some pounamu toki have a straight bevel, or cutting edge, while others are slightly hollowed or curved. The proportions vary from short and wide to long, narrow blades. Many of the stubby examples show that they were once longer and have become shorter through repeated sharpening. Numerous examples of toki have an unfinished longitudinal saw cut that shows the intention of making two narrower tools. The reason for this would have been that the toki had become too short through sharpening; its critical ratio of width of cutting edge to weight would have reached a point where it would be difficult to operate. In other words, as the toki wore out it was recycled into two whao. There are overwhelming numbers of flat whao with a ground edge on one side and a saw scarf on the other. Another reason for this could be that chisels for carving wood were in high demand in the North Island, and a toki could be sacrificed into several whao for trading. Nothing of the precious pounamu was wasted (see photo page 158).

To some degree the method of manufacture by sawing dictated the overall shape of the pounamu toki; they are generally quite quadrangular, and tend to lack the sweeping compound curves and the pronounced hafting shoulder on the butt that are so evident with the early basalt and argillite

LEFT / Selection of toki pounamu, showing both top and bottom sides. These adzes would have been secured to wooden handles and used like the present-day adze. Canterbury Museum.

01 / Woolston.
02 / Flea Bay, Banks Peninsula.
03 / Christchurch.
04 / Arowhenua.

ABOVE RIGHT / The cutting edge of the blade of a toki pounamu from Waikouaiti, Otago, showing distinctive striated use-wear marks. Otago Museum.

RIGHT / A series of notches on the shoulder of an adze from Waimate, Canterbury. Their purpose is unclear. Otago Museum.

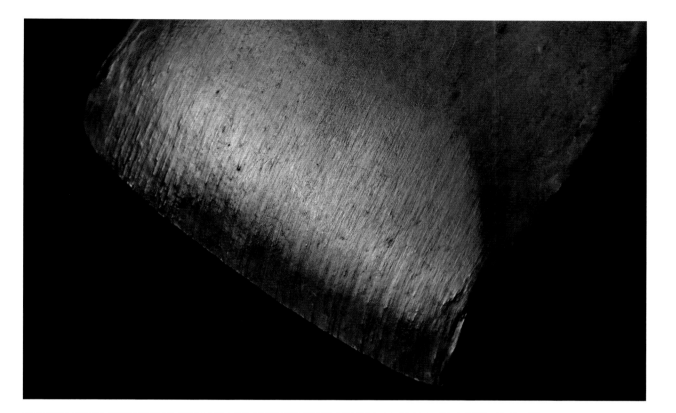

LEFT / Toki pounamu (adze)
resting in an old weathered
tōtara waka (canoe). The
shallow longitudinal scarf
could imply that the adze
was about to be thinned
down. Murray Thacker collection,
Okains Bay Maori and Colonial
Museum.

RIGHT / The beautifully
proportioned, large (370 mm
long) toki pounamu from
Waimate, Canterbury. The typical
quadrangular shape is the result of
the sawing and grinding process.

FAR RIGHT / The mighty tōtara tree
was a favoured timber for Māori,
being valued for its fine even
grain, strength and durability.
With only stone tools, it was a
major task to fell and work these
giants, then hew out a canoe, or
adze into long planks for house
construction. The bark was able to
be peeled off in large sheets and
folded to make food baskets.

FAR LEFT / Toki pounamu displaying, in parts, a brilliant green of the kahurangi variety. It is lying on the eroded stump of a large tōtara tree that was felled long ago by stone tools. Murray Thacker collection, Okains Bay Maori and Colonial Museum.

TOP LEFT / Rare toki pounamu of an early style from Sumner and Temuka, Canterbury. The method of manufacture was by hammering. Canterbury Museum.

BOTTOM LEFT / Whao pounamu (chisels). Cylindrical, hollow-ground gouge, chisel and flat chisel. These would have been fastened to a wooden shaft, but the pointed chisel was probably secured into a socket. Chisels were tapped by mallets to produce amazing wood carvings. Canterbury Museum.

RIGHT / A large toki pounamu from Sandymount, Otago Peninsula. The hole on the top end indicates that it may have been used as a ceremonial adze. Otago Museum.

toki, which were made by hammering. There are a small number of pounamu examples of these early shapes made by hammering, especially from southern sites. Many of these also show weathering or oxidisation on the surface since manufacture – some are completely opaque and chalky; others have a slight bloom or colour alteration to orange/yellow (see page 113). Jade items from very old Chinese tombs display a similar effect. Research on this aging process may assist in determining how old they are. Some very large nephrite toki (in excess of 65 cm in length) were made. These may have been for tree-felling, but it seems more likely that they were for ceremonial use or as a symbol of status.

Pounamu can be sharpened to a razor edge. As well as having a shallower cutting angle of the blade than most other stone types, pounamu toki had the added advantage of being heavier for their size, which gave them more kinetic energy when in use.

The handle was usually fashioned from a secondary branch of a tree; the heavier the better. Hafting or binding the head to the handle was done with flax-fibre cordage – the toki head was lashed to the handle in such a way that the blade wedged itself tighter with use. Different toki types would have required various specialised methods; but much of this detail has not been preserved.

Toki are often mistakenly referred to as 'axes'. There is some debate as to whether the axe as we know it was used by Māori before the introduction of metal tools. There are a few double bevelled pounamu tools that could operate as an axe or wedge for splitting timber.

One may wonder why Māori did not develop the axe, which was common in Europe and other countries for thousands of years. Determined to see just how effective the adze was in felling a tree, I made an argillite toki, hafted it to a handle in the traditional way and began chopping. The downward stroke was aided by gravity and a 60-degree scarf was easily achieved. I developed a technique of bouncing alternative strokes off the back of the adze, which cut off the peeling. By working around the tree, a scarf with a flat bottom evolved in no time and it was only a matter of continuing until the tree fell. For comparison on equal terms, I made a stone axe and handle of similar size and shape to Neolithic axes from Europe. I swung it the same as a metal axe and found that, although it cut well, it was much more labour intensive than the adze. It took more energy to swing it sideways and the cut ended up at 120 degrees, compared to 60 degrees for the adze, which meant it consumed twice the amount of timber. I concluded that the adze was easier and quicker. If I had used a pounamu toki, the difference would have been even greater. The main attribute of a metal axe is that it has more mass.

With the introduction of European metal tool technology such as steel axes, crosscut saws and drills, pounamu tools were eventually replaced, and many once treasured toki were reworked into items of adornment or for trade.

Māori ceremonial adzes (toki poutangata) differed from ordinary toki in that they were designed to be impressive and not for practical use. The blade was preferably made from flawless kahurangi pounamu, frequently thinly ground to take advantage of the translucency of the stone, and usually with holes at the butt for lashing on to the elaborately carved haft. These rare and magnificent taonga were highly prized and associated with chiefly people who exercised spiritual and physical power and authority. Toki poutangata were used exclusively for important occasions such as the initiation of the first chip at canoe-building ceremonies and sometimes as a weapon. Blades frequently have a series of small notches along the edges. The significance of these is unknown but they may simply be a form of decoration or possibly an aid to the recitation of a genealogical record.

01

02

03

05

04

WHAO – CHISELS

Whao and whao whakakōaka (gouges) of all sizes and profiles were developed and used specially for the production of intricate wood carvings. Normally, a whao had a straight, but often slanted, cutting edge and the gouge a hollowed one. Sizes ranged from less than 2 cm to over 18 cm in length, but the average was about 8 cm. Widths varied considerably. A consistent proportion for a flat whao is a 2:1 ratio, i.e., the length is twice the width. Whao were held by hand and tapped with a wooden mallet, or hafted to a straight piece of wood and used in the same way as a modern chisel.

Many whao have a point or blunt bevel at the butt end, which suggests that they were fitted into a socket rather than bound onto the wooden shaft. Constant tapping would then drive them tightly into the shaft, giving a very positive tool. Gouges were usually cylindrical in cross-section and elegantly tapered towards each end like a cigar, with quite a small, curved, hollowed cutting edge. Some were sharpened at both ends, usually at right angles to each other and with differing profiles: chisel at one end, gouge at the other. Many of the more narrow whao made from particularly fine pounamu were perforated at the butt end and worn as ear pendants. This was a convenient method of keeping a valuable tool safe, and was probably the origin of ornamental ear pendants.

Whalebone was an important material to Māori, and many items such as clubs (patu-parāoa), fish hooks and pāua levers, which are held in museum collections at all stages of manufacture, show that they were often shaped by the use of sharp whao. So efficient were these tools that even today they are still used by some Māori wood carvers.

RIPI – KNIVES

Ripi pounamu (pounamu knives and scrapers) are not common but are particularly interesting, as it is possible that some of them are among the oldest pounamu artefacts in New Zealand.

In New Zealand the ripi is generally associated with the Archaic period, when it was used effectively as a knife, probably for butchering and cleaning the skins of moa and seals. The Inuit name for a similar implement is *ulu*, and these are widespread, especially in Arctic America, parts of Asia and Oceania. Ripi could be produced as a flake from brittle materials such as obsidian, but were often made from naturally easily split stones, especially slate. The pounamu examples were made from schistose nephrite or bowenite, which was split into a thin sheet. The overall shape was somewhat oval, with about half of the periphery sharpened for the cutting edge. Additionally, a few have holes bored at the top for securing some kind of hand grip. Ripi were very efficient knives, and were probably also used for cutting fibrous harakeke leaves, which were a vital raw material for cordage and textiles.

The Ngāi Tahu taonga pounamu survey showed that there are a great variety of ripi in museum collections, but they are classified as 'pendants' simply because of a drilled hole or slot. Invariably they showed a sharpened edge, point or serration. I experimented with thin schistose pieces of nephrite and bowenite made as facsimiles of these designs and they performed extremely well, slicing tough flesh, kelp or even a soft tomato. It would appear that as the ripi is used, tiny pieces of the schistose stone flake off, revealing microserrations – a self-sharpening knife (see photo page 149).

OTHER POUNAMU IMPLEMENTS

Although not common, other useful items made from pounamu included fish-hook barbs of several types, awls for making holes in wood and seal skin, hammerstones, drill points, bird spear points and

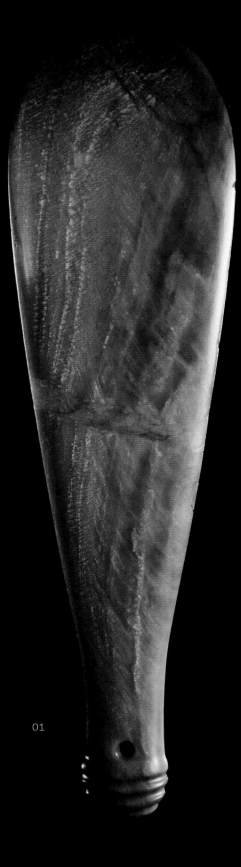

01

leg rings for the native parrot, the kākā. These rings (pōria), which were also made from bone, were often quite decorative and were designed to secure one leg of a tame kākā which acted as a decoy to attract other birds to a snare.

WEAPONS

The ultimate object fashioned by Māori in pounamu was a short, club-like hand weapon, the mere, also termed mere pounamu or patu pounamu. The mere was a highly treasured possession and indicative of the owner's status and position within the tribe. As such, mere symbolised the mana of the tribe and its customary authority over the land they occupied. Mere in the South Island were frequently made from the prized īnanga variety of nephrite. Sizes and proportions vary, but the profile is spatula and most measure about 30–40 cm long, although some are unmanageably long for use with one hand. The butt end is usually oval in cross section and contains a hole for the wrist cord. Where the weapon was grasped by hand it is slightly waisted, but gracefully flattens into a broad thin blade with a rounded end. These edges are quite thin and sharp and, depending on the quality of the stone, can emit a translucent glow around the periphery. A well proportioned mere is beautifully balanced.

As with the toki, a mere was often created from a natural, slab-like piece of nephrite which generally presented any grain longitudinally, and this tended to minimise cross fracturing when in use. The mere was not used strictly as a club – that is, with a downward blow – but as an upward jabbing weapon usually intended for the enemy's head and sometimes the ribs. Similar weapons (patu) were made from greywacke, hard woods and whalebone. While the latter two materials were often elaborately carved or had decorative butts,

Mere were highly treasured weapons and symbols of authority. They were frequently passed down through families or gifted in special circumstances.

01 / A superbly proportioned mere from Ruapuke Island, Foveaux Strait. It is made from the pearly īnanga pounamu, having the characteristics of the stone from Te Koroka at the head of Lake Wakatipu. With a length of 395 mm, it would have originally had a plaited flax wrist cord looped through the hole. Courtesy Topi family and Southland Museum and Art Gallery. BRIAN BRAKE

02 / Te Whānaupani. When a Ngāti Kinohaku pā was ransacked by Ngā Puhi in 1822, a young boy, Rōpiha Te Ketetahi, was taken captive. Rōpiha won the regard of the chief of the war party and was kept as a foster child. He was sent to school in Auckland following his parents' conversion to Christianity, and eventually became secretary to the Governor, Sir George Grey. Rōpiha Te Ketetahi, also known as Hone Rōpiha (John Hobbs), became the holder of Te Whānaupani. When he died, he left the mere to Sir George Grey. Chatoyant bands on the hand grip appear dark because of the orientation of the fibres. COURTESY AUCKLAND MUSEUM, 13924

03 / Te Kihirangi. A Ngāti Tūmatawera (Tūhoe) man, who had married a Te Arawa woman, gifted Te Kihirangi to Ngāti Karenga (Te Arawa). In return, the man was given land for his house, which he named Hurunga-te-Rangi in memory of this gift. COURTESY AUCKLAND MUSEUM, 19433

LEFT / Mere were favoured spoils of war and often their histories were not recorded. The uppermost mere has the black veining and other characteristics of nephrite that has been heated, possibly to enhance the colour. Murray Thacker collection, Okains Bay Maori and Colonial Museum.

ABOVE / J. J. Merrett's painting of Poutairangi, *c.* 1840. He is holding a mere and wearing a hand-woven flax cloak, complemented by a pounamu ear pendant with a hei tiki at his neck. COURTESY AUCKLAND MUSEUM, CN25

RIGHT / Painting of a tattoed chief, Tamati Waka Nene, of the Ngā Puhi tribe, wearing a kiwi feather cloak, pounamu ear pendant and holding a treasured mere. The black and white hūia feathers indicate his high rank. Painting by S. Stuart, *c.* 1840. COURTESY AUCKLAND MUSEUM, B5164

the pounamu mere was not carved except for a few near-parallel grooves on the end of the butt, behind the hole. Most have a distinctive patina, no doubt from continual handling, and the simplicity of design, together with the excellent craftsmanship, made the mere a beautiful but fearsome object.

Although there are many mere in museum collections a number are still held by the descendants of their original owners, being passed down as family taonga. Mere were given names and became legendary objects and obvious prizes as spoils of war, thus many mere changed hands. An example of the importance placed on mere narrated by a member of the Ngāti Whakaue tribe and communicated by George Graham says that the owner of one of two famous mere with the name of Te Kaoreore was defeated in battle and was about to be slain with a bone patu. He presented his weapon to his captor and remarked, 'Nay, slay me not with that base weapon, but rather with this, that I might softly feel the blow, and be slain with dignity.'

FAR LEFT / Two amulets that appear to be reworked hei tiki. The lower example is totoweka pounamu. Canterbury Museum.

LEFT / One of the few hei tiki complete with its plaited neck suspension cord and bird-bone toggle. This hei tiki was obtained by Lieutenant Matthew Flinders on the New Zealand coast about 1797. He took it to England and presented it to Mrs Langsford. She bequeathed it to her grandson, Mr W. P. Palmer who migrated to New Zealand in 1877. Dark kawakawa pounamu, 155 mm long.
COURTESY AUCKLAND MUSEUM, 5587

ABOVE / An unidentified Māori woman wearing a hei tiki, showing that they were sometimes suspended sideways. COURTESY AUCKLAND MUSEUM

ABOVE RIGHT / Īnanga pounamu hei tiki with a plaited flax suspension cord. At one time it was owned by Lady Parry, the wife of Australian Arctic explorer, Sir William Edward Parry. Murray Thacker collection, Okains Bay Maori and Colonial Museum.

PERSONAL ADORNMENT

Items of personal adornment are expressed in every civilisation and were equally important to Māori. Generally both genders wore a wide variety of materials and forms which were suspended by a cord from the neck or ear. Archaeological excavations have revealed that during the early period of settlement Māori possessed beautiful amulets which often depicted a strong association with the whale. There are necklaces of stylised whale teeth cut from whale ivory and moa bone, large single copies of a sperm whale tooth carved in serpentinite, as well as intricate whale-

ivory chevroned pendants. Many other forms carved from serpentinite such as reels, pectoral amulets and abstract symbolic objects were also created. Much later, in the Classic Māori period, completely different amulet forms evolved, and many were rendered in pounamu. These became very fashionable around the period of contact with Europeans. Immediately after, production of pounamu adornments and, to a lesser degree, weapons, grew into a flourishing enterprise largely for the purpose of trade with Europeans keen to collect such items. During this phase several modifications of form, plus a few completely new designs, are thought to have been introduced.

HEI TIKI

Probably the most well-known symbol of Māori culture is the hei tiki, hei meaning to wear around the neck or neck pendant, tiki meaning human – thus, the stylised human neck pendant, hei tiki. The tiki concept originated in Polynesia but evolved to its present form in New Zealand. The few examples which suggest more open features and an erect head are most likely the earlier styles, with the later versions being much more stylised. There are two distinct groups with several variations of design, sometimes characteristic of particular regions, and sizes vary considerably. The early hei tiki were quite small, usually less

05

06

07

08

PREVIOUS PAGES / A selection of hei tiki showing the range of styles, proportions and pounamu varieties. Some show detailed features, others with inlaid pāua shell (*Haliotis iris*) (see page 131) eyes. Two have their suspension holes drilled from the top to back, while on others the hole has worn through, necessitating a new hole.

BACKGROUND / The jagged Fiordland mountains surrounding Lake Quill, the source of the famous Sutherland Falls.

01 / Īnanga pounamu with inset pāua shell eyes and a forked tongue. Canterbury Museum.

02 / An alternative design with the hands on chest and thigh. The pounamu may have been heated. Otago Museum.

03 / Once owned by the famous English collector, W. O. Oldman. His collection was purchased by the New Zealand Government and the artefacts distributed to New Zealand museums. Southland Museum and Art Gallery.

04 / An unusual hei tiki, with notches on the outer edges of the limbs. Kahurangi pounamu from Ruapekapeka, Northland. Otago Museum.

05 / Hei tiki with its head facing the less common way. Īnanga pounamu from Kaiapoi, Canterbury. Canterbury Museum.

06 / Proportionally stunning hei tiki. Darkish īnanga pounamu from Long Beach, Otago. Otago Museum.

07 / Īnanga pounamu with straight sides, suggesting that it may have been made from an adze. Murray Thacker collection, Okains Bay Maori and Colonial Museum.

08 / This fine large hei tiki with a mottled feathered effect was probably heated to lighten the colour. Otago Museum.

LEFT / A very large (180 mm) dark kawakawa hei tiki with an interesting history. In 1844, the Reverend George Clarke Jnr, who was protector of aborigines, was given this hei tiki by Te Āti Awa Māori at Wellington after acting as a Māori advocate for the sale and preparation of the deeds of Māori land in Otago. He gave the hei tiki to Miss C. C. Forsaith in 1862 on her marriage to Mr T. M. MacDonald, who was later the first Crown prosecutor in Invercargill. Southland Museum and Art Gallery.

RIGHT / A hei tiki with straight sides and proportions of an adze on the carved lid of a waka huia box. The eyes have been filled with sealing wax, which was a common practice in post-European times. Kawakawa pounamu. Canterbury Museum.

than 10 cm in length, but later giants of 18 cm and more were made.

The typical hei tiki has a large, angled, rounded or pointed head, usually just slightly less than half of the total length and with the mouth on either the left or right side. The eyes were inset with pāua (*Haliotis iris*) shell but later, after the arrival of the Europeans, red sealing wax was used. Usually the remainder of the body featured a relatively large abdomen and the legs in a squatting position, with the heels together and both hands resting on the thighs, or one hand on the thigh and the other to the head or breast. Numerous have finer features such as the mouth, tongue, ears, hands, feet, ribs and several hei tiki indicate that they are female; the remainder are presumed to be male.

The suspension hole ranges from a cleverly concealed hole bored at a right angle from the top to the back of the head, to rather unsympathetic holes near the eyes or through a projecting tab. A skilfully plaited cord and bird wing-bone toggle often with incised line decoration provided the suspension. Some hei tiki have no holes and appear to have been hung from the slots at the elbows and knees. This would allow the hei tiki to sit sideways with the angled head in a vertical position and would be a more practical way to be worn (see page 127).

The general outline of many hei tiki conforms with the proportions of the toki, and in several cases partly completed hei tiki show that they were carved out of these tools. Certainly in the later period, and probably before that, the toki form thus dictated to a large extent the stylisation and evolution of the hei tiki design.

On his first visit to New Zealand Captain James Cook displayed considerable interest in the hei tiki. They were not common at this time, but when he and others came to New Zealand on later visits, hei tiki were plentiful and freely

offered for barter. Obviously Māori appreciated the wants of the European and were quick to develop the market, for from this time on hei tiki were manufactured by Māori as trading commodities to exchange for metal tools and other articles that the visiting sealers and whalers could supply. The demand was high but fresh supplies of raw stone were not easily obtained, and so with the promise of iron tools many faithful toki were converted to hei tiki. Of course not all were intended for trading, and many treasured heirloom hei tiki have accumulated much mana and have passed through several generations of Māori families to the present day. These are worn or displayed at important occasions.

The production of hei tiki continued well into the nineteenth century, but the quality of craftsmanship declined and the work was finally taken over by European lapidaries. Much has been written about the hei tiki and its magical powers and other properties, but this is unfounded, for evidence suggests that it was a rather late development and simply an ornament in the shape of a human. One early account mentions that hei tiki were neither connected with superstition nor worshipped but were worn in remembrance of their deceased owner or owners. It is interesting that relatively few authentic hei tiki are made from tangiwai, although softer and more easily worked than nephrite, it would have been less durable.

HEI MATAU
The hei matau (hook) was worn on a cord around the neck. It was more common in the south, and is a superb example of Māori art in that it combines fish hook and fish motif in one simple design. This symbolises the relationship of Māori with the sea god Tangaroa, and the importance of fishing in their culture. There are several styles of hei matau, varying from reasonably realistic fish-hook forms to more stylised versions that express fish-like

LEFT / Īnanga hei tiki with sealing wax eyes gazes from within a waka huia box. These elaborately carved wooden boxes were used for the safekeeping of precious items such as pounamu adornments and feathers of the now extinct hūia bird. Fine carving such as this was achievable with pounamu chisels. Canterbury Museum.

RIGHT / Hei matau or hook breast pendant from Haywood Point, Otago. Although the hole is for the suspension cord, it also serves as an eye for the fish theme. Kahurangi pounamu. Otago Museum.

LEFT 01 / An elegant hei matau from Pahia, Southland. The pounamu has a silvery sheen produced by the heating process. Otago Museum.
02 / Hei matau īnanga pounamu. The stone can be sourced to Te Koroka. Murray Thacker collection, Okains Bay Maori and Colonial Museum.
03 / Hei matau with the original hole almost worn through. Kahurangi pounamu. Murray Thacker collection, Okains Bay Maori and Colonial Museum.

RIGHT / Ear pendants (kuru) on a waka huia lid. From left to right, pounamu varieties are īnanga, kahurangi and tangiwai (bowenite). Canterbury Museum.

01

02

03

04

05

themes. Some are beautifully proportioned with perfect sweeping curves, and they are never over-large in size. When carved in the īnanga variety of pounamu – especially from Te Koroka, with the silvery fish-scale appearance – they are, in my opinion, among the finest pounamu taonga. For some unknown reason, this was one form that was not copied by later lapidaries until after 1970.

PENDANTS

Many adornments were worn suspended from holes pierced in the ear. These were made from a variety of materials, including feathers, teeth, bone, fingernails and pounamu. There is strong evidence that many of the ear adornments of pounamu, and particularly tangiwai, were the product of a later fashion.

The quite diverse designs that evolved can be grouped into several types, some of which are peculiar to certain districts of New Zealand. A few designs – especially the long pendant – perhaps owe their origin to the practice of suspending small chisels or gouges from the ear for safe keeping. These ornamental pendants can be straight and pencil-like (kuru); flattish or lens-shaped in section (kurupapa); or have a curve at the lower end similar to that of a hockey stick (kapeu or tautau). These last amulets, approaching 15 cm in length, were frequently made from the finest īnanga variety of pounamu. The slight curve in the shank and more abrupt curve at the end, together with a lens cross-sectional shape allowing light to pass on the thin edges, make these very beautiful objects indeed. Frequently, the straight pendants were made from the rare bluish-green transparent tangiwai, and their attractive appearance was soon noticed by Europeans who often preferred this material because of its translucency. Sizes averaged from 4 cm to 10 cm but longer examples reached 37 cm.

There is a separate group of pendants with bird-like characteristics. These thinnish elegant pendants have a distinctive beaked top with a hole that resembles an eye, and a bottom end that looks like a pointed tail, giving an overall appearance of an elongated bird – although some could also be said to represent an elongated whale-tooth form. Many of these amulets are reasonably long and invariably made from tangiwai, frequently showing oxidisation; I consider them to be early pieces. Their gracefully proportioned shape makes them a most attractive pendant.

There is a rarer group of pendants that have been described as resembling a human leg. These are relatively straight and slender but are kinked at the midpoint, like a knee.

Flat, tabular forms in several abstract shapes, often with serrations, form another group and the meaning or origin of most is not obvious. Some of the larger heavier versions may have been worn from the neck.

Pounamu ear pendants were frequently worn in bunches of several, so that as the wearer moved a pleasant tinkling noise was produced.

PEKAPEKA

Beautiful, intricately carved amulets known as pekapeka and marakihau were made predominantly by northern Māori, though they are relatively rare. The pekapeka is believed to represent the native bat (pekapeka), but H. D. Skinner, who made a comprehensive study of Māori amulets, suggests that it represents two bird forms. Marakihau is a sea monster, but this design also often has a bird-like head. My own interpretation is that the marakihau form is a development of the pekapeka design. The koropepe or kōtuku, a spiral pendant with a head at one end, like a coiled snake or eel, was a form that was regularly produced by the early European lapidaries, and few authentic versions exist. It draws heavily on the spiral koru design that is used extensively in Māori art. Although it is not common, the pōria, or kākā leg ring, was also used as an ear adornment. Like a nephrite version of the mako shark tooth and several other forms, it is believed to have been rare in pre-European times.

There are a number of abstract pounamu ear ornaments that appear to be unique in design and unlike any other in shape. They are possibly experimental pieces fashioned from offcuts or fragments of pounamu to show the individual expression of the artisan.

CLOAK PINS

Bone was the usual material for cloak pins, but some were fashioned from whale ivory and pounamu. These were more for social value and were often worn just for adornment. Pounamu pins were quite long and some have a kink or curve. They are slender and taper to a sharp point, with a hole at the opposite end. Some small versions with very sharp points and tiny holes, regarded as decorative pendants, would have made excellent needles.

REPRODUCTIONS

The manufacture of reproduction Māori artefacts by Europeans began at an early date, and reached a high point during the late nineteenth and early twentieth centuries. As New Zealanders became increasingly appreciative of both Māori art and jade, and as the number of overseas visitors increased, there developed a greater demand for pounamu jewellery, souvenirs and artefacts. By this time Māori had long since discarded their traditional stone tool technology for that of the European. Few Māori artisans remained who could fashion pounamu traditionally, or even pass on the knowledge of how it was done.

The European lapidary industry flourished, and virtually all lapidaries at some time or another produced copies of artefacts. It should be noted that these were not 'fakes' in the true sense, and no deception was intended. The lapidaries were merely meeting the demand by providing reasonable copies. Most reproductions can be identified as such and today are valued as important examples from this era. Details of these lapidaries are given in a later chapter; but noteworthy are the two brothers Andrew and Thomas Devlin of Dunedin, who were responsible for a large number of copies which were sold to North Island Māori. At least once a year the Devlins visited various Māori communities, mainly in the central North Island, with a supply of hei tiki, mere and pendants. Often these were resold to Europeans, who mistakenly believed them to be genuine artefacts; and many have found their way into museums and private collections worldwide. The Devlins – and especially Andrew, who spoke Māori – developed a strong friendship with Māori, and were aware of the need to supply artefacts that were made to order in the styles requested.

Another skilled craftsman was Trevor Lloyd of Auckland, who was a dealer in Māori artefacts. He has been attributed with developing the koropepe amulet design, which became a favourite form.

Copies of hei tiki and other items were also made by overseas lapidaries, especially by the master craftsmen of Idar-Oberstein in Germany. One such company was Jakob Wild XIII, which supplied a copy of a hei tiki to the Leiden Museum in 1908.

Souvenir items are easily distinguished because they are usually out of scale and roughly made; but the more proficiently produced copies can present problems in positive identification. Fortunately, there are a number of general characteristics that usually arouse suspicion. Although they are made by skilled craftsmen, the works often have too straight an edge or wrong curves, are too highly polished and lack the

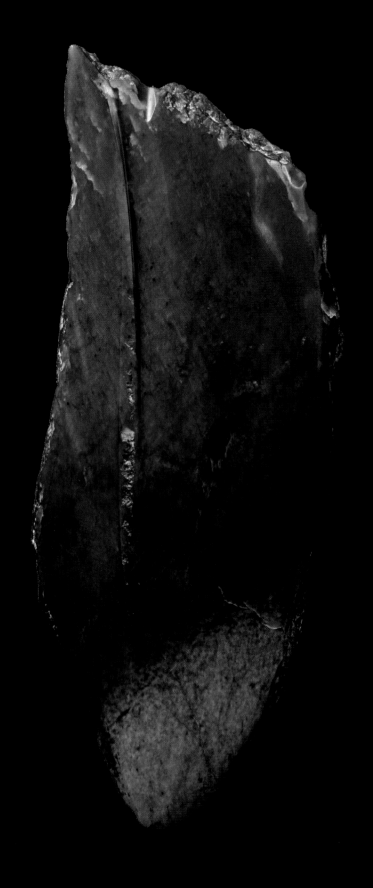

elegance of the originals. Moreover, because the
copies were made from stone reduced to parallel
slabs by mechanical saws, the reproductions,
especially of mere, hei tiki and pendants,
tend to be very parallel. Nevertheless, it must
be remembered that during the early period
European lapidaries occasionally supplied Māori
with sawn slabs and possibly unfinished artefacts
which were completed by Māori craftsmen.

The grain of nephrite in genuine Māori
pieces is invariably orientated lengthwise, with
any foliation parallel to the largest face. With the
European lapidary it was, and still is, customary for
jade boulders to be sawn the most convenient way
– and that often meant across the grain. This wrong
orientation of the stone is a further characteristic to
be examined in a suspected replica. Similarly, holes
drilled by the Māori drill produced blunt cavities
bored from both sides, whereas holes bored in
copies frequently have parallel sides. Sometimes
attempts were made to duplicate the genuine hole
shape, usually by countersinking both sides, but
there is often sufficient of the central parallel hole
left to distinguish it.

The choice of stone variety is also
important. Īnanga was seldom used by the
European lapidaries, who preferred the then-
plentiful rich green kawakawa variety that was
being produced by the goldmining activities in
Westland. Equally, bowenite was extensively used
by European lapidaries for the reproduction of
artefacts such as mere that were not normally
made from this material.

With the growing development of jade carving
in New Zealand since the 1970s, many people
are now capable of producing very good copies
of artefacts. In order to avoid future problems
of identification, legislation has been passed
under the Antiquities Act requiring that replicas
of artefacts must be clearly and permanently
identified as such.

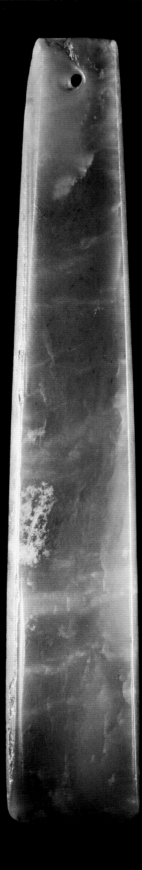

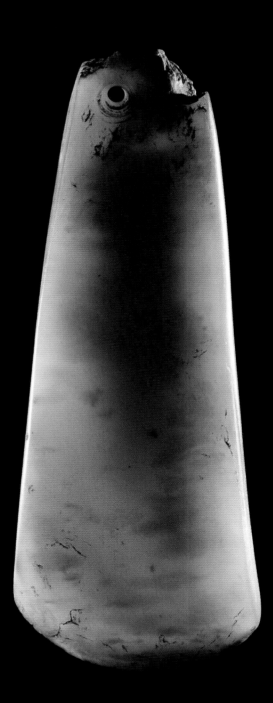

CHAPTER SEVEN/MĀORI WORKING OF POUNAMU

/ TE WHAKAEANGA
From the idea to craft an object
comes ability for grand achievements

Obtaining pounamu was the first step in working the stone. This was not an easy task since pounamu sources were largely located in mountainous areas away from the main habitation sites. There were many different pounamu trails established, and these were the same routes as used by the early European explorers, who renamed them.

To reach the resources, the people living on the east coast of the South Island had a major natural obstacle to contend with: the Southern Alps. This meant travelling at high altitude, with all the hazards that go with typical alpine terrain.

Coastal Otago and Southland communities accessed the Wakatipu source by following the major rivers and overland trails through some very rough and arid country with limited food resources. Southern Māori, who were competent seafaring people who seasonally voyaged to below Stewart Island/Rakiura to harvest tītī (muttonbirds; *Puffinus grisens*), also took canoes around the Fiordland Coast to gather tangiwai at Milford Sound, and further on to the South Westland nephrite source.

Trading with either raw or partly worked pounamu was an ongoing activity, and there were no doubt well established networks. There are several recorded instances of North Island Māori venturing south to trade goods for pounamu. This continued into post-European times, when very high prices were paid for pieces of pounamu big enough to use for manufacturing mere. Likewise, southern Māori travelled north by canoe to trade their wares. The overland treks would have been fraught with obstacles, such as out of season snowstorms and torrential rain with swollen rivers. Pounamu was carried in woven packs – one such pack was found abandoned in a cave in mid Canterbury, undisturbed until the 1980s. Loads of up to 50 kg were possible. Feet were protected from the rough terrain by sandals made from tī

(cabbage-tree) leaves, but as these lasted only a short while, making replacements en route would have been a continual task. Some river valleys were almost impassable, with thorny matagouri (*Discaria toumatou*) and sharp speargrass. Travellers wore specially woven gaiters to protect their legs; and they sometimes set fire to the vegetation to clear the way.

At times the boulders were too heavy to carry so they were broken in two or – in the case of very large schistose stones – a slab would be prised off. According to J. W. Stack, an old Māori chief recalled that a device that sounds like the equivalent of a mechanical hammer was used for breaking pieces off large boulders. The apparatus, which took several men to operate, used a nephrite boulder as a hammerhead fixed to one end of a long pole. It was then raised to about 80 degrees and, steered by two ropes, was allowed to fall down on the target pounamu boulder at a precise place. Clearly, this method would have been more effective if first a groove was cut to weaken the stone, or if it was employed where existing natural fractures were present.

The use of mōkihi laden with pounamu for the return journey down lakes and rivers was common in the south. Flax-flower stems tied together in bundles are remarkably buoyant. An experiment shows that a bundle of 10 stems can support a weight of 8 kg, so a raft of 15 bundles will carry 120 kg. These rafts, reinforced with southern beech saplings, could have been assisted with inflated kelp bags (pōhā). These were made by separating bull kelp fronds, blowing air in and resealing them; and were a versatile, airtight food storage invention that was ideal for travelling.

Important pounamu workshops situated at the mouth of the Taramakau River, Westland; Murdering Beach (Whareakeake), Otago; Kaiapoi, Banks Peninsula area, Canterbury; Foveaux Strait area, Southland; and other coastal localities

developed a significant industry collecting and working pounamu to barter with the North Island tribes in exchange for articles not available in their region. Some of the workshops were extensive, particularly the one at Kaiapoi, known as Hohou pounamu, which was occupied for several hundred years. A recent archaeological excavation on part of the site recovered some 3000 pounamu items as cast-off flakes and partly made tools. Māori at Whareakeake, a village site on the coast north of the entrance to Otago Harbour, were engaged in manufacturing a range of goods such as woodworking tools and hei tiki. Settlements further south at Riverton and west of there at Ōraka and Pahia were active stoneworking centres in argillite and pounamu, and were well endowed with the other ancillary rock types necessary to work stone. These people were well placed to get the pounamu from Te Koroka, which they traded further afield as well as producing beautiful taonga themselves.

Southern and east coast Māori took every opportunity to pre-shape the stone on their long journey home from the sources, and this called for a supply of saws and abrasives that were usually readily available en route.

North Island Māori were also proficient pounamu artisans, working every available precious piece into exquisite taonga, particularly items of adornment. Raw supplies of pounamu were limited and the high demand created a very valuable commodity.

Elsdon Best records an account illustrating the importance placed on working pounamu in the North Island. In the early part of the nineteenth century Māori of the Tūhoe tribe traded a large drove of pigs for two slabs of nephrite to be fashioned into mere, hei tiki and other items. Extensive preparations to cut the pieces included clearing the land to cultivate food and building houses for the pounamu workers. Tribal members visited and shared in the labour, making the task a social occasion.

Nestled in the Southern Alps is the Fox Glacier, slowly grinding its way down to near the Tasman Sea. Rock particles embedded in the moving ice have gouged out a deep U-shaped valley. The same action of producing a groove takes place using a Māori saw with sand, as illustrated in the beautiful sawn block, right, from Okains Bay. The other opposing groove on the underside would have been sawn until the two met. Okains Bay Maori and Colonial Museum.

The technology of working pounamu evolved from a rich and inherent stoneworking knowledge accumulated over a long time. Polynesians developed the art of stone toolmaking to a high level. Their main material was basalt, a fine-grained, brittle volcanic rock prolific throughout the Pacific Islands. Early Polynesians brought this brittle stone technology with them to New Zealand; but here, they were were met with a huge selection of new stone types with different properties.

Māori became proficient geologists, continually exploring and experimenting with rocks that had a whole new range of applications. The manufacture of stone tools flourished – especially from basalt and argillite, which were favoured for toki. These rocks allowed easy flaking to shape the implement, and skilful techniques evolved whereby several by-product tools were created in one process. This hammering or percussion method of manufacture was used by stone-based cultures worldwide for thousands of years.

At Coromandel in the North Island and at Nelson and Southland in the South Island, there are some spectacular stoneworking sites where Māori undertook extensive quarry operations over several hundred years. Using kuru pōhatu (dense hammerstone boulders) they produced large spalls for further working into toki. Roughouts were literally hammered into the various toki styles, and cast-off flakes modified for other tools such as knives, awls and drill-points. The crudely shaped toki were then hammer-dressed – bruised all over to reduce the uneven high spots. Choosing the correct type of hammerstone was very important: a range of tough stone types were used. Rodingite, a heavy and very hard rock composed essentially of a relatively rare mineral, hydrogrossular garnet, was a favourite. It occurs in Nelson, Southland and South Westland, often in association with nephrite. Their use of this material further illustrates the depth of Māori geological knowledge.

The final stage in making a stone toki was to smooth all the dressed surfaces with grindstones, sharpen the bevel and lash the implement to a wooden handle. Many large polished toki are much more than efficient tools. Their unsurpassed design and the standard of workmanship make them pieces of functional sculpture that express the skill and pride of their makers.

We know that very early Māori produced many exquisite items from bone and serpentinite, and they would have been quick to realise that the chipping and bruising technique did more harm than good on these tougher materials. I suggest that the experience gained with serpentinite may have led to the development of the sawing technique that they later used for working pounamu.

It was inevitable that as they explored their new country, early Māori would eventually discover nephrite and realise its potential. The presence of nephrite and semi-nephrite toki from some early South Island sites shows their process of manufacture was the hammer method, most probably using garnet hammerstones. These indicate that nephrite, which was a new

Experiments illustrating the Māori methods of working pounamu.

01 / A greywacke saw is drawn back and forth using sand and water to produce a scarf.
02 / The final grinding of an adze that has been made in the traditional way on a sandstone block with water.
03 / Drilling a hole with a copy of a Māori drill using crushed quartz sand and water.
04 / A ripi made from a schistose piece of nephrite cuts bull kelp easily.
05 / Experiments illustrating the toughness of nephrite. Jade nails, drills and a cold chisel for cutting steel plate. ALL R. BECK

medium, presented some initial manufacturing difficulties, and that the technique of sawing had not at that stage been applied to pounamu. Other pounamu tools show that they were collected as naturally occurring fragments, roughly the shape of a toki, which required only slight modification before sharpening on grindstones. If subjected to prolonged hammering, some nephrite and semi-nephrite with a decided grain or foliation (schistosity) would develop fractures and separate before the tool could be finished. Moreover, compact nephrite, with its extremely tough structure, is very difficult and time-consuming to shape by the hammer technique. For these reasons Māori adopted the more efficient sawing and grinding method of working pounamu. Wastage was kept to a minimum and the process took less time.

It should be pointed out that the main advantage of nephrite over argillite and other brittle stones was not hardness, but toughness. The actual cutting angle of the nephrite blade could be shallower and thus more efficient, and it remained sharp without chipping. Small

chisels and gouges could also be tapped with a mallet and remain intact. The brittle nature of the other stones required a steeper cutting angle, preventing chipping of the blade edge but gave a less efficient result.

With the sudden change to metal implements after the arrival of European technology, a great deal of detailed knowledge on working pounamu was lost. However, from accounts related by early European observers, evidence from the inspection of artefacts, and practical experiments that I have undertaken, a general method of manufacture has been established. This can be separated into several operations: sawing, grinding and polishing, drilling and heat treatment.

MAHI KANIORO – SAWING

Today we associate a saw with a blade and a series of teeth. But the Māori saw (mania or ripi) used for pounamu cutting was a thin slab made of stone, and instead of teeth relied on the effect of abrasion to grind its way through.

The first step was to grind down the surface of the rough stone or boulder to a flat face, both top and underside. This was achieved by rubbing a hand-held piece of sandstone back and forth or in circles with water to remove any weathering and unevenness – which can happen surprisingly quickly. The worked slab was then made secure on a wooden block, or half-buried in the ground, and one or two straight pieces of wood were lashed down as a guide for the next step: sawing.

To cut off an unwanted segment of pounamu, a deep V-shaped groove or scarf was sawn on one side and another directly opposite, until the opposing grooves were close enough to be broken with a sharp blow.

Saws were made in a variety of materials and sizes, depending on the scale of the work intended. Most were palm-size and as thin as practical. Early European accounts and examples in museum collections show that many saws were sandstone or quartzose schist, which are common rocks in Westland and in the south. Greywacke is a very common rock in Canterbury on the east coast of the South Island, and because of its abundance, Ngāi Tahu, who were proficient pounamu cutters, developed and used the greywacke saw extensively. There was an endless supply of water-worn greywacke cobbles from which saws were easily fashioned by striking with a hammerstone, producing a thin round or oval flake with a sharp edge on its periphery.

Using water as a coolant, the narrow cutting edge of the saw was drawn back and forth across the stone with long, slow strokes and an even pressure. To speed up the operation, quartz sand – which is harder than nephrite – was sprinkled into the cut to act as an abrasive saw. This is the same action as the ice of a glacier which traps stone fragments gouging out the deep valleys. Many of these greywacke saws still have remains of the cutting residue adhering to them.

Close-up of a sawn boulder with the broken bridge between two opposing grooves. Wickliffe Bay, Otago. Otago Museum.

RIGHT INSET / Greywacke spall saws from Birdlings Flat, Canterbury. The largest saw still has the cutting residue adhering. Southland Museum and Art Gallery.

Because beach sand consists of rounded grains with less abrasive qualities, quartz pebbles were hammered down to a sharp grit and used as the abrasive. It is also likely that garnet sand, which is slightly harder than quartz and commonly found on the west and southwest coasts of the South Island, could have been used. I have experimented with sawing and found it a satisfying process, dipping the saw in water and sand frequently. If I wedged the saw in a wooden handgrip so I could use both hands on it, cuts were made relatively quickly.

Māori have cut off some very large slabs

by this method, although it must have required considerable time and effort. It is difficult to estimate how long it took, but an account by Charles Heaphy, who observed a mere in the making at Taramakau, said it took one month to saw out the shape. He also mentions that whole families of men, women and children were engaged in sawing, grinding and polishing pounamu.

Sawing was a favourite pastime for the older men of the tribe, and several accounts relate that every spare opportunity was taken to continue the work. With thinnish, slab-like boulders or

cobbles, saw cuts were made on the flattish faces, and this usually produced tapered quadrangular section blocks suitable for toki and mere. As mentioned earlier, most nephrite has a decided grain – not unlike wood – and this gives the stone directional properties; the softest face is the flattest and the hardest is on end grain. This provides distinct advantages: the surface that requires the most work from sawing and grinding is the softest and the hardest requires the least work, being at the cutting edge where it is needed most. In the case of thicker, non-

PREVIOUS PAGE / A slab of īnanga pounamu from an archaeological site in Southland that has been ground down to flat faces on both sides prior to sawing. The stone is typical Te Koroka pounamu. Southland Museum and Art Gallery.

ABOVE / Found in Timaru, this īnanga pounamu cobble is still in its natural shape, but with an unfinished saw cut on both sides. The intention may have been to make a toki and whao. Canterbury Museum.

schistose boulders or blocks, deeper saw cuts were necessary; and in some instances toki were made with the saw cuts parallel to their fronts or backs rather than to the edges as with the previous method, but always along the grain (see page 156). The smaller items, such as chisels, gouges and pendants, were generally made from previously sawn slabs or offcuts.

Many large blocks of partly sawn pounamu in museum collections are very sculptural, and have evidently consumed a large amount of labour. Most have rounded, typical U-shaped grooves that are straight or sometimes twisting, cambered or undulating; and the highly polished surface of these grooves makes the specimens quite irresistible to the touch. Judging from the polish, it is obvious that their makers thought so too, and they would have had little incentive to complete the cuts.

A completely different type of saw, developed particularly in China and Central America, was the bow-like wire or string saw, where an abrasive was fed into the cut; this was used for general sawing as well as for fine fretwork. There is no recorded evidence of this technique being employed by Māori, yet it would not be surprising to find that it was used in a limited capacity to smooth or polish the interior of bored holes. This principle is illustrated by the many hei tiki and other ornaments with oval holes worn in them by the natural abrasive action of grit and dust in the suspension cord. In some cases the hole has migrated upwards and worn completely through the end, so that a fresh hole had to be added lower down.

MAHI HŌANGA – GRINDING

One of the most important tools for the production of objects from stone, bone and, to a lesser degree, wood, were grindstones. The final stage of manufacture was to smooth the item by grinding down all the rough portions and irregularities and then polishing. This was done with hoanga (grindstones) and rasps, usually sandstone or occasionally quartz schist of different grades – from coarse (hōanga matanui) to fine (hōanga matarehu).

Like the sawing process, grinding was a slow but satisfying task. The rhythmical nature of the work appealed to older Māori craftsmen. The Rev J. F. H. Wohlers, a missionary at Ruapuke Island in Foveaux Strait, observed an old man working pounamu in 1844.

. . . sitting and doing nothing, his nerves will not be quiet; so he takes in hand a piece of raw greenstone, looks at it, and thinks what can be made of it. By-and-by he begins to rub it on a suitable stone. It takes a long time before a bright smoothness appears; but even a very slow progress cheers his mind, and the monotonous rubbing quietens his nerves.

New Zealand is well endowed with suitable rocks for grindstones, and Māori procured the raw material from numerous localities. Through working, the grindstones become angular or brick-shaped with shallow hollows on all faces, varying in size from hand-stones to blocks measuring 40 cm × 20 cm or more. As Māori were frequently travelling, grindstones had to be portable, and although much larger examples exist, they were confined to the permanent workshops.

Water was an important ingredient when using grindstones and this either came from a drip supply, or the block was partly immersed at a slight angle in a pool of water. Sandstone suitable for grinding is composed of small grains of quartz sand with other minerals that cement them together. If this bond is very tight, the stone glazes and ceases to cut, whereas if the bond is loose, the tiny grains are freed before they become blunt, exposing a new sharp surface. So the choice of stone was critical for the intended task. To grind a piece of pounamu it was rubbed back and forth on the grindstone; but in the case of smaller hand-stones, the position was reversed.

The earlier, brittle stone toki tended to have compound curves on the faces and were more likely to have been smoothed by hand-stones or rasps. Pounamu toki are squarer in section as a result of the sawing process and of being worked down on the larger grindstone blocks.

Finally, when the article was ground to shape, it was polished with fine whetstones such as mudstone and pumice. The polish on some artefacts, especially mere, was continually improved by constant handling and rubbing with shark oil. It was recorded at Temuka by Herries Beattie that, to give carvings that typical smooth patina, they were secured by a cord to rocks in the sea, where the action of the waves achieved the desired effect. I would have thought that it would have been the sand or seaweed that did the polishing. On examining many hei tiki under a microscope, I have observed red kōkōwai (hematite) residue in the cracks. Knowing that hematite, or rouge, is a common polishing compound, I experimented by applying it on a split, soft flax-flower stem and, rubbing this briskly against a jade carving, produced a reasonable polish. I also applied the hematite to the tough, leather-like leaves of the muttonbird scrub (*Brachyglottis rotundifolia*) with a similar result. Dog skin and seal leather would have been ideal materials for polishing, although this use is unconfirmed.

The technique of carving is associated with grinding. The finer features achieved on the hei tiki and other ornaments were made largely with the use of small sandstone and schist rasps suitably shaped to carry out the work. Rasps were used in a fashion similar to the modern European file; and the stone was frequently dipped into

The mighty braided Waimakariri River. East coast Māori followed this and other Canterbury rivers into the Southern Alps and across mountain passes to the Westland pounamu sources, returning with heavy loads.

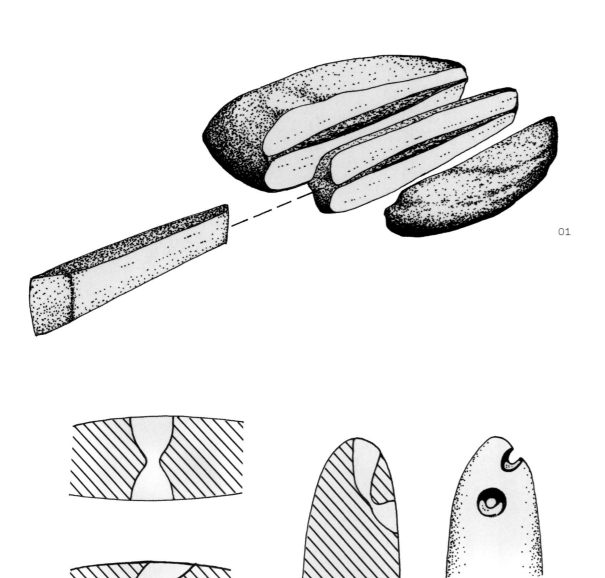

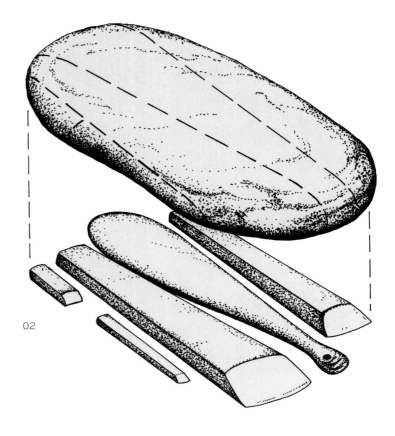

01 / An alternative method to sawing with the faces parallel to the sides of a more rounded boulder.

02 / With three main cuts in a flattish boulder, several items with their faces parallel to the schistosity plane could be achieved, which orientated the grain of the stone to best advantage.

03 / Cross sections of drilled holes from both sides, or at right angles, and the eye effect produced from a countersunk hole.

RIGHT / A collection of Māori tools for carving pounamu, from Pahia, Southland. The kit composes of sandstone rasps, abraiders and red kōkōwai (hematite) for polishing. Rasps were made by grooving sandstone fragments.

water to aid their cutting ability. It should be mentioned, however, that the manufacture of the rasps themselves was not an easy task. Flattish slabs of abrasive rocks were selected, and a shallow furrow was made on both sides, often by hammer pecking, then snapped off. The rasp blank was shaped to the desired profile on a grindstone block. Little has changed, as the various abrasive rasps used by present-day carvers for finishing work are identical in shape to the Māori examples,

the only difference being their composition.

Sharp flint or quartz burins were used for engraving fine detail. Although there is no decisive evidence, it is possible that some kind of core drill, perhaps a portion of tubular bird bone mounted in a drill and used with sand, was employed to achieve the almost perfectly round shape of the eyes in some hei tiki.

It is obvious that the grinding of pounamu was a considerable task for Māori, yet it was

accomplished with a great deal of satisfaction. From my experience as a carver, many satisfying hours can be spent smoothing down a piece of pounamu by hand, even though progress is slow. This love for the work is well illustrated by Heaphy's observation on the West Coast:

> A native will get up at night to have a polish at a favourite *mere*, or take one down to the beach and work away by the surf. A piece of *pounamu* and some slate will be carried when travelling, and at every halt a rub will be taken at it.

MAHI TŪWIRI/MAHI PĪRORI – DRILLING

Many very early stone-based cultures successfully achieved making a hole through stone. The process involved two techniques – pecking with a sharp hammerstone or boring with an abrasive drill. Māori used both methods, but favoured the drill and became very proficient at this work; they were able to perforate pounamu and other materials with great accuracy, achieving holes as small as 1 mm in diameter. The Māori drill (tūwiri/pīrori), sometimes known as the cord drill, was of simple construction and easy to operate, but it took considerable time and effort to produce a hole. It consisted of a vertical wooden shaft, a flywheel, an attached drill point and two pulling cords. Usually the flywheel was made either from twigs bent around with spokes in a cartwheel fashion, or from two or more equally weighted stones lashed to the shaft. In one reported case, a whale's intervertebral cartilage disc was fixed to the spindle; it would have been a very effective flywheel provided it was balanced.

The drill points (matā) were made from several different stone types, the most common of which were obsidian, quartz, argillite and flint. Many

points were angular in shape, while others were merely chipped, tapered flakes. The drill points were fixed to the bottom end of the shaft and the cords were wound around the upper end of the spindle. When the operator pulled the cords apart and downwards, the drill rotated; then, as the fully extended cords were relaxed, the momentum of the flywheel rewound them ready for another pull which, of course, rotated the drill in the opposite direction. Sand and water were added to the point and slowly the drill, with its reciprocal motion, ground its way in. This produced a blunt, tapered cavity, and it was necessary to drill from both sides to make a hole (see page 156).

To place the hole in the exact position, and to prevent the drill from wandering, small starting-off grooves at right angles were made with a pointed rasp. An alternative method was to place a piece of perforated wood over the desired position to guide the drill. A drill without a point could be used on stone and relied on the action of the rounded end of the wooden spindle together with sand and water; the abrasive grains would embed themselves into the wood and cut successfully.

I constructed a drill and found it to be a simple and efficient device to operate. The gyroscopic action of the rotating flywheel, together with the balanced pull on the cords, keeps the drill in an upright position from which it can be steered to any desired angle while spinning. Furthermore, speed is easily controlled and the pressure on the point can be adjusted by simply altering the downward angle of the cords.

The early accounts frequently mention the use of sharp drill points which, when blunted, were replaced with fresh ones. Using sand as an abrasive I have found cutting is more effective by constructing a small clay dam around the hole to contain the sand and water slurry. As the very centre of the drill bit has little cutting action, if the drill is angled slightly, more of the sides of the

point are in contact and grind more effectively. This technique may explain the off-centre or diagonal holes evident in quite a large number of artefacts. One particular style of hei tiki probably owes its design to the drilling of some 10 holes to quickly achieve the profile. The pump drill widely used by other cultures appears to be unknown to Māori in pre-European times.

Once the two opposing bored depressions met, the hole was reamed out with small rasps to smooth off the sharp edges. This resulted in a hole that was countersunk on both sides and hourglass-shaped in section. This effect was used to advantage in many artefacts of fish-like form, for the countersunk hole served the dual purpose of suspension hole and a realistic eye, with the inner hole as the pupil. In effect, the hole became a necessary part of the design – something that the modern carver could learn from. In many artefacts, especially the hei tiki, the artist's sensitivity and skill were such that, where a hole would obviously spoil the design, it was ingeniously bored at right angles, from the top to the back (see page 156).

HEAT TREATMENT

The general Māori methods for working pounamu were widespread in New Zealand, but various refinements and technical skills were developed independently. Some of these have been recorded; others have been lost – but one technique that has become apparent is the practice of heat treatment. I first became aware of it when trying to trace the sources of nephrite used by Māori.

Complicating the sourcing task is the presence of a group of artefacts that have changed their physical appearance through natural weathering or perhaps as the result of heating in a fire.

In an attempt to duplicate the appearance of these artefacts, I prepared a selection of nephrite

and semi-nephrite samples from known sources and placed them in an open fire. After reaching red heat they were then left to cool in the atmosphere. The heated samples presented a black to brownish outside appearance, but when this dark skin was removed by grinding, the inside colour had changed dramatically. A few samples had turned completely brown while others went silvery-white, resembling unheated specimens from different sources. Furthermore, several heated specimens from a known source resembled some prehistoric artefacts that were previously believed to be natural and from an unknown source. More surprising was the fact that during the grinding off of the black coating after firing, the softer semi-nephrite specimens appeared to have increased in hardness.

It was clear that these preliminary results had important implications, and I carried out further experiments. Over a period of several months, a large number of test pieces were fired, using both an open fire and an electric kiln.

Samples were exposed to heat for varying periods of time up to two days and at temperatures of up to 1000°C. The higher temperatures destroyed the structure of the stone, causing myriads of tiny fractures (crazing), and the piece became opaque. The low-fired specimens (300°C) showed a small change, mainly in colour. I found that a temperature of 650°C for a short period of time was the most effective: it did not damage the specimen too much, yet it produced an appreciable change in colour and an apparent increase in hardness.

Many heated samples showed a veining effect where the structure opened, forming tiny cracks which were made conspicuous by the presence of a dark residue. Correspondingly, a huge number of Māori pounamu artefacts show this characteristic black veining effect (see page 161).

Another diagnostic characteristic was a series of concentrations of large, circular feather fractures,

LEFT / As toki were sharpened, they became shorter and less efficient. These examples from Little Papanui and Papanui, Otago, are in the process of being sawn into whao (chisels). Otago Museum.

LEFT / Enlarged surface of a toki pounamu found on the Otago Peninsula. It has been heated to produce these feather fractures, giving it the appearance of scales or feathers. Otago Museum.

TOP RIGHT / Experimental samples of Westland nephrite showing the effects of heating. The natural oxidised specimen on the left has its segment changed to red. A dark green example has developed the typical black veining with a lighter green colour.

RIGHT/ A Māori example of a partly sawn slab of heated pounamu from Okains Bay. It appears as if it has been heated before it was worked, but still carries the characteristics of black veining and silvery green colour. Canterbury Museum.

and experiments on samples from several sources revealed that this effect could be simulated by uneven localised heat or partial quenching in cold water. Nephrite often contains naturally produced feather fractures, but generally does not have this circular fish-scale or bird-feather effect.

There is no doubt that a considerable number of nephrite artefacts have been heated, and it is certain that Māori were aware of the resulting effects and took advantage of them.

There are some indications that a predominant reason for Māori to heat nephrite was to bring about the change in colour; but why transform an attractive, translucent green object to a milky-white colour? Māori regarded the rarer, silvery-pale green īnanga variety with reverence. It is interesting that a fish theme was an important part of Māori mythology on pounamu. This feature, together with the beauty and relative rarity of īnanga, makes it hardly surprising that artefacts of this material were among those held in great esteem.

With suitable specimens we have seen that the firing technique can produce a material closely resembling īnanga in appearance, and Māori would have taken the opportunity to do this with other colours. The increase in hardness provided a dual benefit. Undoubtedly many artefacts suffered heating accidentally, and a few show overheating to the point of destruction. A number of unworked and partly worked blocks of pounamu show heating and this could explain why delicate finished artefacts with heated characteristics have avoided damage. Some show signs of slight heating, and it is possible that valued pieces were fired carefully in stages to obtain the desired colour, because there was no guarantee that the anticipated effect would be achieved. Other colours, such as an attractive orange and a variety with reddish markings, were possibly caused by heating. It would appear that other minerals were also heated to effect a colour change – for example,

Māori village sites where pounamu
was worked occupied many of
the bays and inlets of Banks
Peninsula. This idyllic view of
Akaroa, so peaceful now, has been
the scene of conflict between
Māori tribes. .

brown iron oxide (goethite) was altered to red hematite and used as a paint pigment.

Early communications with Europeans about the source of nephrite refer to nephrite being soft when first found, and needing to be worked before later hardening. These may or may not relate to the heating process; but essentially they illustrate that Māori were aware of a hardening effect for nephrite. There were obvious advantages in working a softer semi-nephrite, then heating it to a hardness equalling a compact nephrite, even though there was some loss of toughness.

The heating of jade in China is well documented; examples are known as chicken-bone jade. These have usually been fired to relatively high temperatures, but comparing the characteristics produced from lower temperatures I have found that many Chinese carvings in collections are very similar and appear to have been heated slightly to produce subtle colour effects. Several other jade cultures were also aware of the effects of heating.

The traditional Māori methods of working pounamu were very similar to those of other jade-possessing cultures, except for one factor: Māori remained a stone-based culture until the introduction of metal by Europeans. Thereafter they quickly took advantage of the new European technology and, for a short while, adopted many refinements to their methods of working pounamu. Among these were the pump drill, metal core drills, rotary grindstones and metal saws. In terms of metal saws, fencing wire in a frame or the two-handled crosscut saw were used with sand abrasives, which made it quicker and easier to saw pounamu, speeding up production.

Considering that the basic tools available to Māori for working pounamu were a wooden drill, sandstone and quartz sand, we must marvel at the outstanding technical and artistic talent they demonstrated in creating their pounamu treasures.

ABOVE LEFT / Granite outcrops near Pahia, on the shore of Foveaux Strait. Several Māori villages in this vicinity were workshop sites where pounamu and argillite tools were manufactured.

LEFT / Whareakeake or Murdering Beach, near the entrance to Otago Harbour, was a major Māori settlement specialising in working pounamu. In 1817 the village was burned by European sealers.

RIGHT / Browning Pass area, under snow, in the Southern Alps. It is one of the many passes used by East coast Māori to cross the Alps in their quest for pounamu from Westland.

THE RETURN OF POUNAMU

The most significant event affecting pounamu in recent times has been the settlement of the Ngāi Tahu land claim and the restoration of ownership of the resource to Māori hands.

The background to this issue began in 1860 when Poutini Ngāi Tahu sold the lands and waters of Poutini/Westland to the Crown. They sought to reserve for themselves the Arahura River and its catchment from the source at Lake Browning/Whakarewa to the sea. Pounamu was their greatest treasure and they were insistent that it should remain in their possession.

James Mackay, the Crown agent, agreed to the setting aside of a large reserve that included the Arahura River, but the Crown subsequently failed to honour the agreement and set aside a smaller reserve. The owners of the smaller reserve continued for five generations to pressure the Crown into meeting its obligations. Finally in 1976 the three titles to the Arahura River bed were transferred to the proprietors of Mawhera Incorporation, a Māori authority that was set up to administer and manage the reserve lands of the West Coast that included the Arahura Reserve MR30.

However, the matter did not end there as the ownership of pounamu was constantly in dispute as a result of a Crown agency continuing to grant pounamu licences within the Arahura River catchment.

In 1985 the Ngāi Tahu Māori Trust Board was preparing to file a tribal land claim to the Waitangi Tribunal. An essential part of the preparation included consultation at the regional level to identify possible breaches by the Crown of the Treaty of Waitangi. The board approached the proprietors of Mawhera Incorporation and offered to include their long-standing grievance of the perpetual

leases over the Māori Reserved Lands of Westland. During the discussions Maika Mason raised the issue of the ownership of pounamu within the Arahura River catchment being included as a clear breach of the Treaty. He was prepared to allow the perpetual lease issue to be included, provided the ownership of pounamu also went forward. It was agreed with the chair and deputy chair of the board, Tipene O'Regan and Maurice Pohio, that both be included subject to the provision that, if successful, ownership of pounamu in the Arahura River catchment would be restored to the proprietors of Mawhera Incorporation – that is, the Māori owners. In 1986 Ngāi Tahu filed the claim and the hearing commenced in 1987 and continued until 1989.

At the Tribunal hearing in Greymouth, Maika Mason presented the traditional evidence regarding the ownership of pounamu. The evidence was so compelling that the Waitangi Tribunal, after seeking more information on the issue of licences, recommended to the Government that it place a moratorium on the granting of pounamu mining licences. This was realised and negotiations were commenced with Ngāi Tahu on the return of pounamu within the tribal area to the tribe. This included the resources in Westland, South Westland, Otago and Southland.

Parliament passed the Ngāi Tahu (Pounamu Vesting) Act on 25 September 1997 as part of the interim settlement of the larger claim. The Crown acted honourably in resolving the issue and Ngāi Tahu once again owned its pounamu (defined as nephrite including semi-nephrite, bowenite and, in some defined areas, serpentinite occurring in its natural condition). Ownership was vested in Te Rūnanga o Ngāi Tahu, the tribal body that replaced the Ngāi

Tahu Māori Trust Board.

Te Rūnanga o Ngāi Tahu then fulfilled the obligations of the claim process by on-vesting the ownership of all pounamu that lies within the catchment of the Arahura River in the proprietors of Mawhera Incorporation. No further mining licences were issued and the current licences were allowed to run until they expired. All royalties from those licences were paid to Ngāi Tahu.

Today, pounamu within the Arahura River catchment is the property of the Mawhera Incorporation. Only its shareholder–owners have access to pounamu from the riverbed. All other persons require a permit. Pounamu outside that area, but within the ancestral land boundaries and adjacent territorial sea, is now the property of Te Rūnanga o Ngāi Tahu. A tribal pounamu protection officer has been stationed at Hokitika.

Ngāi Tahu rūnanga have taken a prominent role in the tribal management of pounamu. As mentioned in the Introduction, each of the nine rūnanga who have deposits of pounamu within their boundaries manage their resources. Some areas are shared, based on traditional usage. Several hīkoi to the various pounamu sources have been organised by these rūnanga to acquaint their people with the importance and history of the resource.

Te Rūnanga o Ngāi Tahu held public consultation meetings throughout the regions and sought submissions from the industry and interested people, from which they prepared an initial pounamu management plan that explains the tribe's position and intentions in respect of the resource.

The return of the stone met with little resistance and generally has public approval. Ngāi Tahu is aware that pounamu is a national treasure and dear to most New Zealanders.

Protecting the natural and cultural values that attach to the stone has been a common thread in all tribal discussion about pounamu management, as has the kaitiaki (guardianship) responsibility for future generations. Only by careful management of the resource will this esteem be maintained and enhanced.

Pounamu has a high monetary value and unfortunately the goodwill has been marred by instances of illegal mining. Two lengthy trials have attracted considerable public attention and resulted in jail terms and hefty fines for the offenders.

Since the pounamu was handed back, it has undergone valuable scientific investigation, especially through a working partnership between Ngāi Tahu and GNS Science geologists, with assistance from the universities of Canterbury and Otago and the Department of Conservation. This has involved surveys of some known deposits to understand the geology, quantitive surveys, exploration and discovery of new occurrences, analytical studies and archaeological surveys. This research is continuing.

With this body of expanding knowledge a comprehensive understanding of the extent, cultural significance and future reserves of pounamu will assist the various rūnanga in their respective management policies. It is a huge responsibility to manage a national icon on behalf of future generations, and representatives have to consider far-reaching options such as the preservation of natural, cultural and archaeological values, research potential and the sustainability and utilisation of resources. Other possibilities are to interpret areas as visitor attractions.

An example of telling the pounamu story is Aoraki Bound, an educational and development course introduced by Ngāi Tahu in collaboration

with Outward Bound, an adventure-based self-improvement organisation. It takes the form of a 20-day journey-based course that builds leadership, cultural awareness and personal development. An important component of the 'journey' is a pounamu experience where students undertake a 12-day hīkoi to Westland, where they are shown traditional sites and learn about the history of pounamu, how it was collected and worked. A small pounamu boulder secured in a kete made of harakeke is carried in turns by every student during the hīkoi on the Arahura River pounamu trail to its source at Browning Pass, high in the Southern Alps. The team of 14 people

then retrace their steps. This course has become very popular and rewarding for students.

Currently the only places from which the general public are permitted to remove pounamu are specified sections of the tidal zone on the West Coast beaches. This is restricted to what one person can physically carry at one time in one day unaided. Because management policy is developing and rulings vary on each area, for any permissions or accidental finds of pounamu, contact should be made with Te Rūnanga o Ngāi Tahu or one of the nine rūnanga concerned and Mawhera Incorporation for the Arahura River.

The Aoraki-bound īnanga pounamu in its kete, which has been carried by many students into the mountains up to the Browning Pass and back. R. BECK

CHAPTER EIGHT/
NEW ZEALAND'S
JADE INDUSTRY

NGĀ PAKIHI
MAI RĀ ANŌ
Development will always
continue to occur

From the 1860s the traditional role of Māori as masters of pounamu working was gradually overtaken by European lapidaries and their new technology. The goldrush in Westland was exposing steady quantities of high quality nephrite, and there was an increasing appreciation of pounamu jewellery among the growing settler population.

Lapidary businesses sprang up on the West Coast and in Dunedin. With the discovery of rich gold deposits in Otago, Dunedin was becoming the centre of commerce. It had the necessary infrastructure to support a lapidary industry that soon developed into the jade-cutting centre of the country.

Nephrite from Westland found its way to Idar-Oberstein, where it was fashioned into many different articles of jewellery and reproductions of Māori weapons and amulets. Much of it returned to New Zealand for resale and this two-way trading, assisted by German settlers living in Westland, initially flourished between the 1860s and 1914, when the First World War interrupted the trade. Between the two wars, Harry Joosten, originally from Flensburg, set up a trading business with New Zealand which included the export of nephrite. As a young man he worked for Ernest Nichol & Co., a shipping agent in Bluff who frequently arranged for Westland jade to be exported to Hamburg.

Another German jade buyer, Otto Jerusalem, (later Williams), came from Herborn near Idar-Oberstein and was based in Wellington. Apparently he copied patterns of hei tiki from the museum for his contacts in Germany to make souvenirs in 10,000-piece lots. He gave up the jewellery business after the outbreak of the First World War, initially going farming before taking up a journalism career including editorship of *The Mirror* and founding *New Zealand Woman's Weekly* magazine.

This trade was finally extinguished in 1947 when the government introduced an act prohibiting the export of raw nephrite. The act still stands, but does allow small specimens to be exported with a permit.

William Dalheimer established a lapidary business at Idar-Oberstein in 1896, specialising in nephrite and 30 years ago his family still had stocks of New Zealand stone that was taken there over 100 years ago.

A considerable amount of New Zealand nephrite was worked by German lapidaries, mostly into items for New Zealand consumption. In both countries, lapidaries tended to produce similar fashionable items and it can be difficult to identify their origin. They were mainly jewellery, watch-chains and fobs, knife handles and small hei tiki. The Dalheimer family, in particular, produced many thousands of souvenir hei tiki.

The earliest example of the jade trade between New Zealand and Germany for processing was that of Joseph Klein, who settled in Hokitika in 1865 and began a business as a watchmaker and jeweller. He collected nephrite and other New Zealand stones and purchased large quantities from local Māori, sending them back to his homeland in Germany to be cut and polished. This was apparently a successful venture and an advertisement in the *Hokitika Evening Star*, January 1868, advises of an expected shipment of 'greenstone' crosses and earrings, among other items. Although Klein was a lapidary by

PREVIOUS PAGE / Strongly veined nephrite from South Westland.

LEFT / Jade cobble from Arahura River Westland.

RIGHT / During the goldmining era, many jade boulders were saved and stockpiled for buyers. These two boulders near Kumara were photographed by Rudolf Veek, a German lapidary, c. 1905.
COURTESY M. VEEK

Apparently William Dickson was the pioneer of jade-working in Dunedin, followed by John Murdoch and John Laing; all three are believed to have established businesses during the 1860s. Dickson specialised in the production of copies of mere. Eventually his business was taken over by his son Andrew and it closed down in 1910. William Dickson trained several people in the trade of lapidary, including Andrew Devlin, who was to remain in the trade the longest. Dickson also supplied the stone for the Māori political prisoners from the North Island who were incarcerated at Dunedin in the early 1880s. Chapman observed that more than a hundred Māori prisoners were working pounamu by hand, but using European metal gang saws and rotary grindstones. They made ear pendants and mere in the gaol yard at the bottom of Stuart Street.

John Murdoch's business appears to have ceased about 1900, and his machinery was purchased by Andrew Devlin. Murdoch trained several men who later worked for other lapidaries, including George Chisholm, who started his own business.

The other early lapidary, John Laing, came to Dunedin in the 1860s with experience gained in Scotland and established a workshop at 40 Great King Street. He retired in about 1906, having spent most of his life as a manufacturing jeweller and lapidary. His son, George Bell Laing, also became a lapidary. He went to Auckland, where he continued to work nephrite part-time until about 1913, when he gave it up completely for a career in the wool industry.

George Hyndman began in 1878. From the 1880s there was a flurry of lapidaries being established, including the Devlin Bros, George Chisholm, Arthur E. Jones and William Bertram, who operated the Milford Sound Greenstone Co. and probably supplied bowenite pendants to the jewellery firm of Frank Hyam, who marketed these. Many trainees went on to establish

trade, it appears that he did not have a workshop in Hokitika. He sold up in 1870 and moved to Melbourne, where he died 14 years later.

The first lapidary on the West Coast was probably C. Chilcott, who advertised his business in March 1867 at the back of the Post Office Hotel, Mawhera Quay, Greymouth. He purchased nephrite, cut and polished it to any design, and he even offered a half-price deal for people who supplied their own stone. He opened a new workshop in Hokitika in June 1868, but five months later sold the business, plant and property. He next appeared

in Wellington in 1869, selling his stock of jade jewellery. He died in Dunedin in 1874.

William Clarke presented himself in July 1869 as a watchmaker, jeweller and lapidary in Revell Street, Hokitika. His business seemed to be mainly watch repairs, but mentioned that 'greenstone is cut and mounted on the premises'.

The early Dunedin lapidaries played an important part in the New Zealand jade story. Fortunately Thomas Conly, in 1948, spoke with many of the people involved and recorded a valuable insight to this remarkable industry.

LEFT / The blasting of nephrite was difficult owing to its toughness. Holes for the explosives were drilled by hand using a hammer and punch, a slow arduous task. COURTESY WEST COAST HISTORICAL MUSEUM

RIGHT / A presentation casket of polished nephrite panels with gold nuggets from the Wakatipu district. It was presented to the Minister for Mines to commemorate the firing of the first shot for the construction of the Kawarau Dam near Queenstown in 1924. It is likely that one of the Dunedin lapidaries made the jade panels. Courtesy Hamilton collection. R. BECK

separate businesses themselves, and as some closed, they were taken over or the machinery sold on to new enterprises.

The early lapidaries began working with hand-cranked or foot treadle machines, usually rotating horizontal cast-iron or lead wheels with emery grit for shaping, grinding and lapping flat surfaces. Polishing was done on felt wheels with polishing rouge and water. Boulders were usually halved on big mud saws, then any rind was broken off with heavy hammers and the core of gem-grade stone was then sawn into thin slabs on smaller mud saws, known as 'slitters' or 'knickers'. Later, these businesses attached themselves to factories to utilise their steam motive power, often via a maze of overhead belts which drove their machinery.

Their products were all much the same: a selection of jewellery and trinkets such as hearts, bar brooches, necklaces, watch fobs, cutlery handles, paper knives and, of course, replica Māori mere and hei tiki. Many of these lapidaries specialised in certain items and sold their work to jewellery shops and wholesalers throughout the country. Interestingly, fashion at the time favoured

LEFT / A selection of the typical items produced by early New Zealand and German lapidaries from the finest quality Westland jade. In many cases lapidaries cut and polished the stone, with jewellers doing the gold and silver smithing.

01 / Bar brooches with gold mountings. This was a fashionable design of the times.
02 / A large flawless cabochon with an ornate gold mounting.
03 / Intricately carved cameo brooch.
04 / Delicate necklaces and gold mounted fish.
05 / Paper knives mounted in silver. These were popular gift and presentation items.
06 / Heart pendant and watch chain fobs. These were very popular.
07 / Two salt cellars with silver spoons, carved thinly to allow the light to penetrate.
08 / Set of jade handled gilt and silver spoons featuring Māori woman with child made in Birmingham, 1924.
09 / Jade handled silver spoons with Māori and kiwi, dated Birmingham, 1899, with Frank Hyam's mark. Jade handled silver knife, Souness and Gamble mark. Courtesy Hamilton collection.
VAHRY PHOTOGRAPHY LTD

the rich green kawakawa variety rather than īnanga, which was not popular with Europeans as it was regarded as too pale.

The best known of the Dunedin lapidaries were the Devlin brothers. Andrew Devlin Snr, a brass moulder from Glasgow, Scotland, financed his two sons, Andrew Jnr and Thomas, into a lapidary business situated at the rear of their home in Duncan Street, which later became Wesley Street, South Dunedin. The precise date of the establishment of their factory is not clear, but it was some time between 1891 and 1898. Andrew Jnr is thought to have begun as a lapidary at the age of 20. His occupation – and that of his older brother, Thomas – is given as 'lapidary' on Andrew's marriage certificate in 1894. The business was known by several names – Devlin Bros; N.Z. Steam Lapidary Works (A. Devlin) and A. Devlin & Co. – and survived until 1941. The brothers built up a remarkable enterprise, at one time employing 12 staff, including young women who did the polishing.

The workshop, which was not a large building, was partitioned into several areas. The equipment was driven by a small steam engine, later replaced by an electric motor. There were six mud saws for cutting the boulders. These were soft, mild steel saw discs, up to 75 cm in diameter, that rotated in a slurry of mud, water and emery grit. The stones were clamped in frames pivoted above the saw blades. The emery abrasive was picked up by and became embedded in the soft steel of the rotating blades, which slowly cut their way through the stones over a period of several days. Grinding and polishing was done on horizontal grinding wheels and lead-based metal laps charged with emery and felt polishing wheels. Holes were usually drilled using small rotating tubes and abrasive grit, but for the very small holes, the brothers used diamond drills which they had made themselves.

As mentioned earlier, the Devlins developed a thriving trade in copies of Māori artefacts, especially the production of mere and hei tiki. The mere were usually made to order as they involved considerable work, and in one case an old Māori chief drew his own pattern and commissioned the Devlins to make 13 of them as gifts for his descendants. Different styles of hei tiki were preferred by particular Māori communities and the Devlin brothers obliged, keeping patterns of the various types.

Andrew became very skilful at carving. His daughter relates that his fingernails were always ground down as a result of it. Thomas operated the saws and grinders, leaving the more intricate work to Andrew. Thomas retired from the business in about 1926 because of ill-health.

The Devlins' factory became quite an attraction in Dunedin, and among the many visitors were prominent overseas dignitaries. The company was commissioned to made several works in jade, among them a large casket that was presented to the Duke of York (later King George V) when he visited New Zealand in 1901. The Devlins were also involved in making a gift that was presented to the Duke of Gloucester when he laid the foundation stone for the Wellington railway station, and a gift from the nation to the Prince of Wales in 1920.

Although the main stones used were nephrite and, to a lesser extent, bowenite, other materials such as pāua shell and ornamental stones of the quartz family were also cut and polished.

It is difficult now to distinguish the Devlins' work. Heart shapes were popular, as were gold-capped jade bar brooches, often with gold lettering 'KIA ORA' or 'N.Z.' or 'MOTHER' mounted on top, and certainly the Devlins produced a large number of these.

Andrew Devlin finally retired from the business in about 1941 after some 50 years' experience as a lapidary. He kept some stone, and continued carving jade as a hobby until he died in 1951.

A. G. (Alex) Passmore set up a lapidary business at Musselburgh Rise in 1943, with new premises and modern machinery, including diamond cutters and drills made by him. The factory employed a staff of five. Passmore made frequent trips to the West Coast to buy pounamu from Ngāi Tahu and off the dredges. He produced mainly items of jewellery and other articles such as cutlery handles, serviette rings, hei tiki and occasionally mere. Several presentation pieces and trophies were commissioned; this was the work he enjoyed the most. When his business closed in 1949, it brought an end to the 80-year-old lapidary industry in Dunedin.

Over this long period, some ten lapidary workshops were established, most around the turn of the century. A 1902 Dunedin directory lists five lapidary businesses trading at one time. Presumably all of these businesses were employing staff, and if the flow-on numbers of stone buyers, retail jewellers and others are included, the industry supported a relatively large number of people.

During the period when the Dunedin lapidaries were operating so successfully, there was little incentive for factories to start up elsewhere. However, the jewellery firm of W. Littlejohn & Son Ltd in Wellington advertised in the 1921 *New Zealand Index*: 'We cut and polish New Zealand Greenstone in our own workshops.' In 1922 the managing director, P. Denton, won the design for a wedding gift to Princess Mary from the women of New Zealand. It was an ornamental inkstand made from nephrite, gold and wood, and was produced by the firm. There were other lapidary enterprise: H. J. Freeman, Wellington; J. Rolf, Napier, and two Auckland firms, H. A. Neilson & Sons, and Heinrich Kohn & Son. Many early New Zealand manufacturing silversmiths and jewellers incorporated jade in their designs and would

01

02

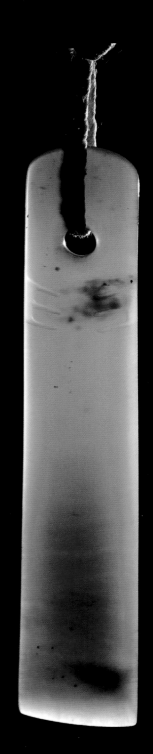

Selection of nephrite carvings by contemporary New Zealand artists. They show a wide range of styles, including fine delicate examples, works based on traditional Māori motifs, fondle pieces and carved boulders.

01 / *Compass*, John Edgar. New Zealand jade, 101 mm. The relief design is carved on both sides. COURTESY MUSEUM OF NEW ZEALAND TE PAPA TONGAREWA, 1993-0038-13/1-2

02 / *Ohomairangi*, Alan Brown, 1987. A stylised adze of kahurangi jade, Westland, 190 mm. Southland Art Foundation, Invercargill.

03 / *Loop*, Joe Sheehan. This necklace is made from Siberian jade and consists of many separate pieces. N. BARR

04 / *Pekapeka*, from 'Kaitiaki' series, Lewis Gardiner, kahurangi jade, Westland. KENJI NAGAI/SPIRIT WRESTLER GALLERY

05 / *Netian*, Robin Lynes, 400 × 270 mm. The almost flawless jade from Marsden area still has a little of the boulder's oxidised rind on the base. The work was spread over several years and weighs 50 kg. D. SALT

03

04

05

have contracted the cutting and polishing work to lapidaries in New Zealand and Germany.

In 1947 Jim Lamont, son of a Greymouth jeweller, began a lapidary section in the business. He worked exclusively in nephrite and at one time employed a staff of five. Although sawing was still being done on mud saws, he introduced small diamond saws and other tools. The workshop continued until 1973 when Lamont retired. His several commissions for dignitaries included the base for a wedding gift to Princess Margaret and a brooch for the Queen Mother.

Between 1949 and 1963, Lamont at Greymouth and later two Auckland firms, Auckland Greenstone Co. and Master Crafts Ltd, were processing jade.

During the early 1900s, the lapidary industry was producing fashionable jade dress jewellery. It wasn't until several decades later that the burgeoning tourist industry sought something distinctively New Zealand as souvenirs.

With the extraction of the jade deposits at Olderog/Waitaiki Creek beginning in 1962 a factory, Westland Greenstone Ltd, was set up at Hokitika – and this business still operates. Factories are now located in many centres, including Greymouth, Hokitika, Riverton, Arrowtown, Queenstown, Christchurch, Rotorua and Auckland. The methods and equipment used in these modern lapidary factories involve fast-cutting diamond tools geared to mass production – a far cry from the Māori workshops. Modern carved versions of hei tiki, mere, and other artefacts that were never originally made from jade are produced commercially, but these are easily identified as recent. On the market there is also an increasing number of New Zealand-style carvings and souvenirs made overseas from foreign nephrite.

For a long time New Zealand jade has been downgraded by the desire to satisfy the souvenir market – and here the use of the word 'greenstone' rather than 'jade' has not helped. However, in the last 20 years the standard of merchandise has improved dramatically: whereas personal mounted jewellery, bookends and cheap souvenirs used to be the main offerings, now most factories produce carved items that reflect a distinctive New Zealand style, even if they still often ignore the important property of feel, with intricate designs and highly polished finishes.

An increasing number of skilled professional jade carvers, both Māori and European, have now established themselves as single or cooperative enterprises at various locations throughout the country. Their work is exciting, producing superb original New Zealand carvings that incorporate all of the attributes of jade. They work in New Zealand stone as well as in jade from overseas sources, and so in a way they are repeating the story of the German lapidaries in Idar-Oberstein.

Many of these carvings are true works of art, and because jade is so durable they will become valued heirlooms for generations to come. There is a steadily growing domestic demand from private and public collectors, local and overseas. The Left Bank Art Gallery in Greymouth has taken the initiative and has for some years held a national biennial jade carving exhibition. They also have an expanding permanent jade collection of contemporary work and an acquisition policy that specialises in jade carving by New Zealand artists.

These carvers are, at last, carrying on the rich heritage of Māori working in pounamu before they were interrupted two centuries ago. In some respects these innovative New Zealand carvers are ahead of their colleagues overseas, where all too often the designs and creations of earlier indigenous cultures are either copied or ignored. Drawing on the Māori legacy, New Zealand has become the leading jade-carving nation.

01 / *Flame Series*, Raymond Ansin, 1979, Westland jade. Originally produced in collaboration with Cliff Dalziel. This design, and variations of it, has become a popular form reproduced by the industry. Left Bank Art Gallery, Greymouth.

02 / *Celtic Throwdown*, John Sheehan Jnr, Siberian jade. Two separate interlocking elements carved from one piece of stone. Left Bank Art Gallery, Greymouth.

03 / *North Beach Taniwha*, Paul Bradford, South Westland jade. A large fondle piece. Left Bank Art Gallery, Greymouth.

01

02

03

01

02

03

04

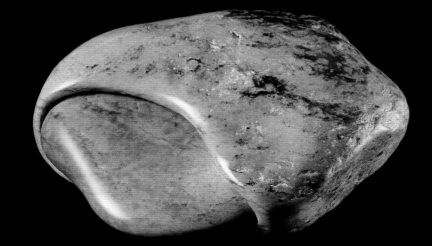

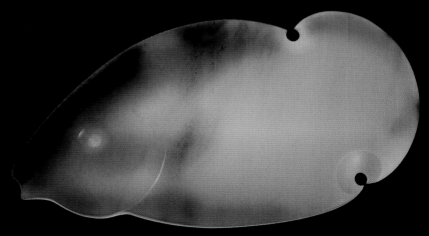

A PHILOSOPHY OF JADE CARVING

Carving is the ultimate in lapidary art, and jade is the ideal medium. No other material can provide the artist with such a comprehensive range of properties. Jade carving can be very satisfying work.

Naturally, carvers are all different. Many are true artists who, in effect, create pieces of original sculpture, while others are more content to rely on existing designs or to model direct from nature. I make no attempt to classify carvers or to comment on their styles – time will do that more effectively – but I offer the following philosophy based on my own experience.

Basic requirements for jade carving are: a deep understanding and respect for the medium, the creative ability to conceive the design and, finally, the technical skill to execute the work. Because jade has a wide range of properties and because each artist has their own individual mode of expression, there is still unlimited scope for original design

and development. A sense of heritage and appreciation of the mauri (spiritual essence) of pounamu are also important for many Māori engaged in working with pounamu and for others who have a respect for Māori culture.

Jade begs to be fondled, and the artist should utilise the property of feel. Likewise, both toughness and translucency can be exploited, though not to excess. This difference is exemplified by a comparison between the simple but superb archaic Chinese carvings and the later ones, which often sacrificed feel and good design to become intricate but untouchable examples of craftsmanship.

Jade's ability to maintain an edge was the original attribute, and not just for Māori. So long as the design allows for it, I occasionally try to incorporate this aspect of the stone into my own carving. An appropriate edge or edges may be ground quite sharp (but not too sharp) so that, when the piece is fondled, you are reminded that the stone commands respect. The remainder of the carving may be soft in appearance and

feel, and this is accentuated by a satin polish. It is also good to take advantage of the natural markings, colour and shape of the stone (especially river pebbles) to inspire a design with the minimum of modification. The ultimate is to search for and find the pebble in its natural environment, and then to work it into a unique, very personal object.

The property of sound is often overlooked by lapidaries, and carvings made specifically to ring when struck offer a whole new sphere of design and skill. Some pieces will retain a note for many seconds, depending on the shape and quality of the stone; for flattish carvings the grain of the stone needs to be parallel. The tone, which is governed by the size of the carving, is usually a distinctive ting that can be quite piercing but also pleasant and haunting.

Although modern technology has given the carver many new advantages with sophisticated diamond tools, it is possible to carve jade by the traditional Māori method using very simple tools – it just takes longer (see Appendix One).

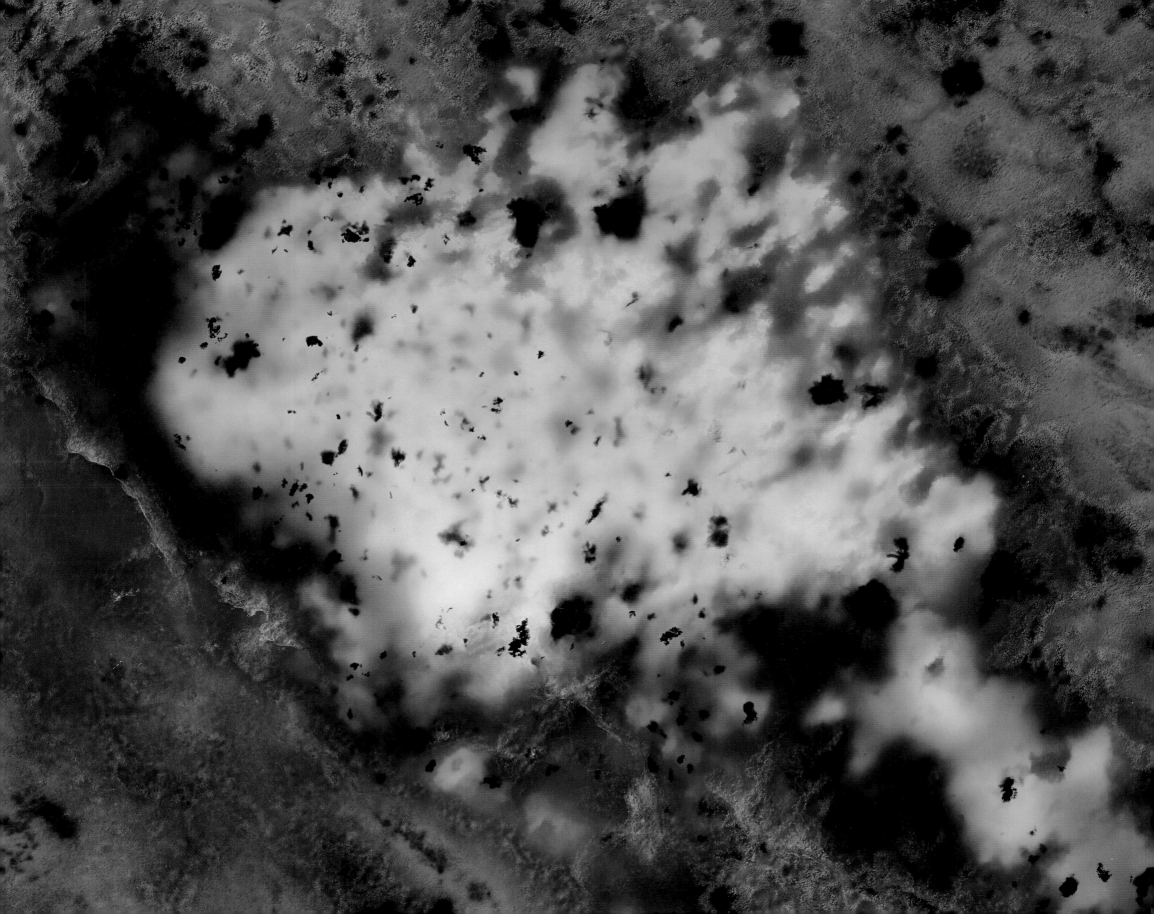

CHAPTER NINE/ TECHNICAL ASPECTS OF NEW ZEALAND JADE

WHAONGIA
KA TAUĀKĪ

Opening and exposing the
stone and also one's mind

THE ORIGIN OF NEPHRITE

Nephrite owes its compactness and toughness to the microscopic, needle-like tremolite crystals that have been twisted and entangled with each other. This is known as a felted or nephritic structure, and its formation requires just the right conditions. Many theories exist for the process of nephrite formation. These tend to vary from one geological formation to another. New Zealand nephrite has formed in association with several separate geological sequences, the three main ones being the Pounamu Ultramafic Belt in Westland; the Dun Mountain Ophiolite Belt in Nelson, South Westland and Southland; and the Greenstone Mélange in Otago.

Circumstances common to these rocks are the presence of fault-bounded serpentinite in contact with other igneous or siliceous sedimentary rocks or their altered equivalents such as schist, together in an active tectonic environment, and the presence of fluids such as water. Provided the right conditions are present, the contact reactions between these rocks cause changes in composition, known as metasomatic and metamorphic alterations. Reactions are driven by both the movement of fluids along contact zones and chemical gradients caused by differences in chemistry between the different rock types. They generally occur when the rocks are buried deep in the Earth's crust where temperatures are between around 250°C and 450°C and pressures may be about 2–6 kbar. The result of this process can be the production of zones of calc-silicate rocks such as rodingite, tremolite, talc and so on. These can also form at relatively low temperatures, but in different circumstances.

Although tremolite is formed, this does not necessarily mean that nephrite is produced. The process of achieving the characteristic felted structure of nephrite is not fully understood, although many theories have been presented.

A popular concept is that tectonic movement is a contributing factor. Many nephrite occurrences are lenticular in shape, bounded by faults, and there is evidence of their having suffered high pressure at some stage of their formation. The relatively small size of nephrite deposits suggests that the environment and circumstances that cause felting are localised and essential. When these conditions are met only in part, semi-nephrite is probably the result.

Ortho-nephrite and para-nephrite are terms suggested by D. Nichol to identify the two different rock associations in which nephrite has formed: 'ortho' when it is derived from an igneous source such as ultramafic rocks, and 'para' from dolomitic sedimentary rocks. Alternative terms introduced by various writers are metasomatic nephrite, metamorphic nephrite; serpentine type, carbonate type; apohyperbasite nephrite and apocarbonate nephrite. My preference is ortho-nephrite and para-nephrite.

The Canadian geologist S. F. Leaming suggests that the texture of nephrite could be inherited. He has noted that the texture of serpentine in some cases is very similar to that of nephrite and that with the metasomatic alteration to tremolite the original texture is preserved. A completely different process, proposed by Nichol, is that the nephrite was produced by dynamic metamorphism with a sudden release of pressure and recrystallisation of tremolite rock to fine-grained nephrite.

G. E. Harlow and S. S. Sorensen state: 'All nephrites occur at moderate to low pressure (<2 kbar?). Supersaturation of interacting fluids, or fluids and solids at low temperature, appears to yield the fibrous-mat crystallisations characteristic of nephrite.'

A. F. Cooper, describing the Makarora occurrence, attributes the texture of nephrite to 'recrystallisation of metasomatic tremolite rocks

during late or post-metamorphic shearing'. He also mentions this happening as a two-phase process, which appears to be the situation in some other New Zealand occurrences.

In many cases tectonics provide the mechanism for the production of nephrite, where sections of suitable rock can encounter the necessary extreme conditions while being carried down deep in the Earth's crust then forced to the surface along faults.

The formation of nephrite is obviously a complex process that varies with each occurrence. One thing that is certain is that it expresses the active geological history of this planet.

PHYSICAL PROPERTIES OF NEW ZEALAND NEPHRITE

Physical properties such as chemical composition, crystal structure, colour, relative density, hardness, optical characters and texture provide means of identifying rocks and minerals.

CHEMICAL COMPOSITION

Nephrite is essentially a calcium magnesium hydroxy silicate with small varying amounts of iron, termed tremolite or tremolite-actinolite:

Tremolite $Ca_2Mg_5Si_8O_{22}(OH)_2$

Actinolite $Ca_2(Mg, Fe)_5Si_8O_{22}(OH)_2$.

The division between the two is fixed by the amount of iron present. Tremolite is white to dark grey in colour. Iron is often present in small amounts, but as this content increases to substitute magnesium, tremolite becomes green and eventually grades into actinolite. With further substitution, the mineral is known as ferroactinolite. Actinolite comes from the Greek word *aktinos*, ray or radiate, because it commonly forms as bunches of radiating crystals; and tremolite has this habit also, with its radiating fan-like fibres.

CHEMICAL COMPOSITIONS OF A TYPICAL GREEN, NORTH WESTLAND NEPHRITE IN BY WEIGHT (%)

CaO	MgO	SiO_2	FeO	Fe_2O_3	Al_2O_3	MnO	Na_2O	K_2O	LOI*
13.25	22.9	57.0	3.65	0.14	0.23	0.11	0.40	0.06	2.2

*Loss on ignition = hydroxyl content

Source: W. C. Tennant *et al.*

Nephrite can grade between these minerals but is more commonly referred to as tremolite.

STRUCTURE

Nephrite is a microcrystalline monomineralic rock made up of minute twisted and tangled crystals or tufts of tremolite that belong to the monoclinic system of crystallography. Thus, we cannot talk of a single nephrite crystal. The texture of nephrite varies widely and has been classified by several researchers, who recognised many varieties from studying world deposits. The five grades introduced by F. J. Turner in 1935, based on his investigations into New Zealand nephrites and related rocks used by Māori, ranged from true nephritic structures to tremolite rocks with little or no nephritic structure.

Semi-nephrites are an intermediary stage between nephrite and tremolite rocks. They are a stage below nephrite, in that the felting process has not completely developed. Tremolite rocks are just that – bunches of radiating or parallel crystals with absolutely no nephritic structure. They cannot be called nephrite or jade, yet have the same chemical composition as nephrite.

Two further types that are also represented by New Zealand specimens and described by Leaming are:

Botryoidal nephrite: composed of microfibres in groups arranged in radial fashion giving roughly spherical surfaces up to about 25 mm in diameter.

Chatoyant nephrite: composed of microfibres in more or less parallel arrangement in alternating bands.

Chatoyancy varies considerably depending on the parallelism of the fibres. If they are completely parallel the effect is at its best, but in this specific case the term nephrite cannot strictly apply as the structure is not nephritic. New Zealand examples are more knotty, with fibres in wavy bands or pod-like lenses. Viewed end grain, these appear as darker areas.

Some nephrites can look quite globular, and C. J. Wilkins describes a specimen with

closely packed and strongly coherent spheroids, which suggest a rolling movement under pressure. Infilling between the spheroids can be actinolite of the same dark green colour, or white tremolite that may arise through depleted availability of Fe.

TRANSLUCENCY

This is a very difficult property to quantify as it depends on the intensity of the light source. White nephrite can transmit light much easier than green; and black nephrite allows very little light to pass. Generally, New Zealand nephrite is renowned for its high translucency.

THE FIVE GRADES OF NEPHRITE

01 / Non-schistose nephrites: characterised by uniformly small size and unoriented arrangement of the component tufts of fine tremolite fibres, and by perfectly developed nephritic structure.

02 / Schistose nephrites: the distinctive feature is the presence of plentiful parallel tufts of tremolite fibres set in a base composed of finely felted unoriented tufts.

03 / Semi-nephrites: while consisting partly of fine-grained interfelted fibrous tufts of tremolite with true nephritic structure, the semi-nephrites also contain abundant, relatively coarsely crystalline tremolite, which takes the form of well defined acicular prisms or relatively large sheaves of parallel unfelted fibres.

04 / Tremolite rocks with linear schistosity: rocks in which fine-grained, truly nephritic fibrous tufts are absent or present in only minor amounts.

05 / Tremolite rocks with plane schistosity: the majority of the tremolite rocks of this group are composed mainly of fibrous or prismatic crystals of tremolite.

RIGHT / Thin sections of New Zealand nephrite showing the textures magnified through a microscope with crossed polars.

01 / Black oxide grains that have acted as a nucleus for the growth of radiating green chromium diopside enclosed in a matrix of nephritic tremolite.

02 / High-quality nephrite with sub-parallel and unorientated tufts of tremolite and a cross-cutting tremolite vein marking a fossil fluid channel.

03 / Aggregates of fine-grained tremolite fibres with some tufts having a sub-parallel alignment giving an imperfect schistosity.

04 / Uniform and random orientation of very fine-grained tremolite. A. COOPER

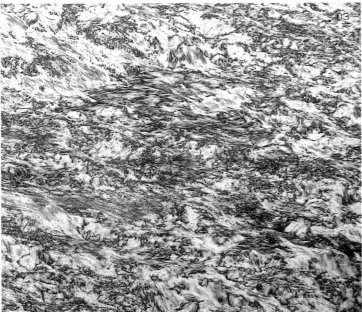

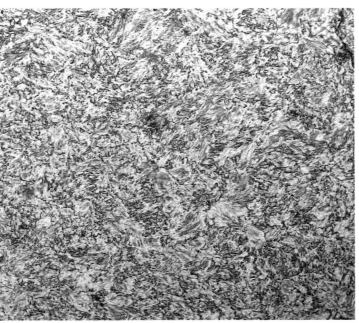

COLOUR

Whether specimens are translucent or opaque alters the colour to some degree. New Zealand nephrite comes in all shades of green except the strong emerald green. Together with the green hues, white, grey, bluish-grey, brown, orange and yellow specimens with flecked, marled or patchy combinations are common.

The green colour owes its presence to iron. The general rule is that higher concentrations of iron give a darker green, but iron is also present in some very pale green varieties.

Weathered hydrated iron oxide can produce a brown or whitish outer rind. Spots are usually black, and veins are occasionally reddish or white. Specimens that appear almost black are, in fact, a very dark green.

Some varieties of īnanga can alter their colour over time from bluish-grey green to an olive shade. I have observed specimens cut more than 10 years ago that clearly show this colour alteration, which appears to be about 1 mm thick. A process has been developed, pioneered by Russian jade researcher V. Y. Medvedev, for changing the exterior colour of olive or dark green nephrite to attractive paler shades of green.

RELATIVE DENSITY

The relative density or specific gravity of a substance is measured by the ratio of its weight to an equal volume of water. This test is possibly one of the best for identifying worked nephrite and for distinguishing between bowenite and nephrite. For medium-sized specimens such as articles of unmounted jewellery and small Māori artefacts this simple test is easy to perform using electronic scales. First, weigh the specimen normally; then place a beaker of pure water, ideally at 4°C, on the scales and zero the reading. Suspend the specimen on a fine thread and completely immerse it in the water without touching the beaker. Take the new reading and divide this into the original reading: this will give you the relative density or specific gravity.

The relative density of New Zealand nephrite varies between 2.95 and 3.05, but is normally about 2.99 and is often quoted in round figures as 3.00. Bowenite is lighter, at 2.61. A cubic metre of nephrite weighs nearly three tonnes on dry land but in the water is one-third lighter. One can take advantage of this fact when trying to move heavy boulders in the sea or rivers: they are manoeuvred much more easily if kept completely immersed.

HARDNESS

Hardness is gauged by the ability of a material to resist abrasion or scratching. The Mohs scale, a scale of comparison from one to 10, begins with one of the softest minerals, talc (1), and ends with the hardest, diamond (10). Nephrite is not a particularly hard material and is often given as 6 to 6.5. Most New Zealand specimens are 6.5 but hardness varies a little depending on structure and sometimes approaches 7, especially on the end grain of some schistose nephrites or on highly polished surfaces. A pocket knife will not scratch nephrite and this test is a good, simple one when in the field: semi-nephrites are softer.

As previously mentioned, some nephrites achieve an apparent increase in hardness when they undergo heat treatment. Another interesting point is that some lapidaries have noticed that when they are working stone recovered a long time ago, it is often decidedly harder than the material available today. It could be that these stones are inherently harder but this discovery also supports the Māori belief that nephrite increases its hardness after being taken from the water.

The hardness test should not be conducted on worked stone such as artefacts, carvings and so on, as a scratch will spoil their appearance.

TOUGHNESS

Nephrite is an extremely tough material, which is why it was so highly valued for implements. This exceptional toughness makes it virtually impossible to break off a sample piece, especially from a large, well rounded boulder, even when using a sledgehammer.

An investigation into the toughness of jade was carried out by R. C. Bradt *et al.*, who concluded that nephrite was much tougher than jadeite and most of the synthetic, commercially produced ceramics. It is, however, exceeded in toughness by the ultra-high-strength hot-pressed oxides and nitrides developed for cutting tools and turbine vanes. Experiments made by D. J. Rowcliffe and V. Fruhauf showed that nephrite is an extremely tough material which, because of its interwoven felted fibrous structure, has a high resistance to crack propagation. They also found that samples sustained at the maximum loading, just prior to cracking, fractured as soon as water was applied to the stress area – yet the same samples did not fracture when lapping oil was applied instead of water.

The strength of Russian nephrite was measured by L. A. Yachevskiy (cited in Y. N. Kolesnik) as 7759 kg/cm^2 and preliminary results from compressive tests that I have carried out on New Zealand nephrite are comparable, if not a little higher, although others were lower, depending on the orientation of any schistosity or the quality of the stone. Put in a more understandable way, a teaspoon-sized piece of nephrite can withstand the weight of 37 family cars stacked on top.

SOUND

The audio property of nephrite is variable and relies on the compactness of the stone and the shape and size of the item. Specifically designed carvings, when struck, give a sharp metallic ring

for a reasonable time, but some continue for 30 seconds or more. This attribute can be a useful guide in evaluating the quality of nephrite. This can be easily tested if a sawn slab is balanced horizontally on the ends of the upturned fingers of one hand while the other hand taps the slab from the underside with the knuckles. Semi-nephrite seldom rings, but I have noticed that after heat treatment specimens lose their dull sound and assume a decided tinkle when handled.

OPTICAL CHARACTERS

The refractive index – a reliable test for all gemstones – is measured by an optical instrument known as a gemmological refractometer. This instrument measures the amount of bending (refraction) that light rays undergo when they enter a polished flat surface of a stone. For accurate readings, sodium light is necessary, but for nephrite and some other microcrystalline minerals that give fuzzy readings, ordinary white light is sufficient. The refractive index for nephrite is usually given as 1.62, and I have found that New Zealand nephrite is no exception.

INCLUSIONS

Nephrite in the form of artefacts, carvings or jewellery can be tentatively identified by specific gravity and refractive index, but the microscope is necessary for determining the structure and identifying the numerous small inclusions of other minerals that are often present. To study the structure of nephrite, a specially prepared thin section of the stone is viewed under a petrological microscope. Using polarised light, the size and arrangement of the fibres become apparent and the specimen can be identified according to the classifications mentioned.

The identification of any accessory minerals can provide an insight into the formation of nephrite and, if characteristic, can help in sourcing the

MATERIAL	RELATIVE DENSITY	REFRACTIVE INDEX	HARDNESS [†]
Nephrite	2.95–3.05	1.61–1.62	6–6.5
Diopside*	3.2	1.67	6
Bowenite	2.61	1.56	4.5–6
Hydrogrossular	3.44–3.50	1.71–1.72	7–7.5
Prase	2.58–2.64	1.54	7
Jadeite	3.3	1.66	7

† Mohs hardness scale units *Quoted from M. M. Wood & J. E. Weidlich

origins of an artefact or specimen. New Zealand nephrite is well known for the small black specks that occur throughout many specimens. These inclusions are usually composed of chromite, or less commonly picotite or magnetite, and often appear fragmented or crushed. Turner identified several accessory minerals in New Zealand nephrite and semi-nephrite, and in addition to the more common chromite and picotite he noted chrome diopside, chlorite, serpentine, diopside, magnetite and garnet (grossular-uvarovite).

Petrology is a very specialised science, and I am grateful to Dr W. A. Watters and Dr A. Reay for their assistance with identifications of accessory minerals. Some Westland nephrite contains soft dark spots that appear to be remnants of relatively coarse-grained tremolite in association with chlorite. These softer areas present difficulties for the lapidary. Nephrite from South Westland may include chromite, chlorite, pyrite and possibly magnetite and talc. Some specimens from this area have numerous ragged crystals of sulphides (pyrite) sprinkled throughout the stone, and these are usually visible with the aid of a 10x hand lens. Other specimens, when viewed with transmitted light, show a darker shade of green or, less frequently, a purplish colour surrounding the dark spots. These spots in some cases appear to be made up of numerous tiny grains of chromite set in a transparent, fibrous chlorite. Similar inclusions, along with small grains of nickel sulphide, occur in Wakatipu stone. Nephrite and semi-nephrites from the Livingstone Mountains have been shown to contain inclusions of picotite, chromite, diopside, garnet (grossular-uvarovite series) and possibly manganese oxide. The green spots and splashes that are so distinctive in some specimens from this locality appear to be fibrous diopside.

Examining slabs of nephrite under low magnification, especially with a stereo microscope, can be most interesting and beautiful. By immersing the specimen in a light oil and using the low powers of 20–40, you can see into the stone, so that any inclusions and patterns become easily visible. Specimens that have a partly oxidised surface display brown to cream-coloured, often plume-like inclusions that penetrate from the borders of feather cracks. These give a picturesque effect – as do inclusions arranged in groups surrounded by different shades of colour. Bowenite and some Westland nephrite occasionally have tiny ring fractures just like a ghostly halo, usually parallel with any foliation.

Over recent years, the scientific study of nephrite globally has advanced the understanding of the stone tremendously. This work has been carried out by many individuals and organisations who have been involved in all aspects, including exploring occurrences in extreme locations. There are still many questions to be answered about this intriguing rock, and exciting new research projects are in progress here and throughout the world.

NEPHRITE SUBSTITUTES

A few other minerals and rocks resemble jade in appearance. Some are poor substitutes, but others are closer to the genuine stone when worked, and many people find it difficult to distinguish between them. For this reason it is fortunate that New Zealand does not have a great number of stones that can be mistaken for nephrite.

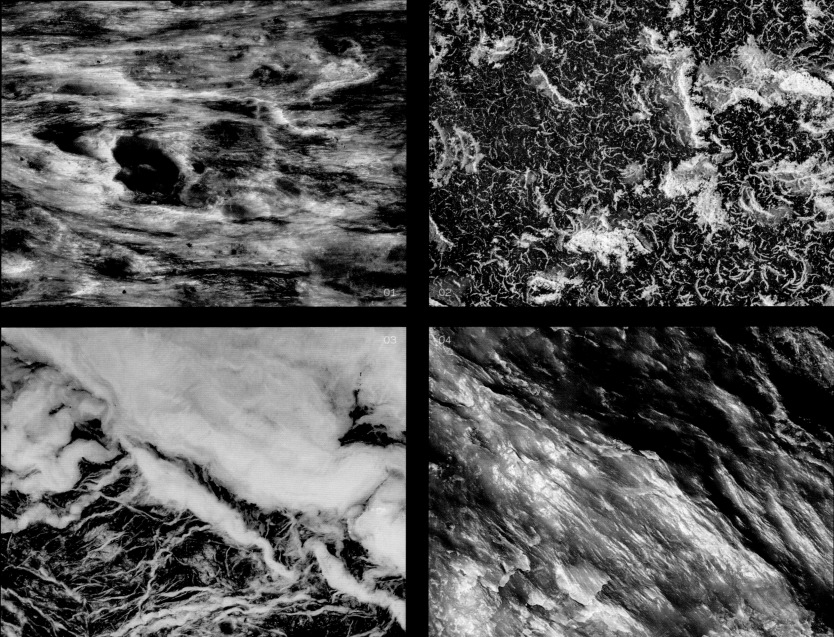

Some rocks and minerals that are known to occur in New Zealand that might be confused with nephrite.

SEMI-NEPHRITE WITH DIOPSIDE

Semi-nephrites from the Dun Mountain Ophiolite Belt in Nelson, South Westland and Southland frequently contain fibrous diopside in varying amounts. Relative density tests are a good indication of its presence. New Zealand nephrite does not appear to exceed a density of 3.05; and I have found that semi-nephrite containing diopside has a relative density above this, varying up to 3.2 – which probably has very little, if any, nephrite present. Just where the term semi-nephrite stops and diopside takes over, I am not sure – this requires more research. Diopside is a calcium magnesium pyroxene and is commonly white, grey or green.

BOWENITE OR TANGIWAI

This is a variety of antigorite serpentine, also known as Milford greenstone. It is olive green, dark green and greenish-blue in colour. The stone is felted or fibrous, often schistose, and translucent to transparent. It is easily fractured and softer than nephrite. Tangiwai occurs at Anita Bay and Poison Bay near Milford Sound, Arahura River in Westland, South Westland, Nelson and other minor localities associated with serpentinite.

SERPENTINE

Several massive forms of serpentine (antigorite, lizardite, etc.) are also frequently confused with nephrite, but are much softer, especially as river boulders. Serpentinite frequently has inclusions of chromite or magnetite.

HYDROGROSSULAR OR RODINGITE

This is a massive form of lime garnet, also known as Transvaal jade. It has a waxy lustre; is white, grey, yellow, brown, pale green or olive green in colour; is quite translucent; and is frequently mottled or fractured and with inclusions of diallage crystals and other minerals. Harder and heavier than nephrite, it occurs in the Roding River (hence the name rodingite) and other rivers in Nelson, the Red Hills Range in South Westland, Eglinton Valley and Orepuki Beach in Southland, with minor occurrences at other localities.

Occasionally associated with these occurrences of hydrogrossular are specimens of massive translucent vesuvianite or idocrase. These tend to be olive green and are usually more translucent. Southern Māori recognised the attributes of the hydrogrossular pebbles – toughness, weight, hardness – and used them as hammerstones for the production of stone tools. Translucent specimens, especially from Orepuki Beach, are very attractive and are sought-after by collectors; although they are quite hard, they are excellent for carving.

PRASE

This is a green variety of chalcedony (cryptocrystalline quartz), also known as green jasper. It has a waxy lustre. The colour is various shades of green, but usually dull. Prase is slightly harder than nephrite; it is easily fractured, and large specimens are rare. It occurs associated with chalcedony in the volcanic rocks of Canterbury and Otago (plasma variety) and other minor occurrences.

OTHER POSSIBLE SUBSTITUTES

Some fine-grained peridotites, especially ones with a rusty, weathered exterior, may resemble nephrite but have a glassy, granular structure. Massive talc or steatite can be similar to nephrite in colour alone but it is very soft and easily scratched, even with a fingernail.

Some green brittle rocks (commonly termed argillite), which were used by Māori for adzes and flake tools, are frequently identified as jade, especially when in artefact form. These are quite opaque and flinty in appearance.

01 / Small, dark nephrite 'eyes' in schistose semi-nephrite from Muddy Creek, Makarora, Otago.

02 / Small crescent-shaped fractures on the surface of a Westland nephrite boulder caused by bruising against other stones in a river.

03 / Folded small veins of semi-nephrite in black serpentinite from the Mararoa field.

04 / Small parallel crimp folds of Te Koroka nephrite that have been naturally polished by earth movement (slickensided).

CHAPTER TEN/JADE OF THE PACIFIC RIM

KEI A IA TŌNA
AKE ANŌ

I possess this treasure,
as do others

Many of the countries that more or less border the Pacific Rim either have deposits of jade or have had a jade culture at some time. Generally this is because of the geology where suitable rock types have undergone change, frequently through ocean floor spreading and its consequences.

I have had the privilege of visiting many of the places where jade occurs, some in fairly remote areas, with memorable experiences. The following is a brief account illustrating only a small portion of the rich human and natural jade history in this region.

AUSTRALIA

It is interesting that Australia is one of the few places where nephrite occurs but does not seem to have been used by the indigenous people. There are two main areas where nephrite is found – one in South Australia, the other in New South Wales – and all of these occurrences are, or have been, prospected or mined. Without a jade culture and with fierce competition from other more colourful gemstones, most Australians are generally unaware of their jade. The South Australian deposit, located near Cowell on the Eyre Peninsula, is vast with huge reserves and was discovered in 1965 by a farmer, Harry Schiller, on his property. He had an interest in minerals and noticed unusual rocks holding down the rabbit-proof wire netting fence; also nearby were very jagged outcrops of the same rocks. He had great difficulty in chipping off a sample and was amazed at the toughness, so much so that he sent a sample away for analysis. To his surprise, it proved to be jade. The quality of Cowell jade is from a superb fine-grained black (really very dark green) grading to olive shades, and both can have beautiful markings caused by weathering. The black is among the finest in the world and is sought after by serious carvers. In 1986, jade carvers Alf Poole,

John Edgar and I visited the mine and were able to collect some rare natural pieces. A remarkable feature of Cowell jade is that the stone is very old, of pre-Cambrian age, about 800 million years old – perhaps the oldest nephrite anywhere. It was formed in association with dolomitic marble.

Nephrite occurs as narrow pods in New South Wales at several locations associated with the Great Serpentine Belt. Nephrite is exposed in outcrops near Tamworth, between Weabonga and Dungowan. It was apparently discovered in the early 1970s by a New Zealand sheep-shearer when he went for a walk up a small creek. The general appearance of the jade is quite different from the Cowell stone and is more like New Zealand nephrite, with pale green and olive hues. It also has interesting lace-like markings from weathering.

When Alf Poole and I visited in 1981, mining had ceased but stones were being cut up onsite. Of the other few known nephrite occurrences within this belt, Spring Creek has received renewed interest.

Since there are a number of Australian jade occurrences it is just possible that Aboriginal use of nephrite for tools may yet be discovered – perhaps hidden away in a museum collection, unidentified.

Tasmania features in a report by H. D. Skinner, who records that in 1927 near the Mersey River at Devonport, a dark green ground nephrite adze or axe was discovered in a gravel pit by a policeman. Apparently it was about one metre below the surface in what seemed to be the remains of an Aboriginal camp. Skinner points out that the features of the tool were typically New Caledonian

PREVIOUS PAGE / Sawn section of nephrite from the Tamworth area, New South Wales, Australia.

LEFT / The Pacific Ocean dwarfs an atoll in Tetiaora, Tahiti. Geological forces have produced jade in many countries around much of the rim of this great ocean.

RIGHT / *Anchor Stones* by New Zealand carver Andrew Ruskin, made from dense black jade from Cowell. Left Bank Art Gallery, Greymouth.

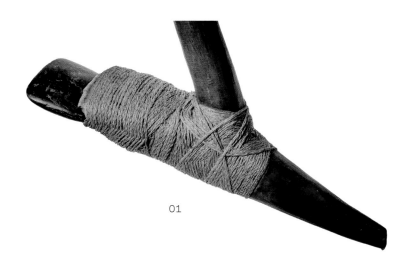

01

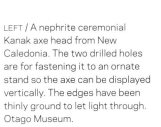

02

– and I agree – but how it came there is a fascinating mystery. There are no known nephrite occurrences in Tasmania and the Tasmanians did not shape their stone tools by grinding. Skinner does not rule out that it may be a relic of the first people to reach Tasmania, but modern sourcing tests of the artefact compared with nephrite from Australia and New Caledonia could, at least, confirm its origin.

NEW CALEDONIA

New Caledonia has a geology very similar in many respects to New Zealand, so it is no surprise that nephrite is present. Just about every major museum in the world with ethnological collections has examples of Kanak nephrite artefacts from New Caledonia and the nearby Loyalty Islands. These take the form of adzes, axes, beads and ceremonial axes known as monstrance axes. Some of these are genuine early pieces, but many, especially ceremonial axes, are later examples made as trade items with Europeans during the nineteenth century.

Studying New Caledonian material held in New Zealand museum collections, I was intrigued at the range of colours and markings of the stone and the similarities, in many cases, to New Zealand pounamu. My first visit to the island of New Caledonia was in 1990 when I met Dr Christophe Sand, a local archaeologist who has specialised in New Caledonian prehistory. With his comprehensive knowledge and our mutual interest in jade, we have, over several years, prospected a number of locations in search of sources of the nephrite from which the Kanak people fashioned their jade articles. The literature frequently quotes the French explorer Jules Garnier, who located a quarry on Ouen Island off the southern tip of the mainland (Grande Terre). We visited this site, and found that the stone there is an attractive green rock composed mainly of anorthite with some tremolite/actinolite, which cannot be labelled jade. It certainly was used by Kanak, but mostly for their ornamental bead necklaces. It does not have the properties suitable for tools. A similar rock also occurs on the mainland in the Bay of Prony and the Blue River area.

In 1995 I corresponded with Professor Philippa Black at the University of Auckland, who had studied the geology of New Caledonia and noticed nephrite rocks in the Tiwaka Valley. That same year, my wife Ann and I travelled around the island and drove across to the east coast at the mid section through the Tiwaka Valley on a newly formed road with few bridges. The road cuttings were freshly dug with clear exposures of the geology, and we found numerous narrow veins of nephrite and semi-nephrite beside the road. We later teamed up with Christophe and visited the local Kanak chief to ask for the necessary permission to prospect the rivers and walk over the land. The greeting ceremony involved the giving of gifts, which included tobacco, cigarettes and money, and the traditional custom of presenting a length of fabric. We were well received and were granted authority to begin our search, accompanied by an elder of the tribe, Anton. We had a wonderful day, up and down the rivers and among the rocky landscape, finding several nephrite occurrences. Anton was a very gentle and knowledgeable man, 77 years old, and could recall assisting the New Zealand troops when they were stationed on New Caledonia during the Second World War. He guided us, barefoot, along tracks, pointing out sacred places and old village sites and leading us to other places of geological interest. We returned to the chief to pass on our gratitude, and showed them our samples. I gave the chief a small fish that I had carved from New Zealand jade and conveyed a greeting from the Murihiku people.

Eleven years later I visited New Caledonia, accompanied by a party of French and New Zealand geologists and Christophe Sand. We revisited the Tiwaka Valley to find that the road had been rebuilt after it was damaged by a typhoon; all the roadside jade outcrops had been completely covered over; and, sadly, Anton had died some years earlier.

New Caledonia has been inhabited by Melanesians for at least 3000 years, originally by the Lapita culture. The museum in Noumea and the magnificent Tjibaou Cultural Centre show rich examples of the early and contemporary art and way of life of the Kanak people.

In many ways the New Caledonian nephrite is similar to New Zealand nephrite that occurs in the Dun Mountain Ophiolite Belt rocks, especially the Mararoa field where the semi-nephrite contains diopside. This stone is quite distinctive, with a higher relative density, and is probably the stone that used to be called oceanic jade. There is much work still to be done to localise all the nephrite sources. Also, I have not ruled out the possibility that a few New Zealand specimens may have found their way there during the early part of the nineteenth century, when New Zealand traders supposedly took nephrite into the Pacific.

The most spectacular Kanak jade object is the ceremonial axe. It comprises an oval lens-shaped polished thin slabs of nephrite, and occasionally other rocks. Axes vary from palm size to 40 cm in diameter, usually with two holes to attach to an ornate handle or stand. The edges have been ground to a thin edge to allow light to pass through, giving a glow around the periphery. They were used for ceremonial purposes and as symbols of authority. Tradition records that there was a circular system of trade for the axes, beginning from where the raw material occurred then across through the Loyalty Islands to the top of Grande Terre. Trade went the other way in the form of goods and women.

Woodworking tools such as adzes, chisels and axes are generally not large, and are secured to wooden handles. Unlike Māori, Kanak did not saw their jade; rather it was ground down with sandstone, which must have taken a long time and contributed to its value. The holes were either pecked or drilled from both sides. Necklaces made up of many small pea-sized beads were delicately drilled and shaped and were regarded as an extremely valuable commodity. Judging by the high number of artefacts – in particular adzes – that exhibit heating characteristics, Kanak stone workers, like Māori, practised the technique of heating nephrite. From archaeological excavations carried out by Christophe it would appear that the use of nephrite was relatively late, probably no more than 1000 years ago.

On Vanuatu, especially the island of Tana, the inhabitants have a tradition of wearing small nephrite amulets. These are much treasured heirlooms and most likely originated in New Caledonia long ago.

OTHER PACIFIC ISLANDS

There have been a few unconfirmed reports of jade artefacts found on some other South Pacific Islands. These present some problems as to their origin, since these islands are composed of volcanic rocks. Skinner mentions a find of a nephrite adze in the Cook Islands group on the island of Puka Puka. It was recovered in 1905 by an islander who was planting taro. Another example was a ground piece found in a creek on Aitutaki Island, which was analysed in 1933 at the University of Otago by Dr F. J. Turner, who found that it was bowenite identical in every way to the Anita Bay material. Was this a piece from Captain Joss, who apparently traded pounamu in the Pacific, or a much older specimen taken back to the Cook Islands by early Māori voyagers?

PAPUA NEW GUINEA

Several 'jade' artefacts in museum collections are labelled as from New Guinea. Early reports mention artefacts of dark green jadeite (chloromelanite); others nephrite. Dr A. B. Meyer, a jade researcher of the Dresden Museum, describes in 1893 a green hatchet from Collingwood Bay in Oro Province, on the northeast coast of the southern peninsula. Professional analysis confirmed that it was nephrite, and resembled New Zealand nephrite. In the Adelaide Museum, South Australia, is a small, pale green adze from the same location, which appears to be nephrite. The geology of this part of Papua New Guinea is favourable for the presence of nephrite, especially where the ultramafic rocks have undergone shearing along major faults. A further collection of PNG artefacts in the Australian Museum, Sydney includes an unconfirmed, green, nephrite-looking axe head from Milne Bay and a mottled perforated disc from the Central Districts.

Another possible source for nephrite in this region is further east at the Solomon Islands, where there is a discontinuous belt of ultramafic rock associated with green schist exposed for a length of 450 km. The belt is described as similar, in some respects, to rock belts occurring in New Zealand. To my knowledge, no nephrite has yet been reported.

The same rock belts (ophiolites) with nephrite possibilities continue northwest into the Indonesian Island of Borneo and Sulawesi, but at the northwestern tip of Sumatra near Aech nephrite has recently been found in gravels and possibly in situ.

PHILIPPINES

Some intriguing nephrite artefacts have been found on the Philippine islands. In 1953 Skinner

RIGHT / The glacier-fed Yurungkax River (River of White Jade) flowing from the Kunlun Mountains in Xinjiang, Western China. The high terraces on each side of the river contain boulders of nephrite.
R. BECK

visited Manila and viewed a collection of more than 1000 ancient nephrite adzes and chisels from southwest Luzon. These had been excavated by an American archaeologist, Ottley Beyer, during the 1930s and 1940s. They are unusual in that their colour is white to grey and quite oxidised. The original source of the stone is unknown, although it is suspected to be local.

Several small, unusual green nephrite ear ornaments known as *lingling-o* have been found throughout the Philippines, Borneo, South Vietnam and the Thailand peninsula. This wide distribution of the lingling-o forms prompted a comprehensive research project by geoscientists at the Academia Sinica, in collaboration with many other institutions, to study the mineralogy and archaeology of these artefacts to ascertain their source. Remarkably, they found that the nephrite could be sourced to Taiwan, as the pieces all have the common characteristic of manganese and zinc-bearing chromite inclusions, revealing a 3000-km-diameter sea-based trade network dating 1000 years from 500 BC. It was also shown that older amulets found their way from Taiwan to the Philippines and Borneo. This important research signifies that there was considerable contact between different prehistoric peoples over a large area – and further investigation may establish that it was even more widespread.

As yet, no nephrite deposits have been found in the Philippines; however, the geology certainly indicates that it is possible.

In 2008 Ann and I visited Manila and viewed a selection of the white nephrite tools of the Beyer Collection. I spent an absorbing morning with Willie Ronquillo and his archaeologist colleagues at the National Museum of the Philippines, discussing these enigmatic artefacts. In the afternoon I gave a public lecture on New Zealand jade.

So many exotic places to investigate – the jade story just gets bigger.

CHINA

China has a rich jade appreciation extending back some 8000 years. No other culture has revered nephrite continuously, so extensively, for so long. Although there are several nephrite occurrences in China, the main source that has been used for at least 3000 years lies in the province of Xinjiang in Western China, from several of the rivers that drain the Kunlun Mountains on the southern edge of the Taklamakan Desert near the famous oasis city of Khotan (Hetian) on the Southern Silk Route.

Like Māori, Chinese treasured both nephrite and bowenite and some other stones, which they called *yu*, but nephrite was the favourite from the Neolithic period to the eighteenth century, when the more colourful jadeite from Myanmar (Burma) was introduced and took centre stage.

Early Chinese jade workers were confronted with the same problems that later cultures were to experience – nephrite's toughness demanded a new technology to shape it. These early artefacts show that the basic grinding processes were implemented with a great degree of skill, and developed into sophisticated techniques involving metal tools and specialised abrasives that produced some outstanding art objects. Initially jade was used for tools and weapons; but it then expanded into a remarkable range of items as communities, kingdoms and dynasties evolved. Religious and spiritual beliefs were expressed in jade as funerary pieces, and at one time nobility were buried totally encapsulated in 2500-piece suits of jade.

Although metals superseded jade for tools and weapons, the appreciation of jade has remained an integral part of Chinese culture into the twenty-first century.

Around the early 1960s at an antique shop in Christchurch I purchased a small Chinese nephrite figurine carved from a pebble. I was captivated by

the translucent white colour and subtle purity of the stone, and it sparked a desire to visit its origin. A few years later, when researching my first book on jade, I came across an article by Ferdinand Stoliczk on the source of Chinese jade. In 1873 he visited the mines high in the Kunlun Mountains in Turkestan, now Xinjiang, where nephrite veins had formed between dolomitic marble and gneiss. His account inspired me to get to this incredibly isolated place one way or another. I partly realised this goal in 1986, but it was not easy as the area had been closed to foreigners for a very long time. After one and half years of correspondence (before the days of email) with Chinese authorities here and in China and with New Zealand Foreign Affairs staff, I was able to make contact with the Ministry of Geology and Mineral Resources people in Beijing. Eventually they agreed to my proposal for a jade study group to visit the jade region in Xinjiang. It was not possible to visit the abandoned jade mines described by Stoliczk, as they were too remote. Instead, the ministry organised a full itinerary which included visiting the glacial-fed jade-producing rivers Urungkax and Karakax, and the jade mecca Khotan, as well as other places of interest.

I gathered together a group of jade enthusiasts to join me: Stan Leaming, Canadian authority on nephrite, Alf Poole and Brian Ahern, John Edgar and his friend Murray Gray. It took a lot of organising, so we thought we should squeeze in as much as possible and included visits to jade sources in Taiwan and Korea after our China sojourn.

Our four Chinese hosts consisted of geologists, a curator and interpreter. We spent a week in Beijing, which at that time was just developing, and were taken to a jade carving factory with over 1000 carvers, museums, temples and tombs and the Great Wall; and in return we gave slide lectures on New Zealand jade and spent an interesting hour with renowned New Zealand journalist Rewi Alley.

A three and a half hour flight across China

ABOVE LEFT / A portion of a very large carved jade boulder in the Forbidden City Museum, Beijing, China, which tells a story of quarrying and transporting jade from its source in the Kunlun Mountains to the eastern coast. R. BECK

BOTTOM FAR LEFT / Green and white cobbles of nephrite found in the Yurungkax River. R. BECK

BOTTOM LEFT / Brian Ahern, a member of the jade study group, reads a greeting from southern Māori to our Chinese hosts on the banks of the Yurungkax River. R. BECK

RIGHT / An elegant carved Chinese jade vase. The stone has the characteristics of the nephrite occurring in the rivers draining the Kunlun Mountains in Western China. Otago Museum.

brought us to Urumqi, the capital of Xinjiang Uyghur Autonomous Region, China's westernmost and largest province. We were welcomed by city dignitaries and we had our first experience of the colourful Uyghur culture.

That evening an orange moon rose above the distant snow-capped mountains: it was almost full, and timely, as according to an old Chinese legend, the moon was responsible for the jade in the rivers. The next day we flew across the Taklamakan Desert. As we approached Khotan we could see through the desert dust the flashes of sun reflecting on the two large rivers that originate as glaciers in the Kunlun Mountains and run out into this forbidding sea of sand, to be totally consumed and evaporate in the heat.

We met our hosts for the next week – members of the 10th Geological Brigade. Khotan is a very

old and exotic city at the base of the Kunlun Mountains. Everything in the city was covered with a fine dust from the desert because it seldom rains and dust storms are frequent, halting all transport for several days or weeks. One elderly resident said he could remember that it once rained in 1945. The friendliness of the Uyghur and Chinese people made our stay there very pleasant.

Next morning we were impatient to get up the river, and boarded our convoy of four jeeps. The road soon turned into a rough track and we bounced along for about an hour following up an old river terrace. We stopped where the river had cut a deep gorge between the high mountains, and began to look for jade on a boulder terrace. The Urungkax River means 'river of white jade' – although other colours occur there as well – and it was not long before we had all found pebbles of jade. The altitude was about 2000 m and the atmosphere incredibly dry, so we had to guard against dehydration. Towards the end of the day I found a 40 kg boulder of green jade and was sorry to have to leave it, but felt satisfied with just the thrill of finding it. It was thought-provoking to be able to look up this spectacular valley and trace the exact route that Aurel Stein, the British archaeologist who rediscovered the Silk Route, took in his incredible exploration of this area in the early 1900s, where he described the jade diggings. Doubtless little had changed since then.

During the next two days we went on field excursions up both sides of the Karakax River, the 'river of black jade'. These were unforgettable experiences as we penetrated deep into the mountains, passing through small villages where the local Uyghur people collected jade to supplement their income. The children were obviously keen-eyed jade pickers and were eager to show us their finds. The language here was jade and we did not need an interpreter. These people had not seen Europeans before – especially Kiwis

in shorts – and we were the focus of attention wherever we stopped. They were very friendly, helpful and gentle, and welcomed us into their homes for treats of fruit and melons.

Back at Khotan we spent a morning giving and receiving jade lectures. Hearing about their nephrite occurring in pods in more than ten major outcrops, and how it was sandwiched between dolomitic marble and gneiss, was most interesting as this mode of occurrence is quite different from New Zealand where jade originates in belts of ultramafic rocks. Mining was extremely difficult at an altitude of 5500 metres, with no roads and only donkeys for transport. Understandably, it was much easier to collect the alluvial boulders in the rivers, transported there by ancient glaciers. Khotan jade is extremely fine-grained and a little less tough, with a hardness value approaching 6.9 in some cases – more than most nephrite at 6.5 on the Mohs scale.

At the government jade-buying station we saw a truck arrive with stones collected from villages. It tipped off its load of several tonnes of beautiful smooth nephrite boulders – you could hear them ringing as they bumped together. The best were destined to be carved in the many jade factories throughout China.

On the last day in Khotan we were treated to the weekly bazaar. This was a colourful industrious mass of people selling everything – from food, clothing, a set of teeth, animals to worn out vehicle parts. This is a very isolated part of the world, so things that we would discard had a value there, and nothing was wasted.

We were sad to farewell our 10th Brigade hosts with whom we had become firm friends. They are dedicated people with a vast, hard-won knowledge of the geology of this extremely rugged region.

Back on the east coast at Shanghai we crossed the Yangtze River and drove to Yangzhou. It was here that the jade carvers of the past specialised

in carving jade boulders of up to several tonnes. It was reassuring to see that this tradition was being continued by a modern factory. We visited the Shanghai Museum and had the opportunity to handle (wearing gloves) superb jade objects over 4000 years old. They also had many other ancient argillite and basalt items that were almost identical to early Māori forms.

In an appropriate sequel to the China visit, with the assistance of New Zealand Foreign Affairs I invited a Chinese delegation – including some of our geologist friends – to visit New Zealand six months later. We spent 10 days travelling around the South Island jade deposits and scenic spots as well as visits to New Zealand geological institutions. This eventually led to a successful liaison between Chinese and New Zealand professionals resulting in several geological exchange visits.

Today, the jade carving industry in China is significant. As in the past, nephrite and jadeite are imported from other countries, supplementing their own resources. Archaeological excavations in China, Vietnam and other East Asian adjacent countries are continuing to reveal exciting new information on the unique jade culture in this part of the world.

TAIWAN

Taiwan is a mountainous island in many respects similar to the South Island of New Zealand. The island has a long human history dating back to Palaeolithic times. By the mid Neolithic period cultures evolved on the east coast, centred on jade. They sourced their nephrite from the rivers draining the mountains to the east coast, where deposits of nephrite occur near the present city of Hualien. These early jade workers developed techniques to shape their tools and ornaments that were identical to the techniques used by

Māori – except for the drilling of holes, which was done with core drills, probably of bamboo. This influenced the design: they produced superb long, hollow, cylindrical tubes, circular earrings and arm bracelets. They also made adzes, chisels, arrow- and spear-heads and necklaces of small beads. Many of these items were ritual or funerary objects, and recent excavations have unearthed great numbers of jade artefacts contained in slate coffins.

The jade study group met Professor Li Ping Tan, a geologist who had specialised in Taiwanese nephrite and who arranged our visit. Together we travelled south by train along the precipitous east coast to Hualien, then drove up into the mountains along a bumpy track to the jade mines. We levered choice samples of rich green nephrite out of the enclosing schist rocks, and also noticed many beautiful boulders in a nearby stream. Hand specimens of Taiwanese nephrite are similar in appearance to New Zealand stone, but can be identified in the laboratory. Back in Taipei we called on several commercial factories and

some contemporary carvers who were working Taiwanese and Canadian nephrite. We concluded our stay in Taiwan with a splendid visit to the National Palace Museum, which houses a fantastic collection of Chinese jade.

Twenty-two years later Ann and I again visited Taiwan, this time with New Zealand geologist, Chris Adams. We were hosted by jade researchers Tzeng-Fu Yui, Hsiao-Chun Hung and Yoshiyuki Iizuka of the Institute of Earth Sciences at the Academia Sinica, Taipei. They organised a seven-day tour to the jade mines, archaeological sites and several museums, and we exchanged lectures on many aspects of nephrite research. The mines had stopped working but we were able to descend into a short adit to get some good specimens for our sourcing research project. The mine manager showed us a jade carving by Taiwanese artist Huang Fu-shou, which was kept in a special carrying case. The stone came from his mine, and the piece was an unbelievably intricate carving of an abstract leaf-like organic form, so fragile and with a delicate beauty.

LEFT / Sawn and polished section of nephrite from the jade mine near Hualien, Taiwan.

ABOVE RIGHT / Members of the 1986 jade study group entering the jade mine deep in the mountains near Hualien, where many tonnes have been extracted. R. BECK

The archaeological sites further south at Peinan near Taitung are spectacular. Here they have kept the excavations as outdoor museums, roofed to protect them from the elements. This huge site was discovered during the construction of a new railway station, and it took 10 years from 1980 to excavate a small portion of it. The adjacent new National Museum of Prehistory holds displays of recovered jade items that are up to 3500 years old – and this was truly overwhelming. Taiwan is regarded as the possible origin of the people who migrated out into the Pacific to become the Polynesians, and the similarities of the artefacts displayed were obvious. We met the museum director and staff, and were introduced to a visiting party of school children who were making small jade trinkets by traditional methods – a wonderful means of generating an understanding of jade and heritage.

Our Taiwan visit has cemented friendships which have led to the establishment of ongoing research projects into nephrite.

JAPAN

The use of jade in Japan began some 6000 years ago and continued until the seventh century, but until relatively recently, the source of the stone was believed to be from outside Japan. The rediscovery of a jadeite source on the northwest coast of central Japan in 1939, with subsequent archaeological excavations, established that jade was collected and worked extensively during the Jomon period (4000–1600 BC). Woodworking tools and ornaments, in particular magatama beads, were produced in large numbers in the Itoigawa region. Magatama are cashew-shaped pendants with a hole for suspension. They vary in size, but average 30 mm long. Their origin and significance is unknown but they eventually became wide-spread throughout most of Japan.

My first visit to Japan was in 1994 with a group of jade-minded people. From Niigata on the west coast of Japan we caught a bus down the coast to the city of Itoigawa. We were surprised to see

that the city had embraced its jade heritage, with boulders and sculptures in jadeite placed on street corners. They had adopted the magatama as their logo, and it was everywhere.

A local retired school teacher, Mitsuo Sunada, who had been to New Zealand and recognised us as Kiwis – I suppose we were rather obvious, wearing boots, shorts and bush shirts – generously offered to show us around. He drove us up into the Kotaki Gorge to photograph the jade reserve and visit lapidary workshops and the internationally recognised Fossa Magna Mineralogical Museum. Mitsuo and his wife treated our group to a traditional Japanese meal in their home and gave an open invitation to return.

At one of the lapidary workshops I was given a small pebble of grey nephrite. This aroused my interest, as I was unaware it occurred in Japan. I surmised that if the early inhabitants were using jadeite, then they must also have recognised nephrite. This tantalising thought prompted me to investigate further and in 2001 Ann and I returned to Itoigawa and spent a week with the Sunadas looking at many places of interest. Near Itoigawa is a Jomon-period archaeological site where the excavation has been left open as an exhibit of how the people lived and worked jade, complete with replica houses and an adjacent museum displaying the recovered artefacts. I was pleased to see that many of the adzes and chisels were made from nephrite and, as expected, some were very oxidised. Sandstone saws and grooved or sawn offcuts confirmed that the methods used to work the stone were again the same as Māori and other stone-based cultures. A few of the oxidised examples showed that they had been shaped by the hammering process and these, I suspect, may prove to be older. Certainly, jadeite was the stone of preference for the production of ornamental items, but the fact that the people had been

ABOVE LEFT / River pebble of grey nephrite from the Itoigawa area, Niigata Prefecture, Japan.

RIGHT /A carving by Korean artist Sun Ryung Suh, using the stone from the jade mine near Chuncheon, Korea. The artist has selected a natural block of nephrite and carved a loose-linked chain emerging from it – all from the one piece of stone. Southland Art Foundation and Southland Museum and Art Gallery.

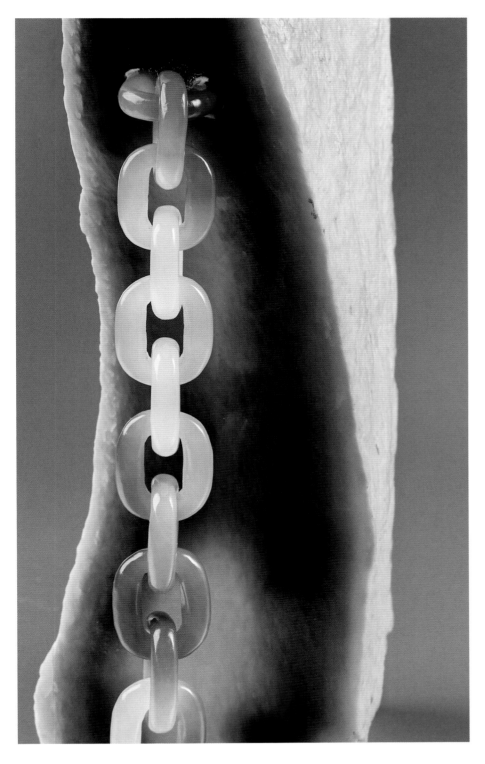

working both nephrite and jadeite is unusual.

We spent an interesting day with geologist Ko Takenouchi from the Fossa Magna Museum, beginning with a visit to the jade reserve in the Kotaki Gorge where huge boulders of white jadeite-rich rocks are in the stream bed. This is a tourist attraction with interpretation panels telling the story of the stone – and, of course, collecting is not permitted. It would be nice to see something similar established in New Zealand with our jade.

On the trail of the nephrite, we travelled inland into Nagano Prefecture, to a tributary of the Matsukawa River, where we found samples of olive green semi-nephrite among huge serpentinite boulders. In this vicinity grey nephrite has been found. It is an area that I would like to investigate more thoroughly as it is possibly a source of the nephrite pebbles commonly found on the sea beach near Itoigawa. Near here is the town of Omi on the banks of the Omi River, and a small special museum is located under the highway flyover where there is only one exhibit: a stunning natural boulder of white jadeite with some delicate violet and green patches, weighing 102 tonnes. A video showed the trials and tribulations of finding the boulder high in the Omi River and transporting it on a specially constructed carrier some distance to the museum. A smaller, 42-tonne boulder is set up in the town of Omi near an outdoor geological museum of giant mineral and rock specimens, among which the visitor can walk.

Walking around the narrow streets of neat houses with their vegetable gardens, I spotted many jadeite boulders and other stones placed on front doorsteps, or even as memorial stones. It was clear from these and the abundance of public stone sculptures that the Japanese have a sensitivity and appreciation for stone, certainly in this part of Japan.

KOREA

Northwest of Japan is the Korean peninsula, which also has a jade culture and deposits of jade. After Taiwan, our 1986 jade study group visited Seoul in South Korea, then travelled 70 km northeast to Chuncheon where, nearby among the mountains and neat rice and corn fields, there is a jade mine. Originally talc was mined here, until nephrite was recognised and in 1976 the mine started producing jade. Malcolm McNamara of the New Zealand Embassy in Seoul had obtained permission from the mine owner, Jun-han Kim, for us to visit the mine. The mine had not been worked for seven years and was consequently filling with water but, knowing we were coming, they had pumped it out some days earlier. It looked a bit dangerous – the timbers were rotten – but Mr Kim was very enthusiastic and led me and some other brave souls down deep into the dripping galleries. We had some anxious moments when I heard a loud rock fall and thought the worst – buried in a jade mine! Apparently a person well behind us had stumbled and set off a rock slide. Then the lightbulb on a cable connected to the generator separated at a joined connection, leaving us in complete darkness until the other end of the cable was found and 'glorious' light was restored.

In the bowels of the mine we finally reached the face, a band of transluscent pale green jade about a metre wide. The nephrite occurs in a range of colours from the valuable white to green and brown, and the reserves are estimated to be extensive. The nephrite has formed in veins and pods up to 3 metres thick from the alteration of dolomitic marble and amphibole schist, and is very similar in appearance to the jade from the Vitim area in Russia.

Back in Chuncheon we noticed a growing lapidary industry making jewellery, and a few carvers producing interesting work.

The National Museum of Korea in Seoul has a beautiful white jade cylinder and other examples of early artefacts found in Chuncheon: their source could be local. It also has many examples of magatama beads of jadeite. These were worn as a necklace or arranged on a crown-like headdress worn by nobility of the Sila Dynasty. Most certainly, the stone and design for the magatama beads would have originated in Japan. Some dark green nephrite examples observed by jade researcher Robert Frey may also have a Japanese origin, or possibly elsewhere – another sourcing project, no doubt.

RUSSIA

Russia has huge deposits of nephrite, chiefly in the Siberian southeastern Sayan Mountains and central Vitim Highlands. Siberia also has a long human appreciation of jade from the Neolithic period, later highlighted by the Fabergé era to the present.

My interest in visiting Russia began in 1979 when Professor Doug Coombs of University of Otago mentioned seeing nephrite artefacts and boulders on a visit to a museum at Irkutsk, Siberia. He subsequently gave me a contact with whom I corresponded several times and, in 1987, sent a copy of my book *New Zealand Jade*, which apparently was of great interest to jade researchers in Irkutsk. They reciprocated with information about Russian nephrite sources, but these were sited in difficult places for foreigners to visit. The possibility did not arise until after 1990 when a fellow researcher, Herbert Geiss of Switzerland, passed on a new contact, Dr Alexander (Sasha) Sekerin of the Institute of the Earth's Crust in Irkutsk. We corresponded and in 1994 received an invitation to visit the Ospin area in the East Sayan Mountains.

Once more I gathered a team to join in this adventure: Stan Leaming from Canada and

ABOVE / Buriat horsemen crossing a river in the Sayan Mountains, near where extensive nephrite deposits are mined. Southern Siberia.

LEFT / All hands to repair our track vehicle when a log became jammed in the tracks while negotiating down a water-scoured slope. Near the jade mines, Ospin area, Siberia. R. BECK

RIGHT / West side of Lake Baikal, the world's deepest lake, Siberia. Far away in the mountains on the other side of the lake lie the deposits of the rare white Vitim jade.

Alf Poole, who had been part of the Asian tour, plus Neil Lewis, an Invercargill adventurer, and Andris Apse, photographer. Because Andris was born in Lapland, there were possible visa delays and he decided to drop out, but he joined another expedition a year later.

We met Stan in Toyko, sped across Japan in a bullet train to Niigata and flew directly to Irkutsk, the major city of Eastern Siberia, to be met by our hosts from the Institute; Sasha and his nephew, Mark, Eugene Sklyarov and Uri Menshagin. There was great excitement during the following morning which was spent looking at nephrite samples and meeting jade researchers at the Institute. Sasha and his wife Nina had studied nephrite for some 14 years. After lunch on board the *Angara*, an old English steamship, we began packing for the 500-km journey into the Sayan Mountains. Our vehicle was a huge ex-army six-wheel drive short bus, loaded to the gunnels with supplies and vodka necessary for 'smoothing the way'. We set out in the late afternoon through densely forested countryside, stopping at a lapis lazuli mine south of Lake Baikal for the night. The route then followed up the Irkut River to its source, passing through the last town, Mondy, on the way then up a spectacular gorge to a high plateau at 2000 m, near the Mongolian border.

Here we were joined by more people and changed our transport for two army track vehicles (like tanks without a gun) designed to carry 20 men over rough terrain. For the next four days we traversed large rivers, passes and valleys on atrocious muddy tracks – bottomless bogs of partly frozen tundra. Occasionally we passed through fields of native rhubarb, then back into forests of pine trees, which apparently have roving deer and bears but none were encountered. It was August, so the snow was gone but the ground was still frozen below the surface; temperatures here in winter reached minus 40°C. Progress

some days was good, others very slow as the rough nature of the route took its toll, causing breakdowns of the vehicles and their worn metal tracks, including getting cast on huge glacial boulders concealed in the mud. We slept in tents and occasionally in log huts, and caught small fish in the rivers to supplement our meals. We finally limped into the Ospin jade mining camp, set among high bare mountains, to be greeted with a stockpile of tonnes of nephrite blocks fresh from the quarry. For the next two days we were occupied clambering over and collecting samples at the various outcrops of jade, one of which was 10 m wide and has to be among the largest anywhere. The nephrite is associated with

albitite and serpentinite and was being prised out manually, so every piece was hard-won. We also located some gem pieces in the creek and talus slopes, but alas, they were too big to take. The comradeship between our group and the Russian geologists and miners was great, with lots of Beatles songs, laughter, stories and experiences shared via Eugene, who spoke good English. His wife Ola accompanied us for the entire expedition and prepared three meals a day, every day, without a kitchen for 10 hungry jade enthusiasts.

The journey back to civilisation was equally fraught with mishaps. There was one incident when our track vehicle became cast on a huge boulder in the middle of the Kitoi River crossing.

Eugene, with axe in hand, jumped in and waded up to his thighs in the icy water to the bank, where he chopped down a reasonable-sized tree and floated it back to the vehicle. It was chained across the tracks and wound under the vehicle, lifting us off the boulder amid cheers – it all comes with the job of being a geologist in Siberia. The vehicle then lurched into a deep pool, filling with water, so when we reached the other side, they backed up a steep bank to drain it. A further complication occurred when Sasha became seriously ill, but fortunately Alf, being a physician, was able to assist although it took an extra day before we could move on. By applying the Russian philosophy 'don't worry and don't hurry', we managed to return safely.

In Irkutsk our hosts had organised a special visit to the museum, where staff had assembled a range of superb jade artefacts dating back 8000 years. Some were identical in shape and method of manufacture to Māori examples. Early ones were dark green, which probably came from the Ospin region, whereas the later white jade ones are likely to have come from further afield, possibly the Vitim area or an unknown source. The white jade pieces were wonderful – the forms were so simple, but perfectly proportioned: delicate rings, half-rings and perforated discs with a soft patina, and all so old. The method of working by rotating a hard stone point from a pivot dictated the basic design. We were also shown drilled jade tablets found near Lake Hovsgol in northern Mongolia. We were privileged to see a collection of carved bone Venus figurines that were some 20,000 years old. We discussed the possibility of touring an exhibition of these ancient treasures and jade to New Zealand, but this eventually proved too difficult.

Seeing these Siberian jade treasures, my mind flashed back to the collections in the National Palace Museum in Taiwan, where we saw carvings made from nephrite that did not fit with known Chinese sources. The demand for high-quality jade in China had been strong and I feel sure that Siberian stone, particularly the vivid green and white nephrite, would have found its way there. Again, sourcing tests will confirm this.

During the late nineteenth century, Carl Peter Fabergé, the famous jeweller to the czars, used Siberian jade extensively, creating lavish jewellery and ornamental items from only the finest nephrite. Today, mining of Siberian nephrite has grown into an active industry. Apart from supplying local lapidaries, most of the raw stone is exported to Asia and other countries, including New Zealand. Contemporary Russian carvers are producing some exquisite works in stunning new designs.

We will always savour our Siberian experience. The jade was the focus, but it was the sincerity and friendliness of the Russian people that made our stay so memorable.

ALASKA

There are several scenarios as to how the American continent was populated. The general belief is that when sea levels were reduced during the last Ice Age, the Bering Strait, which divides Alaska from Siberia, would have been dry land or at least much narrower, making it possible for people in northeastern Siberia to migrate across and spread south and east eventually to all parts of the American continent, even to Tierra del Fuego in the far south.

The Yupik and Inuit people established mainly coastal settlements in Alaska and the Canadian Arctic regions. They utilised a wide variety of rock types, including nephrite, for many purposes, including tools such as hammers, adzes, picks, axes, *ulu* (knives), harpoon and spearheads; and lip ornaments known as labrets. Similar jade artefacts are known from archaeological sites in northeastern Siberia.

An article in the American *Lapidary Journal* by Dan Burlison in 1961 generated my interest in jade in Alaska. He described how the Shungnak jade project was established by the government to assist local Inuit to utilise the extensive alluvial nephrite deposits in the Kobuk area. Large boulders were collected, particularly in Dahl Creek, where they were cut down to manageable sizes, then barged down the river to a factory at Kotzebue on the west coast for processing.

Several other articles on the area published over the next sixteen years tantalised me further, especially one by William Procter, with whom I corresponded and who put me in touch with Ivan Stewart of Anchorage. Ivan was the current owner of the legal jade claims in the Dahl Creek and Cosmos Mountains area, and each summer invited jade enthusiasts to assist him with mining. This was an offer I had to explore. In 1980 Alf Poole and I were invited through the New Zealand Crafts Council to give a jade carving demonstration at the World Crafts Council Conference in Vienna. This was the catalyst, so we took the opportunity to include a visit to Alaska, Canada and California, with Don Wobber, a jade carver from California, accompanying us.

Alf and I flew to Los Angeles where we met Don and drove to his home in the Monterey area. The original plan was to drive up the west coast, visiting as many nephrite occurrences as possible on the way up to Canada, then on to Alaska, but our plans were interrupted by the violent eruption of the Mount St Helens volcano. Instead, we spent several days in the Monterey area checking out museum collections and jade sources, then flew to Vancouver where we concentrated on visits to jade carvers and museums. From there we embarked on our Alaskan adventure.

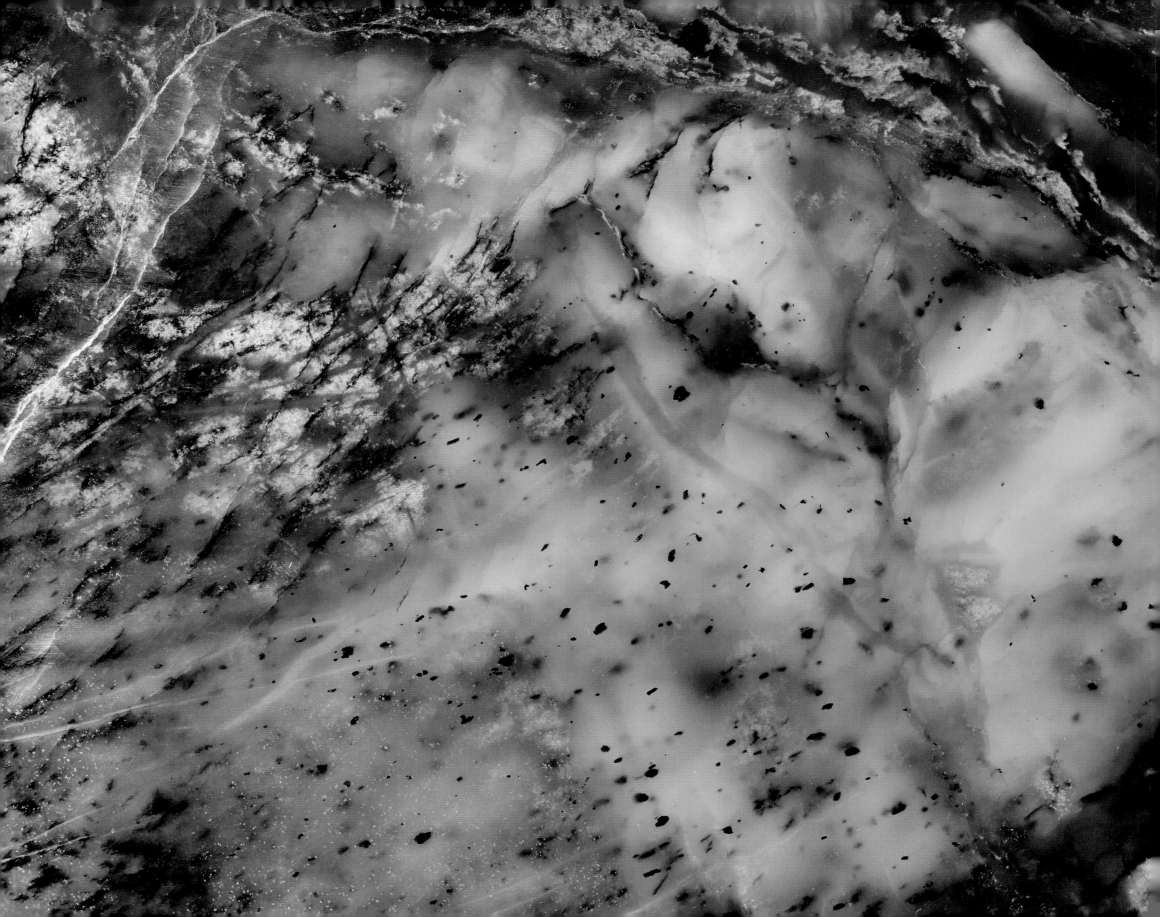

LEFT / Backlit sawn section of nephrite from the Kobuk region of Alaska.

ABOVE RIGHT / Author inspecting an outcrop of nephrite on Asbestos Mountain near Kobuk, Alaska. The enclosing softer rocks have eroded away leaving a spike of nephrite. A. P. POOLE

RIGHT / The famous 15-tonne boulder of Alaskan jade known as the Perón boulder, being gradually cut up by its owner, John Hallay, 1980. His grandson is wetting one end to show the colour of the stone. R. BECK

We were introduced to the Arctic at Fairbanks, originally a goldrush frontier town where we stocked up on food supplies, insect repellent and head nets – the mosquitoes and other biting insects are legendary in Alaska. Gold is still sought after and stores sold all mining equipment, including handguns for protection from bears.

We paid a visit to John Hallay, a double amputee with a 15-tonne jade boulder in his yard. It had a wonderful history, a story that I now wish I had recorded in more detail. The stone was found in Alaska in the 1940s and, with much difficulty, transported to the southern United States. It was destined to be carved into a life-size statue of Eva Perón, president of Argentina. That did not happen, and the boulder remained stored in a warehouse, forgotten for many years, until John tracked it down, became the owner and returned it to Alaska. He was gradually cutting it up, making table-tops, clock faces and other jewellery items, and marketing them as souvenirs of the Perón boulder.

Although there are several small occurrences of nephrite in Alaska, the main one for several hundred years for Arctic people was in the Kobuk region, particularly the Shungnak River and others nearby. Gold seekers in the late 1890s also discovered asbestos and nephrite occurring in the region, and Asbestos Mountain near Dahl Creek became renowned for its deposits of a very pure tremolite asbestos that was mined during the mid 1940s.

Nephrite of varying quality occurs within a 70 km series of outcrops of ultramafic rocks in schist from Jade Mountain in the west to the Kogoluktuk River in the east. The whole area has been spasmodically mined for gold, asbestos and nephrite: many tonnes of jade have been removed, and some was apparently exported to China during the 1940s.

We flew from Fairbanks by bush plane, a twin-engine beach craft, to a bulldozed airstrip at the Eskimo village of Kobuk, some 50 km inside the Arctic Circle. We were welcomed by Dick Chase, one of Ivan's team of four helpers, and he transported us and our packs in a trailer pulled by a farm tractor back to camp on the banks of Dahl Creek. On the way I noticed a small boulder of dark green stone in the old gold tailings by the track. I walked back in the evening and, sure enough, it was jade, and we found several smaller stones nearby, to the amazement of our hosts, who had driven past them every day for several weeks. The camp consisted of several buildings constructed from logs. The food storehouse dated back to the goldrush era and was raised 2 m off the ground for protection from bears. Being well inside the Arctic Circle and summer, the sun did not set, just tracked around us in a huge inclined circle, making our days very long.

The team, which included a carver from England, were welding fluming together from old oil drums for a hydro scheme to generate power for the diamond saws, which they used to cut off thick slabs for jade table-tops. The jade that they were cutting had come from another source in the Cosmos Mountains further to the west.

Ivan gave us a handgun with the instructions, 'Aim for the bear's feet and, if lucky, you might clip an ear.' I must admit the revolver gave us a little more confidence when exploring the area. On one occasion, three bears with cubs startled us but took off into the stunted forest when they saw us approaching; we were thankful that the gun was not required. We walked to the deserted upper mining camp that was used by the Shungnak project to saw the boulders into smaller blocks. Strewn among the remains of large saw gantries were many rejected cut boulders. I was disappointed to see that every boulder had saw cuts: although these were low-grade stones, the natural beauty of the exterior is their best attribute. I hope that some have been preserved somewhere.

The general quality of nephrite in the Dahl Creek area is not high – one estimate was that only 5 per cent was gem grade; however, the pieces that we saw were reasonable, with patches of higher grade material within larger stones. We felt the stone had similarities to some South Westland nephrite, especially the outer waterworn surfaces that were weathered to a beautiful deep orange with rich green patches showing through. The sawn faces often revealed disappointing patchy colour, from pale or olive green to rich green; they contained lots of inclusions, dendrites and fractures, with a relatively schistose texture.

We were determined to visit the source of the jade, and undertook a 16-km return hike up onto Asbestos Mountain (650 m) to the old asbestos mine area. Nearby, where the serpentinite was in contact with schist, we found lots of schistose nephrite float on the screes and two small in situ outcrops, one of which was projecting like a spike and gave off a gong-like sound when tapped. The view from here was spectacular, looking north towards the mountains of the Brooks Range, with the meandering Kobuk River behind us. The weather was fine and quite warm. The snow had gone except for some deep drifts, but the ground was still frozen and the water from the springs was so cold that we could hardly drink it.

On the day of our departure, while waiting for the bush plane to arrive, Don and I were walking along the edge of the airstrip and I noticed a small portion of a jade boulder protruding. We dug frantically with our rock picks and soon retrieved it, and filled in the hole with gravel. The plane landed. It was a small single-engine four-seater instead of the larger one we were expecting. Our stone, at 60 kg, was too heavy to take with us, so we gave it to Ivan to share with the boys. Some months later, Ivan sent me a sample, which I treasure as it brings back so many pleasant memories.

The bumpy flight out over the beautiful tundra, lakes, stunted forest and the mighty Yukon River was a mixture of exhilaration and concern, mainly because the plane had fuel problems and had to make two stops at emergency airstrips for more fuel.

In museums in Fairbanks and Anchorage we perused the collections of jade artefacts that were several hundred years old. The Inuit methods of hafting their tools were very different from those of Māori: they were lashed onto antler handles with seal skin thonging, whereas Māori used wooden hafts and flax cordage. The similarity of the *ulu* to the Māori ripi was striking – both were sharpened split spalls of schistose nephrite. The adzes were also sawn in the same way as Māori adzes; and a few, which I suspect were older, were hammer dressed. There was also some evidence of heating the nephrite. The only personal ornaments we observed were labrets.

WESTERN CANADA

Nephrite in Western Canada occurs in a discontinuous belt of ultramafic rocks associated with major faults that lie between the Coast Mountains to the west and the Rocky Mountains to the east. Jade deposits begin in the south near Hope in British Columbia and extend northwest to the Alaskan border in the Yukon Territory. The various major occurrences are grouped into several mining areas, such as Lillooet, Omineca, Cassiar and Yukon Territory, all of which have been, or are, currently mined commercially. Canada is a major world supplier of nephrite and many thousands of tonnes have been recovered; most of it has been exported, mainly to Asia.

The first jade field to produce commercial quantities was the Lillooet area, beginning in the early 1960s. The area was worked for placer gold. It is said that the Chinese miners encountered jade in their claims, which they shipped back to China.

RIGHT / Brilliant emerald green nephrite from Deas Lake area, Northern British Columbia.

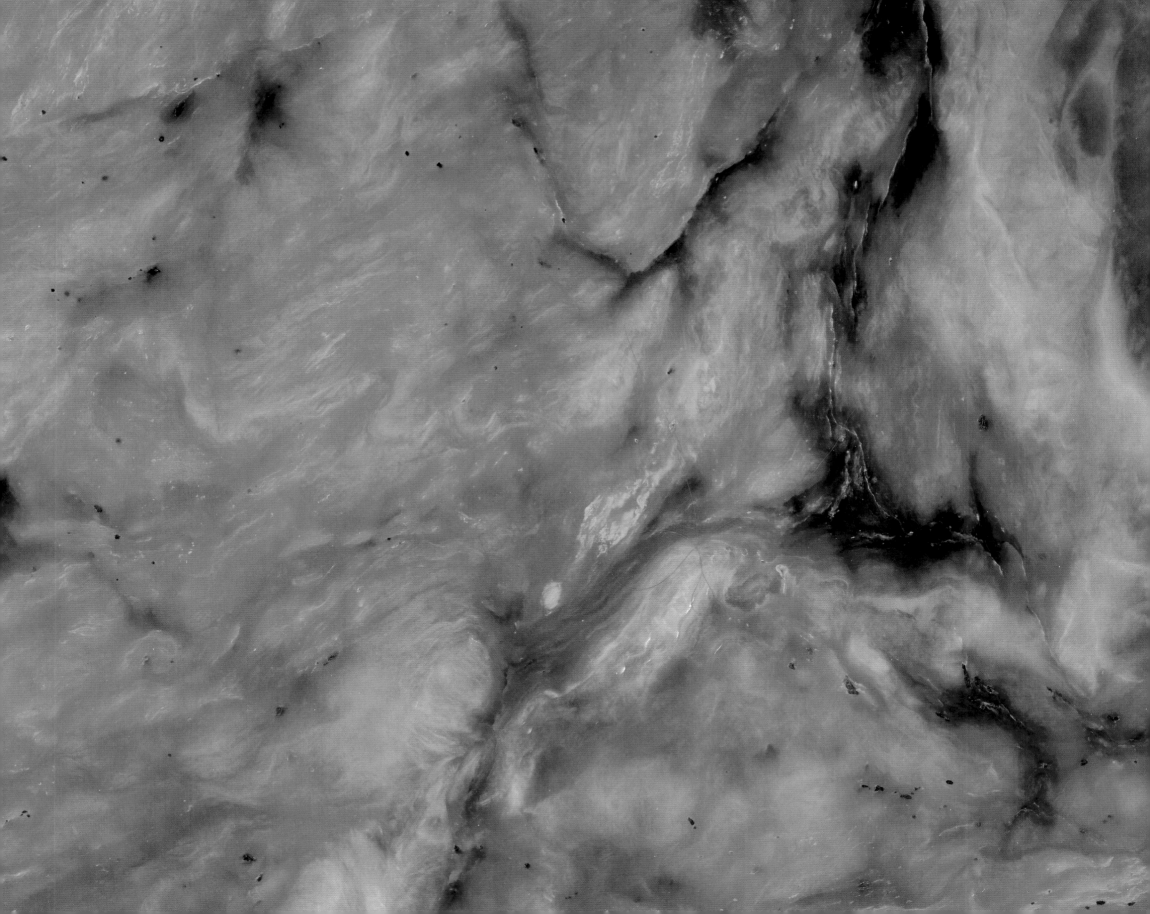

Mining is now concentrated further north, where both in situ and blocks found on talus slopes are sawn into manageable sizes with huge diamond saws of various designs. Some of the blocks are massive: one found in 1992 in southeast Yukon Territory was claimed at the time to be the largest ever found, at 577 tonnes. Some of these occurrences are in remote mountainous areas where mining can take place only in summer, and transport of the stone is challenging.

Canadian nephrite is generally a rich green colour and of high quality; some specimens are similar in appearance to New Zealand stone. A distinctive feature of Canadian jade is the common presence of emerald green inclusions of chrome garnet peppered throughout, which gives a lively contrast.

In 1996 Ann and I accepted an invitation from Stan Leaming to visit British Columbia. Stan, a geologist, has spent many years visiting and evaluating Canadian nephrite deposits and was employed at the Geological Survey of Canada. He took us on a small field trip to the picturesque Bridge River area near Lillooet, on the Fraser River, some 280 km upstream, northeast of Vancouver. Commercial jade production has long since ceased at this source, but sections of the Fraser River have been set aside for the public to prospect for jade after each flood; we were thrilled to find a water-polished specimen there.

Contemporary Canadian jade carvers are concentrated in Vancouver. A popular theme of sculptural works is Canadian animals, birds and sea mammals in both stylised and representational forms, from hand-size to elaborate free-standing pieces.

The bulk jade yards are fascinating to delve through – hundreds of tonnes of beautiful chunks sawn into angular blocks, which come alive when sprayed with water. I purchased some small, choice examples to carve.

The use of jade in British Columbia by Northwest Coast native cultures – now known as Peoples of the First Nations of Canada – is about 3500 years old. The use of nephrite technology

ABOVE LEFT / Lower Bridge River near Lillooet, the area where British Columbia's jade deposits were first commercially mined. R. BECK

ABOVE RIGHT / American carver Don Wobber in discussion with New Zealand carver Alf Poole over a jade boulder that Don has recovered from the sea at Monterey, California. R. BECK

BOTTOM RIGHT / Sea-worn cobbles of Monterey nephrite showing a variety of colours.

flourished some 2000 years ago; and, like Māori, with the advantage of jade they developed a sophisticated woodworking culture and a superb distinctive art style expressing their culture and environment. Main concentrations of nephrite items have been found in archaeological sites along the Pacific Coast and Fraser River area from Lillooet to Hope, extending inland a little to the east. These are centred on the southern local nephrite sources. Similar jade artefacts are also found further south into Washington State in the US.

Several museums in the Vancouver area have extensive collections of indigenous artefacts. Dr Grant Keddie, archaeology curator of the Royal British Columbia Museum at Victoria on Vancouver Island, worked with me on two occasions inspecting the collections. A wide range of stone types were used for various tools, weapons and ornaments, and among these were many nephrite examples. Methods developed for working jade were identical to those of Māori, and the practice of heat treatment was also well understood. The cedar forests were a valuable resource – huge logs were fashioned into massive decorated houses, tall carved totem poles and mighty canoes; but finer work, such as intricately carved boxes and other ornamental items, was also created. Apart from the woodworking tools, adzes and chisels, rarer items made in jade were labrets, war picks and drill points. Exceptionally long adzes, up to 50 cm, are believed to be status pieces and are almost always recovered in burials from about AD 1500 to 1800. These were traded inland from production centres, while the small adzes were traded towards the coast. Also, at a later stage, naturally occurring copper was used to make woodworking tools and ornamental objects. It would appear that jade was not carved into more detailed ornaments, as these were made from softer rocks such as serpentinite, talc, argillite and slate.

WESTERN UNITED STATES

A similar geology to British Columbia, of ultramafic rocks in association with schist, with nephrite lodes and alluvial deposits, extends south into the Pacific United States, but is much less extensive than in Canada.

Nephrite has been found at several localities in Washington State; Stan Leaming gives Puget Sound and Darrington area for alluvial float, and Mt Higgins as the main in situ deposit, which was mined at one time. The only specimens I have seen are from Deer Creek near Oso, and they have quite distinctive marbled markings with sulphides and many other included minerals.

In Oregon State a few isolated nephrite finds of alluvial boulders have been recorded, but to date no commercial reserves are known. The slabbed sample that I have is quite dark green, very fine-grained, and the waterworn surface has small, crescent-shaped fractures similar to some New Zealand Westland boulders.

The best known locality for jade in California is on the picturesque sea coast near Monterey, where nephrite was first recorded in situ in 1941. Further discoveries followed throughout many counties along the coast and inland at isolated occurrences over the northern two-thirds of the state. These occur as alluvial river pebbles to large boulders, beach deposits and a few in situ outcrops associated with serpentinite, which is a relatively common rock in California. An important, sizable nephrite deposit lies in the rugged hilly country near Mariposa, where it has been commercially mined, producing stone of high quality with some specimens close to New Zealand nephrite in appearance.

California has some unusual examples of nephrite, such as a blue or bluish green variety known as vonson blue from Marin County, and a black nephrite with large masses of crystallised magnetite throughout, found near Victorville in San Bernardino County. A distinctive nephrite with diopside rock occurs in the Eel River and Monterey areas; it bears a striking resemblance to a similar rock from the Livingstone Mountains in New Zealand.

Jadeite also occurs in several places, especially at Clear Creek in San Benito County. This is one of the few world occurrences of this relatively rare stone. The general appearance is a somewhat dull green with white ribbons, but in selected areas can be quite attractive. It is found as alluvial boulders and in situ.

Don Wobber is a scuba diver who recovers jade pieces from the seabed in Jade Cove in the Big Sur area, and uses air bags to float them to the surface. Out to sea, he discovered a huge underwater sea cave lined with smooth green jade. The specimens he has obtained range from pebbles to large boulders weighing a few tonnes. Most are encrusted with coralline and other sea life, which has to be ground off or dissolved with acid to reveal the beautiful water-polished green jade. Don carves these treasures into sculptural pieces taking the natural shapes for inspiration.

Don led us down the steep cliffs at Jade Cove in thick fog, and we spent the morning getting thoroughly wet among the boulders and numerous serpentinite outcrops, some with thin semi-nephrite veins. Trying to avoid the breakers of the incoming tide, we found the odd nephrite pebble in the beach gravels. Some of the best examples of botryoidal nephrite comes from this region and Don took us on a hike through the forest to a jade mine near Willow Creek where we collected some examples. On this trail Alf and I experienced our first encounter with the dreaded poison ivy plant and a small rattlesnake slithered across the track reminding us that we were definitely not in New Zealand, where there are no such hazards.

Monterey nephrite is quite distinctive with colours in strong greens to bluish grey containing tiny black flecks. Oxidised stones found in old elevated sea terraces are known locally as vulcan jade because they look as though they were heated, but are just naturally weathered to a rusty red. Some time ago, Don found a special piece weighing over 4 tonnes, which was named 'The Nephripod'. He wrote a book about its discovery, the task of getting it to dry land and polishing it. The Californian state authorities claimed ownership and a long debate ensued, but finally this exceptional stone became Don's legal property. It is now on permanent display at the Oakland Museum.

LEFT / Jade dealer C. McLeod and Stan Leaming, Canada's nephrite expert, with a large jade boulder about to be cut by a breaking-down diamond swing saw at Lillooet. This type of saw has been used extensively in Canada and New Zealand. R. BECK

Native Americans who inhabited the Monterey area collected jade pebbles and used them as cooking stones by heating and placing them in pottery bowls with raw food. The tough nephrite did not shatter on repeated heating, and numerous examples of these are common in archaeological sites in the area. Apparently this was the only use the local inhabitants had for jade.

Since 1992, Big Sur has been the venue for an annual jade festival: carvers from many parts meet to discuss jade recovery and carving and offer their finds and works for sale. New Zealand carver Donn Salt has several times shared his carving knowledge at this event.

Apart from the west coast, there are minor sources of jade elsewhere in the United States; and Wyoming was a renowned supplier of high quality nephrite since the 1930s, but now good finds are rare there. Only a few in situ lodes have been located. Most of the stones are floaters, and many are wind-polished (ventifacted); these are sought-after by jade collectors.

CENTRAL AND SOUTH AMERICA

The Pre-Columbian cultures in this central part of the Americas from Mexico to Costa Rica utilised jadeite to a high degree and it became their most prized possession, far above the appreciation of gold, even though they were expert goldsmiths. This deep appreciation for jade was expressed in the form of a huge number and range of superb jade artefacts. In particular, the Olmec and Maya cultures fashioned jadeite extensively for objects for domestic use as well as ceremonial offerings, funerary goods and personal adornments, dating back some 3000 years.

Not all the Mesoamerican so-called jades are in fact jade. These people appear to have had a preference for green-coloured stones, and they chose a huge variety of rock and mineral species known as 'social jade', the more common of which were green examples of slate, albitite, diopside and quartz. A very small amount of nephrite has also been recorded, but jadeite was their ultimate preference. Much of the jadeite is actually jadeitite.

Although these civilisations possessed gold, they were stone-based cultures. Their lapidary skills were exceptionally well developed, with methods similar to other stone-based societies for sawing, grinding and drilling jade. As with the Chinese, they made use of bow-string saw technology (like a fretsaw) to cut out slots. This technique relies on sand abrasives embedded in the string, and usually requires an initial hole, which was achieved by drilling from both sides to produce an hourglass-shaped hole. Core drills were also used. Carving high-quality jadeite would have presented some problems as the hardness of the stone is similar to that of quartz, which was the common abrasive for working stone elsewhere. Quartz would have made for slow cutting, requiring harder mineral abrasives such as corundum and garnet to produce sharp edges and speed up the operation. Jadeite is easily polished, and many artefacts have a high lustre (some too high; these may have been repolished in recent times to enhance the colour).

Locating the stone sources of the prehistoric artefacts was a mystery until 1954, when deposits of jadeitite were found in the Motagua River valley in central Guatemala, but a source for the high quality so called 'Olmec blue' variety eluded searchers until the beginning of this century when several deposits were discovered south of the Motagua River area. These are now commercially mined for the local lapidary industry. Other sources are suspected nearby and in adjacent countries where a similar geology is present.

Nephrite artefacts occasionally occur in archaeological sites in several parts of the Mesoamerican region, but more so in northern Colombia and Venezuela. In Brazil, nephrite implements and adornments are reported sparingly in many states at coastal and inland archaeological sites extending from the northeast to São Paulo state in the south, but to date no source of nephrite is known south of California. The mention of nephrite on the Pacific side of South America in a brief report by Antonio Carlos Simoens da Silva, who in 1910 inspected an implement in the National Museum in Santiago, Chile, is encouraging, but the provenance of the implement is not recorded. Central American jadeite was extensively traded over long distances and this could also be the case for the nephrite. However, there appear to be several suitable geological situations in Central and South America where nephrite could occur, and I feel sure it will be discovered somewhere, sooner or later.

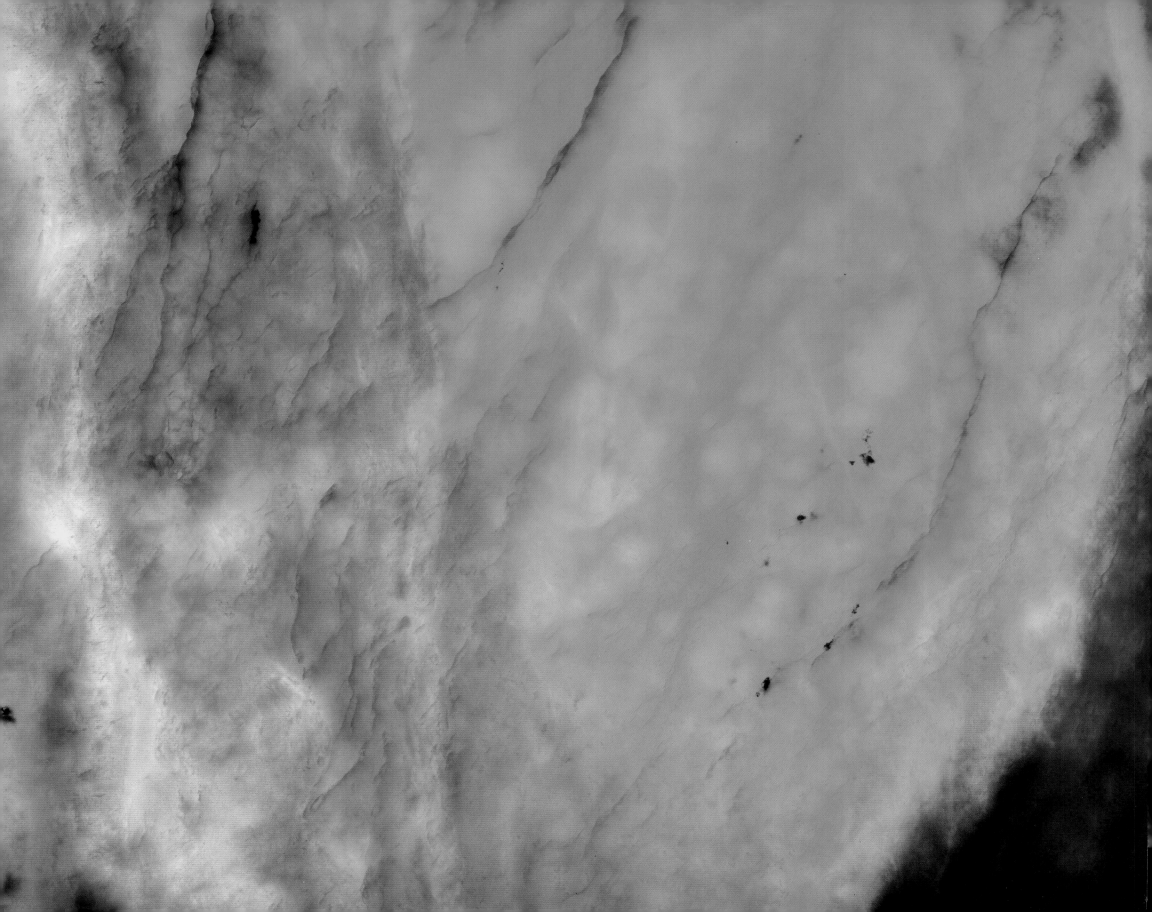

APPENDIX ONE/TIPS FOR CARVING JADE

Every carver soon develops their own technique, innovative methods and style. I have worked with hard stones as a hobby for more than fifty years, but my preference is working with jade. Below are some tips for carving jade that may be useful.

The carving process can be separated into several operations and considerations, and these generally apply to other hard stones as well as jade. The main objective is to carefully remove the unwanted stone to reveal the design intended.

Currently, in New Zealand, tuition is available at Tai Poutini Polytechnic, Greymouth, which offers a comprehensive certificate and diploma in jade and hard stone carving.

DESIGN
Assuming you are fortunate enough to possess some fine jade, you need to be very sure of what you want to carve, for the process may take considerable time and effort.

Try to keep your carving simple, almost chunky, in design, and avoid making weak spots such as spindly legs and projections. Remember that a jade carving can be made to please the hand as well as the eye. Whether you intend to carve an abstract or figurative object, it is a good idea first to construct a plasticine model which you can develop until you are satisfied with its design. Then copy it in stone. If the raw material is a natural boulder or cobble, study its shape,

markings and colour and let the stone influence the design, taking advantage of all the attributes present. This is challenging, but rewarding.

Orientate the stone so that any grain or markings are not going to interfere with the design. Avoid cracks. Plan to work around feather fractures, or use them to advantage by incorporating them in the design. Like wood, work with the grain. Choose a stone colour to suit the design: darker stone will show more reflected light than lighter shades. Try to include some of the rind if a bicolour effect is desired, remembering that sometimes the rind can be quite porous and may not give a consistent finish. Soft inclusions can be troublesome from undercutting, causing an uneven surface, but with diamond abrasives this effect can be lessened. Concentrations of these soft inclusions should be avoided. Marking out the design on the stone can be done with an aluminium pencil or waterproof felt tip pen.

SAWING
If you are working from sawn slabs, these should be cut with the grain and parallel to any schistosity. Probably one of the most useful pieces of equipment is the diamond trim saw. You will be surprised just how much can be done by careful use of this invaluable tool. Trim saws are usually about 200 mm in diameter, mounted on a spindle, with the diamond blade which protrudes through the

bench slot running in water. Quite large areas can be removed by angled sawing, or cutting a series of parallel slots which can be broken out. The stone is held by hand for this operation so take care.

GRINDING
This stage is the most critical one. If too much is accidentally taken off it cannot be put back and you are left with few options – alter the design, make the whole carving smaller or start again on another piece of stone. The objective at this stage is to grind off all the rough projections and to finalise the shape, checking constantly with the model or drawing. This process is best carried out on diamond grinding wheels or laps. Silicon carbide grinding wheels are still available, but wear quickly and require frequent dressing to keep them running true. More carvers now are attempting larger sculptural forms. For this work there is a whole range of diamond cutting wheels available for specialist disc grinders that can operate with water. These can remove a considerable amount of stone in a short time. Usually the larger pieces of stone have enough weight to stay in place while being worked, or they can be made secure with bungy cords or clamps. If the work is heavy and needs to be held against the grinder, support it in a sling using an overhead pulley and counterweight; this eases the strain of holding it in place.

When you can go no further in the grinding stage and the design requires more fine detail, transfer to the flexible handpiece grinder. These tools are very versatile and can be power- or air-driven. A wide range of diamond burrs or cutters with different profiles to achieve complex shapes are available. Water is necessary as a coolant and to flush away the grounds.

Another method developed by the Chinese thousands of years ago is using soft metal mandrels. These can be made from mild steel

LEFT / A section of backlit multi-coloured nephrite from Westland.

in various shapes and secured in a chuck on a rotating horizontal spindle. Loose silicon carbide abrasive grit with water is applied by hand, with the stone being held and worked against the wheel. Although this method has its advantages, most carvers prefer to use diamond tools exclusively. However, from time to time, I still use this process for achieving some special effects.

DRILLING

Drilling is an important aspect of carving and can be achieved using diamond core drills. Making a series of holes is an efficient method of removing stone, and the cores from the centre can be useful for other purposes, which reduces wastage. Holes for suspending pendants should be part of the design and not look as though they have simply been punched through. The hole should not be abrupt or have parallel sides, but should curve or taper so that, in effect, the carving flows into the holes. This effect was achieved by Māori in the past. Jade lends itself ideally to fish-like forms and a very simple shape can be given purpose and life simply by the careful placement of a suitable hole serving as an eye.

SANDING AND FINISHING

The final and often most time-consuming stage is the finishing work . . . and there are few shortcuts. Some of the larger carvings can be sanded smooth by diamond sanding discs or by diamond sanding cloth or blocks rubbed by hand. For more intricate portions such as problem angles and corners, small silicon carbide rasps used by hand with plenty of water are most helpful. These can be made easily by sawing up old silicon carbide grinding wheels on the diamond saw to the required shapes. Finishing with these rasps is usually slow work, and I use hot water so that the carving warms up and dries off instantly and progress is easily checked. Another useful

tip is to spray-paint the carving in a contrasting colour so that any scratches or flat areas show up immediately during the sanding process. To protect finished sections of delicate carvings while working on other parts, the fragile portions can be covered with duct tape bindings or possibly set in some substance that can be dissolved off later.

To preserve a soft appearance and feel, I prefer not to give my carvings a high-gloss polish; this is achieved by finishing by hand with very fine diamond cloth (800 grit) or dry 1000 grit silicon carbide paper. A final brisk rub on a wool carpet will emphasise any relief by providing a slightly higher shine. To achieve a super-soft texture, some carvers sandblast a portion of the surface with a very fine abrasive grit while leaving other areas highly polished. This highlights features that would otherwise go unnoticed. Most carvers apply a light oil or oil/beeswax mixture to enhance the appearance of their work but this should not be overdone. Translucency increases and fractures and scratches will disappear as the oil penetrates. Oiling should, however, be done only after the work is properly finished and should not be done to hide any flaws or scratches because eventually the oil will dry out and expose them. The practice of oiling jade is a very old one and carvings worn next to the skin, and especially fondle pieces, soon absorb natural oils and are enhanced by them. In many ways, the skill of the carver is measured by the quality of finish on the carving. It is not unusual for a carver to take several hundred hours to create a masterpiece.

HEALTH AND SAFETY CONSIDERATIONS

Lapidary work, like many other activities, does demand certain health and safety precautions. The inhalation of dust or water spray laden with stone particles can cause temporary irritation of the eyes, nose, throat and lung passages, but can be prevented by wearing a respirator or mask.

Prolonged unprotected exposure may possibly induce silicosis and asbestosis. Diamond saws, especially the larger ones, and high speed diamond burrs can produce quite harmful noise levels and hearing protection should be used. During trim sawing, grinding and sanding, flying chips, grit and dust are common and safety glasses are a must. Avoid prolonged exposure to vibrations, particularly when grinding. This can lead to a condition known as 'white finger' where the tips of the fingers become white, cold and numb from irreversible blood vessel and nerve damage. In lapping and core drilling, the stone is often hand-held and can sometimes seize onto the lap, or the core drill can jam. This danger can be avoided by using a vice or pliers to hold the stone. Trim-saw collars are sometimes better if not fitted too tightly so that if the saw blade jams the spindle can slip. Remember, too, that although diamond tools will cut stone and not easily your finger, they can take their toll on fingernails: it is best to wear protection such as gloves or finger stalls. When operating electrical grinders and other equipment with water, always use an isolating transformer on mains power. Protective clothing is necessary for the fine spray produced – or be prepared to get wet. To avoid blocked drains, wastewater from equipment should pass into a container or sump to settle the solids, and this should be cleaned out periodically.

In spite of these hazards, jade carving is a most satisfying and worthwhile activity – and one that has been enjoyed for thousands of years.

APPENDIX TWO/WORLD SOURCES OF JADE

The following brief list of known occurrences, except New Zealand, was prepared from many sources, in particular S. F. Leaming, Yu. N. Kolensik and G. E. Harlow and S. S. Sorensen, and from personal visits to many of these sources.

AUSTRALIA – NEPHRITE

South Australia Near Cowell on the Eyre Peninsula. Occurs in dolomitic marble (para-nephrite). Colour: olive to dark green to an intense black of exceptional quality. An extensive deposit and currently commercially mined.

New South Wales Several in situ outcrops along the Great Serpentine Belt, Dungowan, near Tamworth and commercially mined. Spring Creek and other minor localities. Occurs in serpentinite (ortho-nephrite). Colour: light green to olive green.

Western Australia Nephrite is reported from time to time in the state, especially in the Carnarvon region, but unconfirmed.

CANADA – NEPHRITE

British Columbia Occurs in numerous deposits along a belt containing faults and ultramafic rocks between the Coast Mountains and the Rocky Mountains from Hope in the south to the Yukon border in the north. Deposits are in situ and alluvial and can be grouped into three main segments: Lillooet, Omineca and Cassiar. In the Lillooet segment are some 15 sources, including the Fraser River, which was a source for the indigenous people who utilised jade for implements. Significant deposits are in the Omineca segment at Mt Sydney Williams and Mt Ogden and in the Cassiar (northern) segment at Cry Lake and Dease Lake areas. At the latter the nephrite is marketed as Polar Jade and is of high quality. British Columbian nephrite (ortho-nephrite) is of a rich green colour, often with distinctive emerald-green chrome garnet patches. Many of the above localities have been, or are, commercially mined and at present Canada is one of the main producers of nephrite.

Yukon Territory Occurs in several locations, especially in the Frances Lake area.

Newfoundland Has extensive ophiolites, and nephrite has been found at Pistolet Bay on the Great Northern Peninsula, as nodules and botryoidal specimens. There are possible locations also on other parts of the island.

CENTRAL AMERICA – JADEITE

Significant deposits of jadeite are found in Guatemala in the Motagua Valley area and were used extensively by the early cultures throughout Central America. The stone is found as boulders and in situ, in a range of green shades with some specimens bluish and emerald green. Mined commercially for the local lapidary industry.

CHINA – NEPHRITE

North side of the Kunlun Mountains near Khotan (Hetian) in Xinjiang, originally Turkestan. Occurs at 19 different locations both in situ in dolomite (para-nephrite) and as alluvial deposits particularly Yurungkax, Karakax and Keryia Rivers. Colour: light to dark greens and white. Was obtained from this general area for thousands of years, being an important source of nephrite for the Chinese lapidaries. Manus area in the Tian Mountains near Urumqi, Xinjiang in ultramafic rocks (ortho-nephrite). Colour: mid to dark green. Also in Xinjiang in the Altun Mountains, Qiemo County (para-nephrite).

In recent years no less than 14 other nephrite occurrences have been found in China, but the quality of these is generally unknown.

FINLAND – NEPHRITE

Occurs at two in situ localities, Paakkila Asbestos Quarry, Central Finland, and at Stanvik Iron Mine on the Island of Laajasolo in the southern suburbs of Helsinki. Colour: yellowish green (para-nephrite). Pebbles and boulders have been found in glacial deposits at Hakkila on the northern outskirts of Helsinki.

GERMANY – NEPHRITE

Thuringia and Harz area (in situ) Leipzig and Potsdam, eastern Germany, and in Bavaria, western Germany, as alluvial deposits.

INDONESIA – NEPHRITE

Sumatra Alluvial nephrite has been found in the Aceh region and probably originates from the ultramafic rocks present in the area.

Sulawesi Nephrite is reported from the central districts.

Java An attractive jade-like mineral known as 'Java jade' is composed mainly of pumpellyite and is found in the central part of the island.

ITALY – NEPHRITE

Nephrite occurs as nodules and veins (ortho-nephrite) at several places in the Northern Apennines at Mont Bianco and in a belt extending from Sestri Levante on the Riviera Ligure to Monterosso al Mare. Colour: predominantly green shades.

JAPAN – JADEITE AND NEPHRITE

Jadeite occurs at several localities, but particularly Omi and Kotaki districts, Niigata Prefecture. Occurs in albitite, in situ and as huge alluvial boulders. A section of the occurrence has been set aside in the Kotaki Gorge as a reserve and 102-tonne boulder is displayed in a special museum near the Omi River mouth. Colour: mostly white but with emerald green and mauve shades present.

Nephrite also occurs in Japan as boulders and pebbles in the upper Matsukawa River near Hakuba-mura, Nagano Prefecture; the Kotaki Omi area; and as beach pebbles at Itoigawa, Niigata Prefecture. Colour: greyish to olive green. Both nephrite and jadeite from these sources were utilised by the early Jomon culture.

KOREA – NEPHRITE

Dong Myeon near Chuncheon, South Korea. Occurs in association with dolomite and amphibole schist (para-nephrite). Colours: white, browns and light green. An important resource (mined intermittently from 1976) for the local lapidary industry and similar in appearance to nephrite from Vitim River, Siberia.

MONGOLIA – NEPHRITE

Prikhubsugul area as alluvial deposit. The ancient people of Mongolia used green and white jade in the Neolithic and Bronze periods.

MYANMAR (BURMA) – JADEITE

Occurs in situ and as alluvial deposits near Mogaung, northern Myanmar. The world's main source for jadeite and renowned for its quality and fine emerald green and mauve colours. Utilised extensively in China since the eighteenth century.

NEW CALEDONIA – NEPHRITE

Occurs in situ and alluvially in the rivers and streams in the general Tiwaka area on the east side of the island. Also reported from other inland localities. Found in ultramafic rocks (ortho-nephrite). An attractive rock from the Blue River and Ouen Island, composed of anorthite, tremolite and other minerals is known locally as 'jade'. The indigenous people (Kanak) produced beautiful implements and ornaments from their nephrite and semi-nephrite. Similar examples are found in the Loyalty Islands to the northeast of New Caledonia. The origin of this stone is almost certainly New Caledonia.

POLAND – NEPHRITE

Near Jordanów Slaski, lower Silesia district southwest Poland. Colour: greyish green to dark olive green. Occurs in serpentinite (ortho-nephrite). Deposits rank among the largest and most significant in Europe. Appears to have been used from Neolithic times to the present.

RUSSIA – NEPHRITE

Southeastern Sayan Mountains west of Lake Baikal, Siberia, especially the Ospin area; Kitoy, Onoy, Urik, Belaya and Gorlik-gol Rivers. Occurs both in situ with ultramafic rocks (ortho-nephrite) and as alluvial boulders, some up to 150 tonnes. Colour: light to dark green and chatoyant varieties. Used by the early inhabitants 8000 years ago.

Central Vitim Highlands; Vitim, Bambuika and Tsipa river basins east of Lake Baikal, Siberia

(para-nephrite) in situ and alluvial. Colour: exceptionally clean white, browns and light greens, very translucent. The Siberian deposits are vast and both Sayan and Vitim nephrite are renowned for their high quality and are presently mined commercially.

Jadeite also occurs in Russia in the northern Ural Mountains at Levo-kecheplskoe and in the Krasnoyarsk region western Sayan Mountains, southern Siberia.

SWITZERLAND – NEPHRITE

Several small occurrences in the Swiss Alps near Salux, Val da Fallér, Poschiavo and Scortaseo. Nephrite was also encountered while building the St Gotthard tunnel. Some 17 different nephrite sources have been located in Switzerland. Jade was utilised by the Neolithic Lake Dwellers dating back 6000 years.

TAIWAN – NEPHRITE

Main deposits are in the Fengtien area near Hualien, where it is in association with serpentinite and schist (ortho-nephrite). Colour: several shades of green, yellowish and bluish green, some chatoyant. Has been commercially mined. Used by the early aboriginal people for implements and ornaments.

UNITED KINGDOM – NEPHRITE

Northern Unst, Shetland Islands, Scotland, has a large body of ultramafic rocks. Nephrite has been reported from Fetlar Island and semi-nephrite on Balta Island. A few Neolithic nephrite axes have been recovered throughout the United Kingdom, but their source is as yet unknown.

UNITED STATES OF AMERICA – NEPHRITE AND JADEITE

Jade is found mainly in the western Cordillera from California to Alaska.

Northwest Alaska (nephrite) Upper Kobuk River area: Cosmos Hills, Dahl Creek, Shungnak River and Jade Mountain. Found in situ but occurs mainly as alluvial boulders (ortho-nephrite). Original source of jade for the indigenous Alaskan people.

California (nephrite) Found along the coastal ranges, in situ with serpentinite (ortho-nephrite) and as alluvial deposits. The best known locality is Monterey, especially Jade Cove, where some large boulders have been recovered from the sea. Other counties include Mariposa, Menocino, Riverside, Siskiyou, Trinity, Marin, Tulare, Santa Barbara and San Luis Obispo.

Jadeite also occurs in California at Clear Creek, San Benito, and in three other counties – Trinity, Mendocino and Sonoma.

Oregon (nephrite) Curry County and several other localities associated with ultramafic rocks (ortho-nephrite).

Washington State (nephrite) Eastern slope of Mt Higgins and a number of other localities.

Wyoming (nephrite) Occurs in situ but mainly as alluvial deposits in south-central Wyoming, especially near Lander. Wyoming nephrite is renowned for its high quality.

Nephrite is also reported from other states, including a bluish and dark olive green nephrite in Nevada.

UZBEKISTAN – NEPHRITE

Reported from Kansay ore field, Kuraminskiy Mountains associated with dolomite.

ZIMBABWE – NEPHRITE

Near Mashaba. Found associated with serpentinite during mining operations for chromium ore.

OTHER POSSIBLE SOURCES

Jade (chloromelanite) is reported from Papua New Guinea and artefacts made from nephrite also occur there. Nephrite is recorded from Austria, Northern India and Malawi. Nephrite artefacts are found in early archaeological sites in Bulgaria, Balkans and Greece. Rocks capable of bearing nephrite are present, but to date no sources have been found. Some jade artefacts found in Vietnam and the Philippines are suspected to be from local, but undiscovered sources. To date, no sources of nephrite are known from South America, particularly for the many nephrite artefacts from Colombia and Venezuela. Reports that nephrite occurs at Amargoza, State of Bahia, Brazil appear to indicate that this is an archaeological artefact find spot and not a geological source. Chile has ophiolite rocks in the far south, but nephrite has not yet been reported. Jadeite is also found at Itmurundinskoe, Kazakhstan.

GLOSSARY/

A

abrasive minerals or manufactured substances of sufficient hardness for grinding stone and other materials.

accessory minerals minerals that occur in rocks in small amounts but do not affect the classification or definition.

actinolite a member of the amphibole group of minerals being a hydrous silicate of calcium, magnesium and iron. Occurs as green needle-like crystals, often radiating.

adit a horizontal mine passage.

alluvial gravels and sands deposited by water action, such as rivers.

amphibole a mineral group of basically calcium, magnesium and iron hydrous silicates and other elements (Na, K, Mn, Al). Common amphiboles are hornblende, tremolite, actinolite.

anorthite a mineral being a calcium-rich member of the plagioclase series of feldspar.

antigorite a mineral of the serpentine group.

archaeology study of past societies through systematic recovery and analysis of artefacts.

argillite indurated rock derived from fine-grained sediments. Argillites used by Māori for tools are metasomatised. Often referred to as 'baked argillite'.

artefacts objects made or used by humans.

asbestos a general term for various fibrous minerals.

asbestosis a disease of the lungs brought about by the inhalation of asbestos fibres.

Australian Plate the tectonic plate occupying Australia, North Island and west side of the South Island, New Zealand.

B

basalt a fine-grained, dark-coloured volcanic rock of the mafic family.

bleb a small, generally rounded inclusion.

botryoidal the habit of a mineral resembling a bunch of grapes in appearance.

boulder a rounded rock exceeding a diameter of 225 mm.

burin a sharp-pointed tool used for incising or engraving.

C

cabochon a style of cut for gemstones in which the top is domed and the back either flat, curved or hollowed.

calc-silicates a general term for calcium silicate minerals.

chalcedony a compact variety of silica composed of minute crystals of quartz with sub-microscopic pores. Colour usually greyish, but can be several colours which have independent names.

chatoyancy an optical effect caused by parallel fibres reflecting a silky band of light when suitably orientated.

chlorite a group of soft, flaky green minerals, essentially a hydrous silicate of magnesium, aluminium and iron.

chrome-diopside the mineral diopside containing a little chromium. Colour often bright emerald green.

chromite a mineral of the spinel group, which is an oxide of iron and chromium. Colour black, and commonly found in ultramafic rocks.

cobble a rounded rock between the diameters of 64 mm and 225 mm.

core drill a hollow, tube-like drill that drills a hole but leaves a core of rock in the centre.

corundum a mineral composed of aluminium oxide. When coloured red by chromium, called a 'ruby'. Other colours known as 'sapphire'. Used as an abrasive and gemstone.

crush zone an area where solid rock has been crushed by tectonic compression and movement.

D

dendrites branching, tree-like patterns commonly of manganese oxide that often form in fine cracks and joints in rocks and minerals.

diallage a mineral, being a calcium, iron, pyroxene, with a lamellar or foliated structure. Often dark-coloured with a pearly lustre.

diopside a mineral, being a calcium, magnesium, pyroxene. Several colours but often varying from white, to green to nearly black.

dolomitic marble a magnesium-rich marble.

drag saw an oscillating saw for cutting stone with either a diamond-tipped cutting edge or operated with loose abrasive grit.

drift rock material transported by glaciers and deposited by the ice or water.

dunite an ultramafic rock which is a variety of peridotite composed of mainly olivine. Named after Dun Mountain, Nelson.

E

erratic a boulder or stone transported by glacier.

F

fault a fracture or zone in the earth's crust, along which displacement has taken place.

feather fractures somewhat circular fractures resembling the tips of feathers. Often aligned parallel with the plane of schistosity.

felted a tightly interwoven structure like felt.

ferric oxide an oxide of iron (Fe_2O_3).

ferroactinolite a mineral of the amphibole group and end member of the tremolite-ferroactinolite series. A calcium, iron hydrous silicate.

ferrous oxide an oxide of iron (FeO).

fissile easily split along parallel planes, e.g. schist or slate.

flax (*Phormium tenax*) a strong, fibrous, New Zealand native plant used for twine and rope making.

flint a dense, impure form of micro-crystalline quartz that breaks, leaving sharp edges. Various colours.

float pieces of ore or rock that have been separated from their parent body or place of origin by natural processes.

fluvioglacial alluvial deposits resulting from rivers flowing from glaciers.

foliation a layered or laminated structure.

fuschite a mineral, which is a chromian-muscovite mica. Colour emerald green.

G

gabbro a crystalline igneous rock composed mainly of plagioclase and pyroxene.

garnet a group of silicate minerals usually associated with metamorphic rocks. Frequently forms as regular, multi-faced crystals but some varieties also occur in massive form. Used as an abrasive and gemstone. Colour mainly red tones but other colours occur.

gemmology study of minerals and other substances used for gem purposes.

geochronologist a person who measures the age of rocks.

glaciation the covering and modifying the landscape by glaciers.

gneiss a foliated metamorphic rock with fine and coarse-grained bands.

goethite a term for hydrous iron oxide (limonite), colour usually brown or yellow.

GPS Global Positioning System, used in fixing a position on the earth's surface by satellite.

granite coarse, crystalline plutonic rocks consisting essentially of quartz, potassium and sodium-rich feldspars, mica and sometimes hornblende.

greywacke in New Zealand applies to a dark rock of sedimentary origin, and composed of grains of quartz and felspar cemented together.

grinding grits a lapidary term that applies to silicon carbide or other abrasive grits which are graded to size.

H

hammerstone a stone used as a hammer.

hapū Māori term for a section of a large tribe, clan or sub-tribe.

hematite a mineral composed of iron oxide. Occurs as metallic crystals or as a red earthy substance.

hei tiki a Māori neck ornament depicting a stylised human.

hīkoi pounamu to walk in search for pounamu.

hydrogrossular a mineral of the garnet group, being a hydrated, calcium, aluminium garnet. Colour white, greenish and yellow shades.

I

idocrase *see* vesuvianite.

igneous rocks solidified from magma.

inclusion a crystal, fragment or small gas- or liquid-filled cavity enclosed within a crystal or crystalline substance.

in situ in place, in the position that it was formed in.

isotope forms of an element with the same number of protons (atomic number) but with different numbers of neutrons.

J

jadeite a member of the pyroxene group of minerals. Essentially a sodium, aluminium silicate; colour white, mauve and green shades. In compact form it is one of the two minerals known as jade.

jadeitite a rock composed essentially of the mineral jadeite. Other minerals such as albite and diopside are often present in small amounts.

K

kākā (*Nestor meridionalis*) native New Zealand bird of the parrot family.

kūmara a sweet potato brought to New Zealand and cultivated by the Māori. Found over most Polynesia but originally a native plant of South America.

kuru pōhatu a Māori term for a hammerstone.

L

lapidary one who cuts, shapes and polishes precious and ornamental stones.

lenticular lens shape.

M

magnetite an iron oxide belonging to the spinel group of minerals. Colour metallic black, magnetic.

mana Māori term for influence, prestige or power.

manaia a Māori term for a stylised beaked bird form.

Māori indigenous Polynesian race of New Zealand and the Cook Islands. In this book refers to New Zealand only.

marble a rock composed of calcium carbonate, usually as a result of metamorphosed limestone.

massive a material composed of one or more crystals but with an irregular external shape.

mauri a Māori term for 'life force'.

mélange chaotic mixture of rock of a variety of compositions and sources.

mere a Māori club-like weapon made from nephrite.

meta-gabbro an altered gabbro that was originally a basic igneous rock.

metamorphic rocks rocks that have been altered in structure and composition by the effects of temperature and pressure: schist, gneiss, etc.

metasomatic/metasomatised a process by which minerals are replaced by others of different chemical composition.

microcrystalline a crystalline substance in which the individual crystals or grains can be seen only with the aid of a microscope.

micro fibres tiny fibres that can be distinguished by the use of microscope.

mineral a naturally occurring, inorganic, homogenous substance with an orderly internal atomic structure and other reasonably constant physical properties.

mineralogist one who studies minerals.

mineralogy the study of minerals.

moa a giant flightless bird native to New Zealand, now extinct.

Mohs scale for measuring the hardness of minerals on a scale from 1 to 10.

monoclinic system one of the seven systems of crystallography. Three axes of unequal length, one at 90° to the plane of the other two, which intersect each other obliquely.

monomineralic rocks composed of essentially one mineral, e.g. dunite-olivine, marble-calcite, nephrite.

Moriori the indigenous Polynesian people of the Chatham Islands.

moraine a deposit of rock fragments that have been transported by a glacier.

mud-saw a lapidary saw, usually circular and of soft steel, which rotates in a slurry of mud, abrasive grit and water. The grit adheres to the blade and is carried into the cut to grind its way through the stone.

N

nephritic a geological term to describe a felted microcrystalline structure similar to nephrite.

nodule small, more or less rounded rock, generally harder than the enclosing rock.

O

obsidian natural, volcanic glass, usually black or dark green.

olivine magnesium iron silicate mineral also known as peridot (gem variety). Colour yellowish green.

ophiolite a term for mafic and ultramafic rocks – basalt, dunite, serpentinite, etc. – associated with geosynclinal sediments. Considered to be originally oceanic crust.

ortho-nephrite nephrite that has been derived from an igneous source such as ultramafic rock.

oxidised the surface that has been modified by oxygen, soil acids etc.

P

Pacific Plate a tectonic plate occupying much of the Pacific Ocean and the eastern South Island of New Zealand.

para-nephrite nephrite that has been derived from dolomitic sedimentary rocks.

patu a Māori club-like weapon made from bone, wood or stone.

pebble rounded stone varying in size from 4 mm to 64 mm in diameter.

peridotite a rock composed essentially of the mineral olivine.

petrology the study of rocks, including the identification, classification, origin, mode of occurrence, etc.
picotite a chromian spinel mineral.

pillow lava rounded pillow-like masses of lava that have solidified quickly in water.

placer gold gold found in sedimentary deposits, such as sand or gravel.

plasma a variety of chalcedony similar to prase, but a brighter green colour and often with white spots.

pod a geological term for a body of ore or rock occurring in a pod or cigar shape.

Polynesian the race of people native to Polynesia, a group of Pacific Islands occupying an approximate triangle bounded by New Zealand, Hawai'i and Easter Island.

prase a dullish green variety of chalcedony used for ornamental purposes. Also applied to quartz coloured green by actinolite.

pyrite a mineral also known as iron pyrites, being a sulphide of iron with a brassy colour.

pyroxene a group of rock-forming minerals closely related in form. Silicates of magnesium, calcium and iron are prominent and less often Mn, Na, Al, Li. Common pyroxenes are enstatite, diopside, augite.

Q

quartz a common mineral composed of silicon dioxide. Usually white. Many other varieties occur, depending on colour and form – amethyst, citrine, rose quartz, chalcedony, etc.

quartzose made up of grains of quartz.

R

reef a layer of a rock or mineral enclosed within a different rock.

rind outer weathered casing or layer.

ripi a Māori knife or saw.

river bar a ridge-like gravel mass deposited in the bed of a river by water action.

rock an aggregate of usually more than one mineral.

rodingite a calc-silicate rock consisting of mainly hydrated calcium aluminium silicates and pyroxene. Found in association with serpentinite. Named after the Roding River, Nelson.

rouge a red powder composed of iron oxide used as a polishing compound.

rūnanga or rūnaka Māori term for a council of people.

S

sandstone a sedimentary rock, composed of compacted grains of sand. When quartz grains are predominant and loosely bonded it is used for grinding purposes.

schist a metamorphic rock having foliation commonly derived from sandstones.

schistose schist-like.

schistosity foliation due to the parallel arrangement of platy minerals making the stone easily separated along planes.

sediment a rock, mineral or solid particles deposited by natural processes.

sedimentary composed of sediments.

serpentine a mineral group (antigorite, chrysolite and lizardite), being hydrous magnesium silicates. Colour commonly green. Derived from the alteration of magnesium-rich rocks, such as dunite, peridotite, etc.

serpentinite a rock composed predominantly of the serpentine minerals.

shift a geological term pertaining to the dislocation along faults.

silcrete rock composed of essentially quartz, sand and pebbles cemented by silica.

siliceous containing abundant silica (silicon dioxide or quartz).

silicon carbide a manufactured compound (silicon and carbon), which is extremely hard and used as an abrasive.

silicosis a disease of the lungs caused by the inhalation of silica dust.

slabs in lapidary terms refers to parallel slices of sawn stone.

slate a fine-grained metamorphic rock with a well-developed cleavage (fissility).

sluiced sediments washed with water over apparatus to catch heavy minerals.

spall a chip or fragment of stone with sharp edges, produced by striking with a hammer.

steatite a soft rock made up essentially of talc. Also known as soapstone.

strontium an element, Sr.

sulphides a group of minerals that are mainly compounds of sulphur; iron pyrites, chalcopyrite, galena, etc.

T

taiga name given to the cold forest of the lower Arctic regions.

talus coarse debris deposited at the foot of a steep slope or cliff.

tailings waste ore or gravels from mining operations.

talc a hydrous magnesium silicate mineral commonly found associated with altered magnesium-rich rocks. A very soft, greenish mineral with a greasy feel (soapstone, steatite).

taonga Māori term for a treasured item.

tectonic relating to large-scale features and the forces involved.

terrane a defined sequence of rocks tectonically added to a continent.

tohunga Māori term for a priest or expert.

toki Māori term for an adze.

trace elements elements present in only small amounts.

translucent allowing the transmission of light, but diffused.

trap rock applied to dark igneous rocks, such as basalt.

tremolite a member of the amphibole group of minerals, being a hydrous silicate of calcium and magnesium. Colour white, and forms needle-like crystals, often radiating.

trim saw a lapidary term for a small circular diamond saw used for trimming slabs and other work.

tupuna (*pl.* tūpuna) Māori term for ancestor or grandparent.

U

ultramafic (igneous) rocks composed essentially of magnesian and iron rich minerals, olivine, pyroxene, etc.

uvarovite a calcium chromium garnet. Colour dark to vivid emerald green.

V

ventifacted shaped by the abrasive action of wind and sand.

vesuvianite (idocrase) a complex hydrous silicate of calcium, magnesium and aluminium. Also known as californite when in massive form. Often associated with rodingite.

Vickers hardness test an indentation test for gauging the hardness of substances.

W

wāhi tapu Māori term for reserved ground, a special or sacred place.

wānanga Māori term for school or seminar/series of discussions.

watershed the collective area, which supplies a stream or river.

whao Māori term for a chisel.

whetstone a sharpening stone.

BIBLIOGRAPHY/

Adams, C. J. and Beck, R. J., 2009. 'A signature for nephrite jade using its strontium isotopic composition: some Pacific Rim examples', *Journal of Gemmology*, Gemmological Association and Gem Testing Laboratory of Great Britain, London, vol. 31:5-8, 153-62.

Adams, C. J., Beck, R. J. and Campbell, H. J., 2007. 'Characterisation and origin of New Zealand nephrite jade using its strontium isotopic signature', *Lithos*, vol. 97, 307-22.

Anderson, A. and Ritchie, N., 1986. 'Pavements, Pounamu and Ti: The Dart Bridge Site in Western Otago, New Zealand', *New Zealand Journal of Archaeology*, vol. 8, 115-41.

Anderson, B. W., 1964. *Gem Testing* (7th ed.), Temple Press, London.

Anderson, E., 1945. *Asbestos and Jade Occurrences in the Kobuk River Region, Alaska*. Pamphlet No 3-R, Department of Mines, Territory of Alaska.

Ball, R. A., 1980. 'Jade', *The Australian Journal of Gemmology*, Parts 1-3 (Aug-Dec).

Beattie, J. H., 1920. 'The Southern Maori and Greenstone', *Transactions of the New Zealand Institute*, vol. 52, 45-52.

——, 1945 (republished 1994). *Maori Lore of Lake, Alp and Fiord*, Cadsonbury Publications, Christchurch.

——, 1949 (republished 2002). *The Maoris of Fiordland*, Cadsonbury Publications, Christchurch.

Beck, R. J., 1970. *New Zealand Jade: The Story of Greenstone*, A. H. & A. W. Reed, Wellington.

——, 1981. 'A New Development in Understanding the Prehistoric Usage of Nephrite in New Zealand', in Leach, F. and Davidson, J. (eds), *B.A.R. International Series 104 Archaeological Studies or Pacific Stone Resources*, 21-29.

——, 1984. *New Zealand Jade*, A. H. & A. W. Reed, Wellington.

——, 1987. 'Jade in the Pacific', *New Zealand Crafts Council Magazine (21)*, Crafts Council of New Zealand, Wellington.

——, 1991. 'Jade in the South Pacific', in Keverne, R. (ed.), *Jade*, Anness Publishing Ltd, London, 220-57.

Beck, R. J. and Neiche, R., 1992. 'Jades of the New Zealand Maori', in Markel, S. (ed.), *The World of Jade*, Marg Publications, Bombay, 89-108.

Beck, R. J. with Mason, M., 2002. *Mana Pounamu: New Zealand Jade*. Reed Books, Auckland.

Bell, J. M. and Fraser, C., 1906. 'Geology of the Hokitika Sheet North Westland Quadrangle', *New Zealand Geological Survey Bulletin*, 1 n.s.

Best, E., 1974. 'The Stone Implements of the Maori', *Dominion Museum Bulletin* no. 4, Government Printer, Wellington.

——, 1982. *Maori Religion and Mythology* (part 2), Government Printer, Wellington.

Bishop, D. G., 1994. *Geology of the Forgotten River Area*, Institute of Geological & Nuclear Sciences 1:50 000, Geological Map 15, GNS Science Limited, Lower Hutt.

Bishop, D. G., *et al.*, 1976. 'Lithostratigraphy and Structure of the Caples Terrane of the Humboldt Mountains', *New Zealand Journal of Geology and Geophysics*, vol. 19:6, 827-48.

Bishop, R. L., Lange, F. W. and Easby, E. K., 1991. 'Pre-Columbian Jade in the Central and Southern Americas', in Keverne, R. (ed.), *Jade*, Anness Publishing Ltd, London, 316-41.

Blattner, P., 1991. 'The North Fiordland transcurrent convergence', *New Zealand Journal of Geology and Geophysics*, vol. 34, 533-42.

Bottomley, G. A., 1956. 'Seiches on Lake Wakatipu, New Zealand', *Transactions of the Royal Society of New Zealand*, vol. 83:4, 579-87.

Bradt, C., *et al.*, 1973. 'The Toughness of Jade', *American Mineralogist*, vol. 58, 727-32.

Brailsford, B., 1984. *Greenstone Trails: The Maori Search for Pounamu*. A. H. & A. W. Reed, Wellington.

Burlison, D. M., 1961. 'The Shungnak Jade Project', *Lapidary Journal Inc.*, USA, vol. XV:1, 10-15.

Campbell, G. P., *et al.*, 2009. 'Compositional data analysis for elemental data in forensic science', *Forensic Science International*, doi:10.1016/j.forsciint.2009.03.18.

Campbell, H. and Hutchings, G., 2007. *In Search of Ancient New Zealand*. Penguin Books, co-published with GNS Science, Auckland.

Carrick, R., 1900. 'New Zealand's First Mining Speculation', *The New Zealand Mines Record*, vol. III, Government Printer, Wellington.

Chapman, F. R., 1891. 'On the Working of Greenstone or Nephrite by the Maoris', *Transactions of the New Zealand Institute*, vol. 24, 479-539.

Chihara, K., 1991. 'Jade in Japan', in Keverne, R. (ed.), *Jade*. Anness Publishing Ltd, London, 216-17.

Coleman, R. G., 1966. 'New Zealand Serpentinites and Associated Metasomatic Rocks', *New Zealand Geological Survey Bulletin*, 76 n.s.

Colenso, W., 1894. 'The Modern History of a Block of Greenstone', *Transactions of New Zealand Institute*, vol. 27, 598-605.

Conly, T., 1948. 'Greenstone in Otago in Post Maori Times', *Journal of the Polynesian Society*, vol. 57, 57-63.

Coombs, D. S., *et al.*, 1976. 'The Dun Mountain Ophiolite Belt, New Zealand Its Tectonic Setting, Constitution, and Origin, with Special Reference to the Southern Portion', *American Journal of Science*, vol. 276, 561-603.

Cooper, A. F., 1976. 'Concentrically Zoned Ultramafic Pods from the Haast Schist Zone, South Island, New Zealand', *New Zealand Journal of Geology and Geophysics*, vol. 19:5, 603-23.

——, 1995. 'Nephrite and Metagabbro in the Haast Schist at Muddy Creek, Northwest Otago, New Zealand', *New Zealand Journal of Geology and Geophysics*, vol. 38, 325-32.

Cooper, A. F. and Reay, A., 1983. 'Lithology, Field Relationships and Structure of the Pounamu Ultramafics from the Whitcombe and Hokitika Rivers NZ', *New Zealand Journal of Geology and Geophysics*, vol. 26, 359-79.

Coutts, P. J. F., 1971. 'Greenstone: The Prehistoric Exploitation of Bowenite from Anita Bay, Milford Sound', *Journal of the Polynesian Society*, vol. 80:1, 42–73.

Daily Southern Cross, 15 October and 9 November 1866. 'Greenstone Case', paperspast.natlib.govt.nz.

Dalziel, A., 1963. 'A New Find of Nephrite Jade Insitu Made in New Zealand', *Lapidary Journal Inc.*, USA, vol. 16:11; vol. 16:12.

Da Silva, A. C. S., 1915. 'Nephrite in Brazil', *Proceedings of the 19th International Congress of Americanists*.

Davidson, J., 1992. *The Prehistory of New Zealand*, Longman Paul, Auckland.

Davis, H. L., 1968. 'Papuan Ultramafic Belt', *XXIII International Geological Congress*, vol. 1, 208.

Deer, W. A., Howie, R. A. and Zussman, J., 1966. *An Introduction to the Rock Forming Minerals*. Longman, London.

Dieseldorff, A., 1901. *Nephrite in Mother Rock and New Sources of Nephrite in New Zealand*, Centralblatt für Mineralogie and Palaeontologie, Stuttgart.

Duff, R. S., 1977. *The Moa-Hunter Period of Maori Culture* (3rd ed.), Government Printer, Wellington.

Edbrooke, S. W. (compiler), 2005. *Geology of the Waikato Area*, Institute of Geological & Nuclear Sciences 1:250 000 Geological Map 4, GNS Science Limited, Lower Hutt.

Emmons, G. T., 1923. 'Jade in British Columbia and Alaska and its use by the Natives', *Indian Notes and Monographs* (no. 35), Museum of the American Indian Heye Foundation, New York.

Evening Star, 15 June 1868. 'C. Chilcott' advertisement, West Coast Historical Museum.

——, 14 March 1936. 'The Romance of Greenstone', Dunedin.

Finlayson, A. M., 1909. 'The Nephrite and Magnesian Rocks of the South Island of New Zealand', *Quarterly Journal of the Geological Society*, London, vol. 65, 351–81.

Forster, J. R., 1778. 'Observations Made During a Voyage Round the World' (White), in Skinner, 'New Zealand Greenstone', *Transactions of the New Zealand Institute*, vol. 65, 213.

Frey, R., 1991. 'Jade in Korea', in Keverne, R. (ed.), *Jade*, Anness Publishing Ltd, London, 218–19.

Garnier, P. J., 1871. 'La Nouvelle Calédonie', in Chapman, F. R., 'On the Working of Greenstone or Nephrite by the Maoris', *Transactions of the New Zealand Institute*, vol. 24, 537–38.

Giess, H., 1994. 'Jade in Switzerland', *Bulletin of The Friends of Jade*, San Diego, vol. IX.

——, 2001. 'Jade in Khotan', personal report sent to author.

Graham, G., 1943. 'Te Kaoreore', *Journal of the Polynesian Society*, vol. 52:2.

Graham, I. J. (chief ed.), 2008. *A Continent on the Move: New Zealand Geoscience into the 21st Century*. Geological Society of New Zealand, in Association with GNS Science, Wellington.

Grindley, G. W., 1958. *Geology of the Eglinton Valley, Southland*, New Zealand Geological Survey, bulletin n.s.58.

Hall-Jones, F. G., 1943. *King of the Bluff*, Southland Historical Committee, Invercargill.

Hanna, N. and Menefy, D., 1995. *Pounamu New Zealand Jade*. Jadepress, Kamo.

Harlow, G. E., 1994. 'Jadeitites, Albitites and Related Rocks from the Motagua Fault Zone, Guatemala', *Journal of Metamorphic Geology*, vol. 12, 49–68.

Harlow, G. E. and Sorensen, S. S., 2001. 'Jade: occurrence and metasomatic origin', *The Australian Gemmologist*, vol. 21:1.

——, 2005. 'Jade (Nephrite and Jadeitite) and Serpentinite: Metasomatic Connections', *International Geology Review*, vol. 47, 113–46.

Heaphy, C., 1846. 'Notes of an Expedition to Kawatiri and Araura, on the Western Coast of the Middle Island', in Taylor, N. M. (ed.), 1959, *Early Travellers in New Zealand*, Clarendon Press, Oxford, England.

——, 1862. 'A Visit to the Greenstone Country', in *Chapman's New Zealand Monthly Magazine*, October 1862, 107–11; November 1862, 166–71.

Heimatmuseum, 1980. *A General Information on Gems and Minerals*. Heimatmuseum Idar-Oberstein, Germany.

Heinz, W. F., 1977. *New Zealand's Last Gold Rush*, A. H. & A. W. Reed, Wellington.

Herzog, R., 1990. *Tiki Uber Originale und Imitationen von Nephriteobjektin der Maori-Kultur*. Dietrich Reimer Verlag, Berlin.

Hill, E. J., 1995. 'The Anita Shear Zone: a major, middle Cretaceous tectonic boundary in NW Fiordland', *New Zealand Journal of Geology and Geophysics*, vol. 38, 93–103.

Hochstetter, F. von., 1864. 'Über das Vorkommen und die verschiedenen Abarten von neuseelandischem Nephrit (Punamu der Maoris)', in *Sitzungsberichte der Akademie der Wissenschaften, math.-nat. Klasse*, Bd. 49, Wien, 466–80.

Hockley, J. J., 1974. 'Nephrite (Jade) Occurrence in the Great Serpentine Belt of New South Wales, Australia', *Nature*, vol. 247 (8 February), 364.

Hooker, R., 1986. *The Archaeology of the South Westland Maori*. New Zealand Forest Service, Hokitika.

Howard, B., 1940 (1974 ed.). *Rakiura: A History of Stewart Island*, A. H. & A. W. Reed, Wellington.

Hung, H-C., *et al.*, 2007. 'Ancient jades map 3,000 years of prehistoric exchange in Southeast Asia', *Proceedings of National Academy of Sciences of the USA*, vol. 104 (50), 19745–50.

Hutton, C. O., 1936. 'Basic and Ultrabasic Rocks in North-West Otago', *Transactions of New Zealand Institute*, vol. 66, 231–54.

Iizuka, Y. and Hung, H-C., 2005. 'Archaeomineralogy of Taiwan Nephrite: Sourcing Study of Nephritic Artifacts from the Philippines', *Journal of Austronesian Studies 1*, June, 35–81.

Inverarity, R. B., 1950. *Art of the North West Coast Indians*. University of California Press, Berkeley, CA, USA.

Ireland, T. R., *et al.*, 1984. 'The Pounamu Ultramafic Belt in the Diedrich Range NZ', *New Zealand Journal of Geology and Geophysics*, vol. 27, 247–56.

Jacomb, C., *et al.*, 2004. 'Excavations at The Buller River Site (K29/8) January 2004', *Archaeology in New Zealand*, vol. 47:2, 118–35.

Johnston, M. R., 1983. 'Nephrite in the Pounamu Formation, McArthur Crags, Olderog Creek, Arahura Valley, Westland', *Industrial Minerals and Rocks (no.8)*, DSIR Science Info. Pub. Centre, 5–8.

Kawachi, Y., 1974. 'Geology and Petrochemistry of Weakly Metamorphosed Rocks in the Upper Wakatipu District, Southern New Zealand' *New Zealand Journal of Geology and Geophysics*, vol. 17:1, 169–208.

Keverne, R. (ed.), 1991. *Jade*. Anness Publishing Ltd, London.

Kim, W-S., 1995. 'Nephrite from Chuncheon, Korea', *Journal of Gemmology*, Gemmological Association and Gem Testing Laboratory of Great Britain, London, vol. 24:8.

Kinnicutt, L., 1889. 'Nephrite and Jadeite', *Proceedings of the American Antiquarian* Society, in Ruff, E., *Lapidary* Journal, vol. 16:11, 1048–50.

Kolesnik, Yu. N., 1970. 'Nephrites of Siberia', *International Geology Review*, vol. 12:10, Book Section, 1–107.

Lange, F. W. (ed.), 1993. *Precolumbian Jade, New Geological and Cultural Interpretations*. University of Utah Press, Salt Lake City.

Lapidus, D. F. and Winstanley, I. (eds), 1990. *Collins Dictionary of Geology*. HarperCollins, London and Glasgow.

Leaming, S. F., 1978. *Jade in Canada*, Geological Survey of Canada, paper 78-19.

——, 1991. 'Jade in North America', in Keverne, R. (ed.), *Jade*. Anness Publishing Ltd, London: 296–315.

Leaming, S. F. with Hudson, R., 2005. *Jade Fever: Hunting the Stone of Heaven*, Heritage House Publishing Co. Ltd., Surrey, BC, Canada.

Mason, M., 2000. 'The story of Poutini and Pounamu' in Talmont, R., *Legends of the Land: Living stories of Aotearoa as told by ten tribal elders*, Reed Books, Auckland.

Mennell, E. J. O., 1968. 'Midas' Treasure Land, Rhodesia', *Lapidary Journal Inc.*, vol. 22:3, 425.

Merrony, C. J. N., 1985. *The Characterisation of NZ Greenstone by Neutron Activation Analysis*, MA dissertation, School of Physics and Archaeological Sciences, University of Bradford, England.

Mead, H. M. and Grove, N., 2007. *Ngā Pēpeha a ngā Tīpuna, The Sayings of the Ancestors*, Victorian University Press, Wellington.

Meyer, A. B., 1893. 'Nephrite Hatchet from British New Guinea', *Journal of the Anthropological Institute of Great Britain and* Ireland, vol. 22, 398.

Moreton, A., 2008. *Te Wahi Pounamu, The Place of Greenstone*. Alfred Moreton.

Nathan, S., Rattenbury, M. S. and Suggate, R. P. (compilers), 2002. *Geology of the Greymouth Area*, Institute of Geological & Nuclear Sciences 1:250 000, Geological Map 12, GNS Science Ltd, Lower Hutt.

Neich, R., 1997. *Pounamu Maori Jade of New Zealand*. David Bateman, Auckland.

Nichol, D. 1974. *Nephrite Jade Deposits near Cowell, Eyre Peninsula*, Department of Mines, South Australia.

——, 2000. 'Two contrasting nephrite types', *Journal of Gemmology*, Gemmological Association and Gem Testing Laboratory of Great Britain, London, vol. 27:4, 193–200.

——, 2001. 'Nephrite Jade from Jordanów Slaski, Poland', *Journal of Gemmology*, Gemmological Association and Gem Testing Laboratory of Great Britain, London, vol. 27:8, 461–70.

——, 2003. 'Nephrite Jade from Sestri Levante, Italy', *Journal of Gemmology*, Gemmological Association and Gem Testing Laboratory of Great Britain, London, vol. 28:8, 463–71.

——, 2004. 'Nephrite Jade in Finland', *Journal of Gemmology*, Gemmological Association and Gem Testing Laboratory of Great Britain, London, vol. 29:2, 105–8. Orbell, G., 1965. 'Wakatipu Jade Find', *Lapidary Journal Inc.*, vol. 19:9.

Orchiston, D. W., 1972. 'Maori Neck and Ear Ornaments of the 1770s: A Study in Protohistoric Ethno-Archaeology', *Journal of the. Royal Society New Zealand*, vol. 2:1, 91–107.

——, 1975. 'Maori material culture change in early protohistoric New Zealand: the greenstone trade at Queen Charlotte Sound', *The Artefact*, vol. 39, 40–77.

Pashin, A., 1995. 'California Jade', *California Geology*, Department of Conservation Division of Mines and Geology, Sacramento, CA, vol. 48:6, 147–54.

Polack, J. S., 1838. *New Zealand (vol. 1)*, Richard Bentley, London.

Porteners, C., 1987. 'The Search for Pounamu', *Mobil News*, June, Mobil Oil NZ Ltd, Wellington.

Prickett, N., 1999. *Nga Tohu Tawhito Early Maori Ornaments*, David Bateman Ltd, in association with Auckland Museum, Auckland.

Procter, W. O., 1977. 'Jade Beyond the Arctic Circle', *Lapidary Journal Inc.*, vol. 31:2, 598–604.

Rattenbury, M. S., Cooper, R. A. and Johnston, M. R. (compilers), 1998. *Geology of the Nelson Area*. Institute of Geological & Nuclear Sciences 1:250 000, Geological Map 9, GNS Science Ltd, Lower Hutt.

Ray, H. N., *et al.*, 2003. 'Jade', *New South Wales Industrial Minerals Database* (2nd ed.), Geological Survey of New South Wales, Sydney.

Reed, J. J., 1957. 'Use of the Terms Greenstone, Nephrite, Bowenite and Jade', *Journal of the Polynesian Society*, vol. 66:2, 204–5.
Ritchie, N. A., 1976. *New Zealand Greenstone Sources*, MA thesis, University of Otago Library, Dunedin.

Rowcliffe, D. J. and Fruhauf, V., 1977. 'The Fracture of Jade', *Journal of Material Science*, vol. 12, 35–42.

Ruff, E., 1950. *Jade of the Maori*, Gemmological Association of Great Britain, London.

——, 1960. 'The Jade Story', *Lapidary Journal Inc.*, vol. 14:4–vol. 17:10.

Ryan, P. M., 2005. *The Reed Dictionary of Modern Māori*, Reed Books, Auckland.

Salt, D., 1992. *Stone, Bone and Jade: 24 New Zealand Artists*, David Bateman, Auckland.

Schoon, T., 1973. *Jade Country*, Jade Arts, Sydney.

Sciascia, P., 1991. *Aue, He, Atua!*, Learning Media, Ministry of Education, Wellington.

Seitz, R. *et al.*, 2001. 'Olmec Blue and Formative Jade Sources: new discoveries in Guatemala', *Antiquity 75*, 687–8.

Sekerin, A. P., 1996. 'The Problem of Nephrite-bearing Properties of Folded Areas (Siberia)', *The Bulletin of the Friends of Jade*, vol. IX.

Sekerin, A. P. and Sekerina, N. V., 1986. 'Petrology of granites in deposits of light-coloured nephrite in the central Vitim Highland country', *Geologiya i Geofisika*, vol. 27:12, 36–43.

Shaw, J. A. S., Beck, R. J. and Ritchie, N. A., 1976. *Mount Aspiring National Park Special Area*, Mount Aspiring National Park Board.

Sheppard, W., 1995. *Gold & Silversmithing in Nineteenth & Twentieth Century New Zealand*, Museum of New Zealand Te Papa Tongarewa, Wellington.

Shortland, E., 1851. *The Southern Districts of New Zealand*, Longman, Brown, Green & Longman, London.

Skinner, H. D., 1912. 'Maori Life on the Poutini Coast Together with Some Traditions of the Natives', *Journal of the Polynesian* Society, vol. 21:4, 141–51.

——, 1933. 'Greenstone in the Cook Group', *Journal of the Polynesian* Society, vol. 42, 225–6 ('Notes and Queries').

——, 1935. 'New Zealand Greenstone', *Transactions of the New Zealand Institute*, vol. 65, 211–20.

——, 1936. 'A Greenstone Adze or Axe from Northern Tasmania', *Journal of the Polynesian* Society, vol. 45:1, 35–42.

——, 1959. 'Murdering Beach Collecting and Excavating: The First Phase, 1850–1950', *Journal of the Polynesian* Society, vol. 68:3, 219–38.

——, 1966. *Hei-tiki*, Otago Museum Trust Board, Dunedin.

——, 1974. *Comparatively Speaking (Studies in Pacific Material Culture, 1921–1972)*, University of Otago Press, Dunedin.

Smith, W. C., 1963. 'Jade Axes from Sites in the British Isles', *Proceedings of the Prehistoric* Society, vol. 29, 133–72.

Southland Times, 24 January 1951. 'Last Links Broken, Expert of Lapidary Trade Dead', Invercargill.

Stack, J. W., 1935. *Early Maoriland Adventures of J.W. Stack*, A. H. & A. W. Reed, Dunedin.

Stapleton, A., 1987. *Schillers Richest Find: Jade*, Investigator Press Pty Ltd, Hawthorndene, South Australia.

Stein, M. A., 1903. *Sand-buried Ruins of Khotan: Personal Narrative of a Journey of Archaeological & Geographical Exploration in Chinese Turkestan*, London.

Stewart, H., 1973. *Indian Artefacts of the North-west Coast*, University of Washington Press, Seattle and London.

Stoliczka, F., 1874. 'Note regarding the occurrence of jade in the Karakash Valley on the southern borders of Turkestan', *Quarterly Journal of the Geological Society of* London, vol. XIII, 568.

Stones Directory, 1885, 1889 and 1892. *Otago and Southland Directory and N.Z. Annual*, Stone & Son, Dunedin.

Sutherland, R., *et al.*, 1995. 'Pliocene – Quaternary Sedimentation and Alpine Fault-related Tectonics in the Lower Cascade Valley, South Westland, New Zealand', *New Zealand Journal of Geology and* Geophysics, vol. 38, 431–50.

Tan, L., *et al.*, 1978. *A Mineralogical Study of the Fengtien Nephrite Deposits of Hualien, Taiwan*, National Science Council, Taipei.

Tennant, W. C., *et al.*, 2005. 'Structural studies of New Zealand pounamu using Mössbauer spectroscopy and electron paramagnetic', *Journal of the Royal Society of New* Zealand, vol. 35:4, 385–98.

Te Rūnanga o Makaawhio, 2009. 'Pounamu Resource Management Plan', www. makaawhio.maori.nz.

Te Rūnanga o Ngāi Tahu, 2002. 'Pounamu Resource Management Plan', www.ngaitahu.iwi.nz.

Thomas, J. S. and Cox, S. C., 2009. '42 Years' Evolution of Slip Stream Landslide and Alluvial Fan, Dart River, New Zealand', GNS Science Report 43, Institute of Geological and Nuclear Sciences Ltd, Lower Hutt.

Thompson, R. B., 1967. 'Ultrabasic Rocks of the Solomons', *New Zealand Journal of Geology and* Geophysics, vol. 10:5, 1191–3.

Turnbull, I. M., 1979. 'Stratigraphy and Sedimentology of the Caples Terrane of the Thompson Mountains Northern Southland, N.Z.', *New Zealand Journal of Geology and Geophysics*, vol. 22:5, 555–74.

—— (compiler), 2000. *Geology of the Wakatipu Area*, Institute of Geology & Nuclear Sciences 1:250 000, Geological Map 18, GNS Science Ltd, Lower Hutt.

Turnbull, I. M. and Allibone, A. H. (compilers), 2003. *Geology of the Murihiku Area*, Institute of Geological & Nuclear Sciences 1:250 000, Geological Map 20. GNS Science Ltd, Lower Hutt.

Turner, F. J., 1933. 'Metamorphic and Intrusive Rocks of South Westland', *Transactions of the Royal Society of New* Zealand, vol. 63:1, 178–236, vol. 63:2, 237–84.

——, 1935. 'Geological Investigation of the Nephrites, Serpentines and Related Greenstones used by the Maoris of Otago and South Canterbury', *Transactions of the Royal Society of New* Zealand, vol. 65, 187–231.

Wang, C., 1996. 'Jade in China', *Bulletin of the Friends of Jade*, vol. IX.

West Coast Times, 8–10 and 14 August 1866. 'Greenstone Case', paperspast.natlib.govt.nz.

Wilkes, C., 1845. *Narrative of the United States Exploring Expedition* (vol. 2), Lea and Blanchard, Philadelphia.

Wilkie, J. & Co., 1906. *Tangiwai: The Queen of Greenstone*, brochure for the Milford Greenstone Co., Hocken Library, Dunedin.

Wilkins, C. J., *et al.*, 2003. 'Spectroscopic and related evidence on the colouring and constitution of New Zealand jade', *American Mineralogist*, vol. 88:8–9, 1336–44.

Williams, H. W., 1988. *Dictionary of the Maori Language*, Government Printer, Wellington.

Witter, D., 2009. '3½ years' fieldwork archaeology at Pegasus', *Archaeology in New Zealand*, vol. 52:3, 171–82.

Wobber, D., 1975. *Jade Beneath the Sea: A Diving Adventure*, Boxwood Press, Pacific Grove, CA.

Wood, B. L., 1962. *Sheet 22 Wakatipu: Geological Map of New Zealand*, 1:250 000, DSIR, Wellington.

——, 1972. 'Metamorphosed Ultramafites and Associated Formations near Milford Sound', *New Zealand Journal of Geology and Geophysics*, vol.15:1, 88–128.

Wood, M. M. and Widlich, J. E., 1978. 'Diopside "Jade" from the Eel River', *Lapidary Journal Inc.*, vol. 32:7, 1532–5.

Yui, T-F. and Kwon, S-T., 2002. 'Origin of a Dolomite-related Jade Deposit at Chuncheon, Korea', *Economic* Geology, vol. 97, 593–601.

INDEX/

ACKNOWLEDGEMENTS/

I wish to thank the following people for their assistance with research, photographs, information about the jade fields, archaeology, lapidary history and technical aspects:

Chris Adams, Atholl Anderson, Ray Ansin, Dougal Austin, Steve Bagley, Sandi Hinerangi Barr, Sadie and Gerry Barson, Graham Bishop, Ian Boustridge, Paul Bradford, Ken Bradley, Alan Brown, Steve Bryant, Stewart Bull, Gareth Campbell, Hamish Campbell, Yvonne Carrillo, Andy Chapman, Riki Cherrington, Dave Cleghorn, Mick Collins, A. I. Cook, Alan Cooper, Charlie Cross, H. Dalheimer, Jane Davis, E. Dizon, Bill Doland, David Dudfield, John Edgar, Mat Ellison, Amy Findlater, Rena Fowler, Roger Fyfe, Lewis Gardiner, Herbert Giess, Rodney Grapes, Trevor Gray, Murray Gunn, Peter Haddock, Ron Hamilton, Lindsay Hazley, Erima Henare, Pat Hohepa, Hsiao-Chun Hung, Harvey Hutton, Yoshiyuki Iizuka, Chris Jacomb, Nathan Jerry, Mike Johnston, Muriel Johnstone, Richard Jongens, Ross Kawharu, Grant Keddie, Richard Kennett, Jun Han Kim, Margaret Laing, Raymond Lau, Stan Leaming, Rob Lynes, M. McNamara, Marie-Mahuika-Forsyth, Greg and Tony Maitland, Ngaire Mason, Jo Massey, Nick Mortimer, Pierre Maurizot, Mawhera Incorporation, Clem Mellish, D. Miller, Jesse Morin, Daryl Munro, Kenji Nagai, Doug Nichol, J. O'Connor, Gerard O'Regan, Parata family, Tim Popham, Chris Porteners, Kath and Nigel Prickett, Bernie Radomski, Gael Ramsay, Vicki Ratana, Tony Reay, Scott Reeves, Neville Ritchie, Willie Ronquillo, Andrew Ruskin, Donn Salt, Christophe Sand, Rey Santiago, Piri Sciascia, Alex Sekerin, John and Joe Sheehan, Michael Skerrett, Eugene Sklyarov, Gerard Symth, E. J. Soltys, Paul Souman, H. Sujatmiko, Terry Sweetman, Ko Takenouchi, Wilfred Ti Koeti, Murray Thacker, Horiana and Bob Tootell, the Topi family, Tom Trevor, Ian Turnbull, Mia Veek, Richard Walter, Maurice Watson, Bill Watters, Dean Whaanga, Moira White, Roger Williams, Jim Williams, Cyril and Natalie Win, Dan Witter, Don Wobber, Tzeng-Fu Yui.

Those deceased who have contributed to my research are:

Brian Ahern, Brian Brake, Cliff Dalziel, Norrie Groves, Geoffrey Orbell, Alex Passmore, Alf Poole, Naina Russell, Theo Schoon, E. Sibley, Edgar Sixtus, Jim Staples, Li Ping Tan, R. Tucker.

I am grateful to the following institutions and organisations for their assistance and permission to study their collections and reproduce photographs:

Alexander Turnbull Library, Auckland Museum, Canterbury Museum, Department of Conservation – Southland, Otago and Westland Conservancies, Department of Foreign Affairs, GNS Science, Hawke's Bay Museum and Art Gallery, Hocken Library, Invercargill Public Library, Left Bank Art Gallery, Museum of New Zealand Te Papa Tongarewa, Nelson Provincial Museum, North Otago Museum, Okains Bay Maori and Colonial Museum, Otago Museum, Puke Ariki, Rakiura Museum, Southland Museum and Art Gallery, University of Otago, Wallace Early Settlers Museum, West Coast Historical Museum, Whanganui Regional Museum, Whangarei Museum.

Academia Sinica, Taipei, Anchorage Historical and Fine Arts Museum, Alaska, De Young Museum of Asian Arts, Los Angeles, Fossa Magna Museum, Japan, Institute of the Earth's Crust, Siberia, Ministry of Geology and Mineral Resources, China, Museum of Australia, Sydney, Museum of Prehistory, Taiwan, Museum of Regional Studies, Irkutsk, Russia, National Musée Territorial de Nouvelle-Calédonie, National Museum of Korea, Seoul, National Museum of the Philippines, Manila, National Palace Museum, Taipei, Royal British Columbia Museum, Victoria, Spirit Wrestler Gallery, Vancouver, University of Alaska Museum, Fairbanks.

The following rūnanga and groups were consulted regarding research and the taonga photographed:

Arowhenua, Awarua, Hokonui, Kāti Huirapa ki Puketeraki, Koukourarata, Makaawhio, Mawhera Incorporation, Moeraki, Ngāti Kuia, Ngāti Tuwharetoa, Ngāti Waewae, Ngāti Whatua, Onuku, Ōraka Aparima, Ōtākou, Southern Kaitiaki Rūnaka – Pounamu Working Group, Rangitane o Wairau, Te Ao Marama Inc., Te Atiawa Authority Inc., Te Hapuo Ngāti Wheke Inc., Te Ngāi Tuahuriri, Te Rarawa, Te Taumutu, Tūwharetoa Māori Trust Board, Waihao, Waihopai and Wairewa.

I am especially grateful to Te Rūnanga o Ngāi Tahu for their involvement, co-operation and use of photographs. I particularly thank Anake Goodall, and Sir Tipene O'Regan for his foreword. A special thanks to Simon Cox, GNS Science, for assistance with the production of the maps, technical details and comments within the text and his foreword.

I am grateful for the guidance and enthusiasm of Penguin Group (NZ) staff, particularly Geoff Walker and Jeremy Sherlock. I thank Gillian Tewsley for her valuable editing and Gideon Keith for reflecting his sensitivity for pounamu in the design.

My co-author, Maika Mason, has once again been a crucial guiding hand with his vast knowledge and passion and, for this, I thank him.

It has been a privilege to work with Andris Apse, who gave access to his incredible photographic library and travelled hundreds of kilometres to take new photographs in museums, collections and special places. His contributions make this book a true celebration.

Finally, heartfelt thanks to my wife Ann, for her unfailing support and interest in my jade pursuits, and production of the initial draft.

Russell J. Beck
Invercargill
July 2010

VIKING
Published by the Penguin Group
Penguin Group (NZ), 67 Apollo Drive, Rosedale,
North Shore 0632, New Zealand (a division of Pearson New Zealand Ltd)
Penguin Group (USA) Inc., 375 Hudson Street, New York,
New York 10014, USA
Penguin Group (Canada), 90 Eglinton Avenue East, Suite 700, Toronto,
Ontario, M4P 2Y3, Canada (a division of Pearson Penguin Canada Inc.)
Penguin Books Ltd, 80 Strand, London, WC2R 0RL, England
Penguin Ireland, 25 St Stephen's Green,
Dublin 2, Ireland (a division of Penguin Books Ltd)
Penguin Group (Australia), 250 Camberwell Road, Camberwell,
Victoria 3124, Australia (a division of Pearson Australia Group Pty Ltd)
Penguin Books India Pvt Ltd, 11, Community Centre,
Panchsheel Park, New Delhi – 110 017, India
Penguin Books (South Africa) (Pty) Ltd, 24 Sturdee Avenue,
Rosebank, Johannesburg 2196, South Africa

Penguin Books Ltd, Registered Offices: 80 Strand, London, WC2R 0RL, England

1 3 5 7 9 10 8 6 4 2

First published by Penguin Group (NZ), 2010
Published in association with Te Rūnanga o Ngāi Tahu

Te Rūnanga o NGĀI TAHU

Portions of *Pounamu* were previously published in *Mana Pounamu* (Russell Beck with
Maika Mason, Reed, 2002) and in *Jade* (Roger Kererne, Aquamarine – an imprint of Anness
Publishing, 1991).

The Poutini myth text on pages 44–45 was first published in *Legends of the Land: Living Stories
of Aotearoa as told by Ten Tribal Elders* (Reed Books, 2000).

Designed and typeset by Seven
Prepress by Image Centre Ltd
Printed in China by South China Printing Company

ISBN 9780670074884

A catalogue record for this book is available
from the National Library of New Zealand.

www.penguin.co.nz